DATE DUE

Rae Earl was born in Lincolnshire in 1971. She went to Hull University where she won the Phillip Larkin prize and following a brief stint at Parcelforce moved into broadcasting. She now writes full time from her shed in Hobart, Tasmania.

Also By Rae Earl

My Mad Fat Diary
OMG! Is this my actual life?
OMG! I'm in love with a geek!

RAE EARL

my MADDER FATter *Diary*

VOL·2

HODDER

First published in Great Britain in 2014 by
Hodder & Stoughton
An Hachette UK company

First published in paperback in 2014

1

A CIP catalogue record for this title is available from the British Library

Paperback ISBN 978 1 444 75428 5
Ebook ISBN 978 1 444 75429 2

Some names, circumstances and identifying details have been changed
to protect the identity/privacy of the individuals concerned. All of the
events happened to the author as described.

Typeset by Hewer Text UK Ltd, Edinburgh
Printed and bound by CPI Group (UK) Ltd, Croydon, CR0 4YY

Hodder & Stoughton policy is to use papers that are natural, renewable
and recyclable products and made from wood grown in sustainable
forests. The logging and manufacturing processes are expected to
conform to the environmental regulations of the country of origin.

Hodder & Stoughton Ltd
338 Euston Road
London NW1 3BH

www.hodder.co.uk

For

Emma 'Mort' Drury – for ALWAYS being right (bar that train) and for Feint and Margin

And

Sharon Rooney – for your utter brilliance and total talent

INTRODUCTION
THIS IS MY MADDER FATTER DIARY.

IT'S 1990 AND I'M A morbidly obese teenager living in Stamford, Lincolnshire. I live with my mum who, in her late forties, has just divorced her homosexual second husband and is having a sexual renaissance with a Moroccan bodybuilder 20 years her junior. I know. It's a bit Jeremy Kyle but you're going to have to go with it.

I have two older brothers – who are lovely but have their own lives – and a dad who is quite sweet but who I don't see much.

I go to an expensive private single-sex school in a felt navy hat because I passed a scholarship exam at age 11. This fact, combined with my size, doesn't make me particularly popular on the fairly crappy council estate where our house is. All the streets are named after members of the royal family – Edinburgh Road where I live is not palatial and I get teased a lot in Mountbatten Avenue. It's Anne Road though that's the real killer. 'The Anne' and Green Lane are a hotbed of 'Jabba' baiting – where teams of total twats call me every fat name under the sun. I could list them here but it would take up half a page and they were not particularly creative. That said, the day 5 teenage boys started singing 'Hey Fattie Bum Bum' at me at least showed a good knowledge of 1970s lovers rock reggae.

In the absence of getting the REAL thing, food is sex. Most days I down custard creams almost intravenously. Kit Kat multipacks are hoovered away in an instant. I have a full meal at school and then come home to more. I graze like a cow but eat like someone half-starved when big plates of anything are presented to me. Food is a pleasure, food is an anaesthetic, food is dependable. It would be a perfect partner if it didn't push up my waist size to something that relegated me to middle-aged women's clothes shops and the romantic dugout.

This doesn't sound very joyful does it? Thankfully the best humour often grows in the darkest places. Plus my life then is littered with lovely people, good music and great things.

I have a social life to die for. I have a record collection that's been in alphabetical order since I can remember. I'm madly in love with a sculpted piece of testosterone wonder called Haddock. That's his codename because my mum refuses to enter the 20th century and get a home phone so I have to use phone boxes to ring people and I'm concerned this most secret and beautiful of true loves will be exposed to the world. I'm not ready to do that yet – despite the fact that on New Year's Eve 1989 he seemed to be saying some odd and frankly very encouraging things that may mean that he secretly loves me and wishes to 'do' me senseless. I have a fantastic best friend called Mort, school is a safe haven and largely a total laugh and music saves me everyday. It says what I can't say and heals things I can't even express. I live for it.

What else?

Oh I'm crackers.

I'm stark raving loony mad. I know it. My mum knows it. A few other people suspect it and the professionals have diagnosed it. I was in a psychiatric ward at 16 but I'd been crazy long before that. Who knows where being 'nuts' starts? I was always scared of something. I don't remember a time when I didn't think I controlled everything with the power of my thoughts. Thinking you are in charge of world peace is quite a big burden. Thinking that you can stop your mum dying in a horrible train accident by touching things many times or counting or praying takes up a lot of time. It also demands a lot of energy and a need for distraction. For most of the time there were no tablets to calm me down so I took HobNobs. It made sense. My Prozac was oaty and sublime when dunked in half a mug of Tetley. Whatever the worry, a packet of something fatty sugar-coated the mental pain.

The thing is, anxiety is a total bastard. It shape-shifts. It finds a face and things to latch on to then it multiplies the threat. Needles, floods, poisonous plants, rabies, terrorists, nuclear war, Sinitta ruining the charts – from the deadly serious to the really stupid, I've thought my brain could control it all. Then it just all got too much and I totally lost it. I found myself in an adult psychiatric ward with a schizophrenic biker and a woman who kept yelling about her skirt. We did group exercises with beanbags. The walls were brown. It was noisy at night. People who are ill and distressed don't do 9 to 5. They shout and scream at 2 in the morning. I had to get out. I told them I was better. I wasn't but I wasn't going to improve there and mad people still want the same things as sane people do – success, happiness, a man. None of those were going to come to me in ward 4 of the Edith Cavell Hospital, Peterborough.

So in 1990 my head was often on fire. I knew I didn't want to go back to the ward. I knew I had to keep it together as best I could. I had to finish my A levels and get to university. My diary gave me a place to explode. It was a place where all my mental debris could splatter all over the pages privately. That said, I couldn't always fully let go. That would have been too scary, a loss of control. So you'll get phrases like 'trying to appease', 'trying to keep it together', 'maintain spiritual stability' – what I'm really saying is that I don't want to talk to anyone because I'm frightened I'll end up in a psychiatric ward again. But as I get older you'll see I get more honest . . .

I've had to edit this diary a lot. There are pages and entries where I just write 'God Help Me – PLEASE'. You don't want to read that but that IS one of the problems with mental illness. On top of the pain there's the tedium of it. The repetition. That horrible realisation that today is going to be ANOTHER day when you eat a loaf of bread to forget, when you burn yourself with matches to punish your thoughts and find the only relief is in a mangled cassette of Motown chartbusters, a water fight at school and Haddock's arse in a tight pair of jeans.

I've had to rewrite a few things too. They made no sense at all. At times I was very poorly and one of the really evil things that does is strip you of the ability to express yourself with any coherence. No-one gets it. Not even you. Word for word just would not have worked. I've messed around with timings and changed people's names but this is how it happened. This was me in 1990 & 1991.

In 1990 the world is crawling out of communism and repression and new countries are being born, but bloody Jive Bunny are still shitting out compilation singles and I'm still hoping to crawl out of the fat body I'm stuck in and the mad brain I'm chained to. I'm sharing my diary

4

for the reasons I shared the last one – because it makes me laugh and because I want to tell people you can be out of your tree crazy in your teens and things can work out OK. However, there are now new reasons too. Since having my first teenage diary published I know there are young people who still feel mad. There are young people who cut themselves and look in the mirror and despair. I want you to see the terrible things I thought about myself and how I longed to be a 'real woman' like so many of my friends. Then I want you to know that those women I thought had it all sorted wrote to me and told me they had felt EXACTLY the same way as me! Adolescence sucks. Being a teenager is utter shit FOR EVERYONE but life gets better.

Anyway. 1990. The Berlin Wall is down, The Happy Mondays are off their magnificent trolleys, A levels are approaching and Haddock's backside is a national treasure.

I'll handle your questions at the end because you'll have some . . .

Monday 1.1.90

10.12 a.m.

NEW DECADE! NEW YEAR! NEW RAE! It even starts on a Monday. It's like the year already knows what it is doing. Perhaps just the 80s were TOTAL shit.

I CANNOT get over Haddock last night. Seriously though, it did sound like he would proper like me as a girl if I 'just toned up a bit'. That won't take that long. A bit of tone. That's just a bit of walking isn't it? FUCK! If I think about being that man's girlfriend I could orgasmsexplode. That's not even a word. I don't care. It sums it all up.

11.22 a.m.

Just tied a scarf round my head and pulled all my chins off my face. I look a bit Chinese in a good way but there IS something there. There is something not totally rotten and ugly and bollocks.

1.12 p.m.

Just thought, I don't know where everyone disappeared off to last night. I walked from Vine Street to Fraggle's house at 4 a.m. I saw that everyone had gone to bed and came back to Vine Street to sleep. I love Dobber's mum but I wish she had bought a thicker carpet. My cheek looked like a potato waffle this morning. Battered Sausage took the piss then started talking about women and how they were a pain in the arse and how they couldn't decide what they wanted. I said 'Your ex could decide last night – she didn't want you.' It was a bit harsh but he can take it.

Oh I can't stop thinking about Haddock. In my head I've already had sex with him about 15 times this morning. Can men do it 15 times or do they just run out of stiffy? I WOULD LIKE TO TRY.

Dobber says she's heard maximum 7 times in one night and by time 5 they are getting tired.

OK here is the plan for the year 1990.
1) 1990 is literally fraught with looming crises: Health problems reaching a head. What IS wrong with my insides? Will my ovaries ever work? Or have I just got a terrible bloody cancer that no-one has spotted yet?
2) Bloody A levels.
3) Depending on what happens with those leaving Stamford

BLOODY WORRYING

Also . . .

4) Crush (now 5 month crush verging on ridiculous) on Haddock is not actually getting better but steadily worsening. And now there might be some hope that he might like me. In <u>that</u> way.

    No Rae. He actually thinks I'm repulsive in <u>that</u> way.
5) Trying to appease.
Got BAD January blues. I went too mad over Christmas and there are bloody Brazil nut shells on

the landing. I'm not going near the scales. The scales fear me. I fear the scales.

<u>OBJECTIVES</u>
1) Get A levels and get away!
2) Have a bloody good time.
3) Keep cool and calm.
4) Maintain spiritual stability.
5) Try to have some sort of a decent relationship with a real man that exists as a breathing thing.
6) Become a bit of a sex bitch. HA HA HA! Not really. Just a bit.

Anyway here's to 1990. I can't believe this diary is going to take me through A levels and Summer holidays and starting uni. Next year I'M 20!! THAT'S SICK!

I need to take this year seriously and concentrate on the things that really matter.

4.24 p.m.
The *Smash Hits Yearbook* is 'frame that bastard' EPIC CLASSIC this year. They ask Jon Bon Jovi if he's ever been sick in his cowboy boots. HA HA HA! Soft rock furry toss ball!

Tuesday 2.1.90

11.46 p.m.
I'VE JUST BEEN DOWN THE pub. The lads were discussing whether or not you should spray deodorant on your cock to be hygienic when you are with 'a bird'.

Haddock was laughing. Haddock does not need Right Guard on his knob. I just know he doesn't. It's not a question I would ever ask his girlfriend anyway to be fair.

Haddock was lovely to me but I think he's forgotten what he did on New Year's Eve. He only stroked my hair but it wasn't like me stroking White the cat. It was like . . . a bit sexual. A bit.

Oh perhaps it wasn't. Perhaps he was just being kind. That's the trouble with Snakebite – it gives you balls but it makes you talk bollocks.

If it does all come to nothing I will just break in two I think. Oh Rae, that's melodramatic crap. Just masturbate and fuck off. The thing is, it's not just the shagging with Haddock it's the mind connection. He just gets it.

It is lots about the sex though as I'm TOTAL HORN.

Wednesday 3.1.90

9.38 p.m.
I'M LISTENING TO MY SIXTIES Mania compilation. The Mamas and the Papas are singing something about the worst bit being just before dawn breaks. As if you don't know if the day is going to dawn at all. IT'S BLOODY DARK let me tell you.

Mum has just been up. Apparently Mama Cass from the Mamas and the Papas choked on a ham sandwich and died in bed. Thanks for that. It felt like she was giving me a 'Rachel is too fat' lecture disguised as pop trivia so I said 'Why don't you make a public information film about the dangers of eating filled rolls in bed?!' Mum got really cross and said 'There's no need for sarcasm' and the usual 'I'm your mother – give me some respect' shit. I don't care. She hardly says two words to me these days unless it's to have a go. It's ALL about Adnan – the Morrocan bodybuilding boyfriend. It's 'Addy – would you like a beef sausage.' That's another thing, pork is now banned from this house and beef sausages taste shit. And NO I don't know what direction Mecca is either!

Thursday 4.1.90

11.22 p.m.

GOT PISSED TONIGHT AND DID the following:

1) Told Chelsea Dunn I was totally in love with Haddock. Swore her to secrecy.
2) Told Dobber tonight that I was totally in love with Haddock. Swore her to secrecy.
3) Hid the beef sausages and the bloody couscous. Sick of them.

Now THAT was stupid. Not the sausages or the couscous (hidden behind shitloads of yoghurts) or Dobber (she will take it to the grave) BUT Chelsea is a bit of a shit-stirrer and good mates with Haddock's girlfriend. I have to remember if this gets out too early, 1) My body won't be ready and primed for action 2) Haddock's girlfriend – I can't even imagine. She will go ballistic. She's told me EVERYTHING about him. I know stuff that no-one on earth knows. I have a basic blueprint for a completely successful Haddock relationship. I just can't use it yet. It's like Churchill sitting on the plans for D-Day. I've got to wait for the right conditions.

No. Haddock's girlfriend is not Hitler. I repeat, she's gorgeous and sweet and funny. And I feel bad BUT all is fair in love, war and HADDOCK!

I am currently wishing facial hair on someone. That's not good. Hormones send you mad.

Friday 5.1.90

11.34 p.m.
I HAVE DECIDED ADNAN IS the Cookie Monster from *Sesame Street*. For a start, he is incapable of using the word 'I'. He says 'Me hungry!' and 'Me thirsty!' And he eats like the Cookie Monster too. He shoves it in. YET if I make even a tiny noise when I'm eating Mum calls me 'cement mixer'. They are so loved up. I hate living here. I'm so sick of being the only person on earth without someone who loves them and I am SO SICK of being in a house that smells permanently of spicy lamb.

Saturday 6.1.90

LATE. I DON'T CARE WHAT the time is anyway. What does it matter?!

I know I always get so pissed off in early January and this year is no exception. I feel like a total gooseberry at home. I also feel like a TOTAL liability with my friends as well, like an ugly dog that follows them around. Oh that's not fair. I am an ungrateful bitch and I've got

11

some brilliant mates. What have I actually got to moan about?!

I had a chat with Haddock's girlfriend tonight. I feel so immensely guilty because she is so lovely. Haddock wanted to talk to me tonight after I got upset in the pub. It was just about the usual stuff. I HATE ME BASICALLY. He said he wanted to make me feel better. Oh bloody hell – it's so dangerous writing this. I bloody love him but it's absolutely blatantly obvious that we could never properly get on. His girlfriend says he's insecure too and is probably 'insurance salesman material'. Who gives a fuck? He's FUCKING LOVELY AND GORGEOUS. I don't want him to be a stuntman or anything dangerous. I just want him to be IN MY LIFE . . . SOMEWHERE.

I ran off tonight. I cried my bloody eyes out. I feel like such a fat loud cow sometimes. I feel really unwanted and totally unloved. I can't turn off what I feel. When I am loved it's the wrong type of love – 'just friends'. I am so sick of 'just friends'.

At least I don't fancy Battered Sausage anymore. At least I can just be mates with him like I'm mates with Fig. Every time Fig comes back and sings Showaddywaddy songs I think what a brilliant friend he is.

You deserve an explanation and I'm feeling very honest. I am tortured by this head. I am praying night and day thinking I'm the devil. I'm frightened to death of going to hell.

I wish I was attached to someone. It's curiosity more than anything. What could I give someone? If anything? I need some music. I need something to take away all this shit in my head I can't fix. I can't be Satan. God wouldn't give Satan an Atlantic Soul box set.

I'm joking because I'm fucked.

I feel better for screaming it all down. I'd be a useless Italian. I only lose my temper here. I put a face on ALL THE TIME. I pretend to be happy. Just sometimes – like tonight – it all gets too much.

Sunday 7.1.90

9.56 p.m.

I JIBBED AGAIN. I JUST can't fake it at the moment. I'd rather stay in my room and listen to T-Rex and David Bowie. Jasmine Bobbs lent me *Diamond Dogs* over Christmas. It's ace but *Electric Warrior* is better. 'Get It On' sounds like sex is happening in an alley and 'Rip Off' sums up my life at the moment. A massive swizz with a big intro and then an empty stage full of fuck all.

11.12 p.m.

How the HELL does Sinead O'Connor be sexy with no bloody hair? She's MORE bald than Battered Sausage yet she is GORGEOUS. How do these women happen?! Where does their confidence come from?! The only time I had short hair I looked like a bloke with tits. Mum MADE me cut it because I was chewing it and she was worried about fur balls.

A cat does live in this house so it's easy to get mixed up, Mum. We are both white!

If I shaved my head I would just look like Buddha and people would rub me for luck.

Perhaps I DO need to shave. HA HA HA!

Monday 8.1.90

4.13 p.m.

BACK TO SCHOOL TOMORROW. I have A level mock exams and I have done no revision whatsoever. I just need to be in love.

By February it will have been a year since I've had a snog. It's insignificant.

5.49 p.m.

No it's not. It's BLOODY SIGNIFICANT. I'M FULL OF CHOCOLATE BUT SEX STARVED.

11.12 p.m.

Dear Adnan – Please stop singing to Radio 1 in your wailing Arabic way. For all you know I could be trying to do school work.

Bloody hell, if John Peel heard what was currently happening to his show I think he'd die. It should be against the law to fuck up The Fall with shit singing.

Tuesday 9.1.90

7.12 p.m.

BACK TO SCHOOL!
   The following things happened today:

1) Everyone is going on about exams like they are life and death. They are slightly life and

14

death but it's DULL to talk about revision timetables!

2) Daisy has dyno-printed some of her revision timetable in her pencil tin. It's replaced her 'Work Hard Play hard' sticker.

3) Some people are actually using study periods to revise rather than talking shit and having a laugh in the common room.

4) People got CARS for Christmas. CARS. I got the *Smash Hits Yearbook* and two selection packs. You cannot drive to the Showcase cinema in a Curly Wurly.

5) RANK! Daisy went to eat an apple. It looked fine on the outside but when she bit into it . . . it was ROTTEN to the core with maggoty shit in it. Those of us who saw that apple will never get over it. Daisy was nearly sick. Say what you like about Creme Eggs but they don't try to kill you.

Adnan goes back tomorrow. I am hiding upstairs. Menopausal love affairs are not a spectator sport.

10.13 p.m.
Yes I'm a jealous cow. Why shouldn't Mum be happy? She was married to my dad who was married to cricket and beer and then she was married to a man who wanted to be married to other men! HA HA HA! She deserves a break. I just wish she wasn't doing it in my actual A level year.

Wednesday 10.1.90

6.12 p.m.

AFTER A HARD DAY OF studying Stanislavski's acting theory and Phillip II of Spain I DO NOT want to come back to a woman of nearly 50 sitting in a chair looking miserable as shit listening to soppy songs. I can never listen to those songs again without thinking of Mum in relationships. They are DESTROYED.

8.22 p.m.

OH NO YOU DON'T. Mum is listening to 'Nothing Compares 2 U'. That's one of my Haddock songs. She's not hijacking that.

9.24 p.m.

Mum and me have just had a massive row.

> ME: Please can you turn that off. I'm trying to revise (I wasn't but that's not the point).
> MUM: No. I want to listen to it.
> ME: Can you put some headphones on then?
> MUM: No. Not with my tinnitus.
> ME: Well if I fail my A levels we'll know why.
> MUM: If you fail it will be because you haven't done enough work and you keep going out with your mates and . . .

I walked off at this point and she turned it off! Always use the 'you are going to mess up my exams' tactic as it

works every time. I have saved myself and Sinead
O'Connor from death by middle-aged crap soppy romance
shit.

Thursday 11.1.90

5.13 p.m.

ANOTHER PREGNANCY SCARE AT SCHOOL.
CONTRACEPTION – IT'S NOT DIFFICULT. I'm an
expert. Take the pill everyday. If you have antibiotics for
your zits use johnnies too. Johnnies split. Get the
morning after pill if you're worried. If your doctor thinks
you're a slag, who gives a shit – at least you're not up the
duff! Shame all this knowledge is wasted. I have a great
contraceptive device with a 100% success rate – it's called
being really fat. No side effects – except complete
strangers taking the piss and every time you go to the
corner shop gangs of lads chanting 'walrus' at you. Apart
from that – fine!

I feel very angry at the moment.

Friday 12.1.90

11.35 p.m.

UNBELIEVABLE!
No, Mum – Battered Sausage does not want to
see photos of your Moroccan boyfriend when he comes
round to pick me up to take me for a drink. Only
apparently he does! Battered Sausage will sit there,
drink tea and let you tell him all about protein

requirements and muscle mass and laugh at all your jokes. Tell you what Mum – why don't you go down the pub with him! Take over my life completely. You clearly want to.

I was pissed off down the Vaults. Battered Sausage kept asking 'What's up Big Razza?' I said nothing. But here's what was actually pissing me off: 1) Haddock was not there and he hasn't even got exams 2) My mum has a photo album of semi-naked men photos and she thinks it's OK to show them to people.

I need to calm down. I'm going to have to get my Deacon Blue album out or something. Deacon Blue sing about everyone thinking love will fix things and how that's crap.

Well I love Deacon Blue but I think they are wrong. I think it makes everything better. I've seen it does.

Saturday 13.1.90

12.33 p.m.
NO-ONE IS GOING OUT TONIGHT because of exams. What a bunch of jibbers. Not even Dobber who can usually be totally relied upon. So I'm going to use my time productively and go for a massive walk to get me some 'tone' for sex! I might even do the old railway line walk down Gypsy Meadows.

5.12 p.m.
This isn't a big deal but I've spotted my . . . Actually, as I write it IS a big deal. I was just walking down Gypsy Meadows and I saw this massive mound of rubbish and

on it was my old rocking horse 'Beauty'. Mum gave it to the family across the back and now they've dumped the thing I loved the most in the world in a bloody field. It's totally pissed me off. Fly-tipping my memories. They could have given it back to me. I'm too big to ride it but – you shouldn't fuck with people's toys!

Mum is out. God knows where. She's probably throwing away more stuff that matters to me.

8.35 p.m.
As soon as Mum got back I asked her about Beauty. She looked at me for ages and then said . . .

MUM: Rachel – you're 18 years old. Why are you bothered about a bloody broken rocking horse when you've got exams next week?!
ME: Because MUM – that rocking horse was everything brilliant about being a kid and freedom.
MUM: Stop talking such shite and do some work.
ME: Thank you for your sensitivity as ever. You know the photos of Adnan that you've got – I might give them away!
MUM: I've hidden them! (or something – she was going mental)
ME: Good! But my mates don't really want to see some bloke's biceps.
MUM: Actually, Battered Sausage seemed very interested!
Me: No. He was just being polite to a middle-aged saddo (worst thing I've ever said but I was bloody cross).

19

Mum just walked off but it seriously was my favourite horse. My only horse. I used to pretend I was doing the Burghley Horse Trials on it.

10.12 p.m.
I just said sorry to Mum. At least when I am a cow I apologise. And I was a cow. It just seems like everything I love is starting to slip away.

Sunday 14.1.90

6.13 p.m.

> **Goodbye Beauty**
> There lies my horse
> Fallen in a domestic war
> Once ridden, now forgotten
> Goodbye Beauty.
> You are amongst flowers and clover,
> Grass will be with you and the odd cow,
> I rode you once
> There are other things I want to ride now.

Bit pervy but says what I feel!
    Without the pub and my mates I start to feel weird again.

Monday 15.1.90

5.13 p.m.
SPOKE TO MORT FOR AGES today about Beauty.
She gets it. She always gets it.

I've got exams for the next two weeks.

When I hear about other people's parents at school I realise how lucky I am to have Mum as a mum. She just tells me if I fail my exams I will end up having a shit life in a dead end job. Some girls at school have dads that hang over them and nag them to death. Ebony's mum checks on her every 15 minutes, forces her to eat figs and still makes her wear a vest!

Politics tomorrow.

Tuesday 16.1.90

4.57 p.m.
AFTER TODAY'S MOCK A LEVEL U.S. Politics TOTAL abortion I wish I did have a mum who made me work! WHAT IS FEDERALISM?

Wednesday 17.1.90

SHELLBOSS AND ME GOT BOLLOCKED today for singing 'Letter from America' by The Proclaimers full blast in the common room. Yes we did have shit Scottish accents but there was no need for Mrs C to go quite so bonkers. We are 18! ADULTS. Teachers have zero pressure in their lives. They've done all their exams and passed them. GIVE PUPILS A BREAK.

My eating has gone out of control. Tonight – oh too much shit. I just feel panic and have stuff to do and I eat instead. Mum comes upstairs and stares at the plate. So I go to shovel it in at my window and Mrs Bark from the house opposite sees me from her kitchen or someone walking their dog glances up and disapproves. PISS OFF LASSIE MAN! I don't want to be looked at when I eat. I know what people are thinking. You shouldn't be eating. NOTHING. Except lettuce. And air.

Well FUCK YOU world because this brain needs energy. Perhaps that's why I'm off it. My mind is fat.

Why is my lard on my gut and not on my toe. A massive toe would be easier to hide. I could have disabled shoes. I don't think shit feet put off men.

Why I am even thinking about this when I should be revising voting behaviour?!

Thursday 18.1.90

11.30 p.m.

MUM WENT INTO HOSPITAL TODAY for what she calls 'Ladies reconstruction'. It's a bladder repair.

As a woman, your body is either pissing you off or just pissing.

Usually Mum not being here would mean party time but A level mocks mean that is off the list. So I shall just sit here writing you, diary, looking at cabinet collective responsibility and listening to The Beautiful South. I will have to sail my ship alone because no-one wants to be in the boat and they couldn't fit anyway.

Friday 19.1.90

7.12 p.m.

DID THE BRITISH POLITICS EXAM and then a massive row erupted because everyone was having an exam inquest and saying they'd flunked it. They we had an argument about government whips. Shellboss said the maximum whip on a bill was 3. I said no, it was 4 because of the 1979 vote of no confidence against the Callaghan Labour government where they brought nearly dead MPs on stretchers on drips. No-one else remembered this and everybody started telling me I was talking bollocks. I know I'm right though! Though I can't find it in any textbook.

That was the most boring entry in a diary ever recorded.

I should be with a bloke right now not talking about Tories.

I'll ask Mum tomorrow about whips.

Saturday 20.1.90

5.12 p.m.

I WENT TO SEE MUM in hospital. She said 'The only whips I know about Rachel are Walnut!' We both agreed they are the best kind! She is sore but OK.

I'm going out tonight or I will just sit here watching *Beadle's About* feeling depressed.

Sunday 21.1.90

8.02 a.m.
THANKS MR BARK FOR MOWING on a Sunday morning. Your son came round and bollocked me for playing 'Thriller' too loudly one night but apparently it's OK for you to get the Flymo out first thing.

11.34 a.m.
Saturday nights are getting really weird. Last night Ryan Bates cornered me by the toilets in the Vaults to apologise for being 'such a shit' to me on New Year's Eve and calling me a sarky bitch. I told him not to worry about it as I hadn't been. This is true. I am panicked out of my head about lots of things but Ryan Bates is not one of them. Then he said 'Are we mates?' and tried to give me a hug. I sort of shrugged him off and said 'Yeah!' Then he looked at me with this big STARE so I went 'Bye Ryan!'

No Haddock. He is doing shifts. No anyone really tonight but I needed the pub. I needed people.

11.25 p.m.
I just tried to make a shopping list. I can't be fagged. As long as I get tea and milk in for when Mum gets home she'll be happy.

I miss her when she's not here but I can't stand her when she is. I don't make sense to me let alone anyone else.

Monday 22.1.90

I WENT TO PETERBOROUGH AND bought some records. I should be revising but HMV is sex. I'm on my own. I've noticed marked collapse of sanity. Hypochondria creeping in badly. Think I've swallowed glass and it's currently cutting into my liver. It's not. I'm sure *That's Life!* said you should eat cotton wool if that happens but this is NOT a beauty household. We only have cotton buds for waxy ears and feminine hygiene products – I WANT TO SHOUT 'SANITARY TOWELS' EVERYWHERE!!! JAM RAGS!! YES I BLEED – IT'S NATURAL.

English tomorrow – you can't really revise. We are allowed our set books in with us anyway.

Tuesday 23.1.90

5.38 p.m.

T HE GREAT THING ABOUT ENGLISH is that it's actually an A level in bullshitting about books which I am brilliant at!

Mum is home but very sore. She is coming with me to the hospital tomorrow. I've got an appointment to find out what is up with my tummy and why I get in so much pain. They always blame it on stress. As soon as they hear it's exam time they will say it's me worrying and making myself ill. As soon as they see 'psychiatric ward' they say it's my head. I will have this for life now. When I'm 60 and I get run over by a pissed up drunk driver who mounts the pavement the ambulance men will say 'She's batty – it's her fault.'

Wednesday 24.1.90

6.12 p.m.

FUCK.
   Fuck.
  Fuck!

Went to the hospital and saw a new specialist who was lovely and basically blew up my backside with a pump. Then he said 'I'm not entirely happy with what I'm seeing down there. I think we could do with some further investigations.' Basically I've got to come back to hospital and have a massive camera up my arse. My mum looked really worried and kept saying 'What do you think it is?' and the specialist goes 'Nothing too serious or she'd probably be looking a lot more unwell than she is'. TALK ABOUT ME LIKE I'M NOT HERE WHY DON'T YOU?! HE MEANS I'D BE SKINNY NOT FAT.

I'm being mean. He was actually really nice and didn't mention the nervous breakdown once.

I'm worried though. What is it? What is wrong with me? You know what I'm thinking. It would be a-bloody-typical of me to have something rare and horrendous.

Mum has just been up to ask me if I want to talk about anything. When I said 'No' she asked me if I wanted anything. Yes Mum – I'd like Haddock to come in here, hold on to me and never let go because I'm shitting it. But I told her nothing.

26

9.12 p.m.

I just told Mort about my arse. She was brilliant. She doesn't think it's anything to worry about or they would have kept me in.

I'm not staying there. Even the smell of Dettol makes me feel off my head.

I couldn't stay in the phone box long as a bunch of twats had sat down on the old people's flat's wall. They were pretending to ring up the fire brigade and saying stuff like 'Can you come quickly, a fat bitch needs to be cut free from a phone box she's got stuck in.' When I finished I just put the receiver down and ignored them.

I came home. Ate some cheese. Lots of it. Shoved it in. Got under the duvet. Wrote this.

Thursday 25.1.90

8.23 p.m.

THEATRE ARTS THEORY PAPER. I can't tell you how much I don't give a toss about Bertolt Brecht when death could be in my bum. Fuck knows why I'm laughing when I could be on my way out.

Last exam tomorrow. Thank GOD.

Friday 26.1.90

5.32 p.m.

WELL HISTORY, YOU'RE A PILE of shit. I just presented the same point in 400 different ways in every essay.

11.34 p.m.

Battered Sausage picked me up about 8 p.m. He'd already had a bottle of sherry. I have no idea why he's started downing Harvey's Bristol Cream but it makes him really grumpy. We walked into town and he kept moaning about women like I'm not one (actually I'm not to him) then he started saying 'If you come to Exeter you've got to give me some space to pull women.' Er . . . yes . . . what does he think I will do? Cramp his style. What style? TOSSER. He was so busy going on about HIMSELF he didn't ask me ONCE about me. Exams or ANYTHING. Good job though because what do I tell people?! I could be dying?! I have to have my entire anus and colon investigated. Not very sexy is it? Who wants this MESS. A girl at school had a cyst on her breast and no-one laughed at that. Which is right – it was horrible – but why are they laughing at me?!

OK they are not but only because I haven't told them.

And before you ask, no Haddock either because he's working again stacking shelves in a blue overcoat which he no doubt SETS ALIVE with wonderfulness.

He's like an endangered species. A panda. But he shits on a panda's cuteness from a great height.

Saturday 27.1.90

11 something. Who cares. Late.

JUST BACK FROM THE PUB. WHAT A NIGHT! Everyone relieved exams are over and having a laugh. Then I see a back at the bar in a grey cardigan. HOW CAN YOU MAKE A GREY CARDIGAN SEXY but he does!! And when you haven't seen him for a while – he blows your head off. But I act casual and we eventually talk . . .

Haddock: How did the exams go?
Me: OK. Well a bit shit but fuck it.
Haddock: You all right?
Me: Yes I'm fine mate.
Haddock – Really? (EYEBROW UP IN THE AIR – PLEASE PUT IT DOWN IT MAKES HIS EYES LIKE A LASER BREAM)
Me: Yeah fine mate.
Haddock: Good to hear it.

And then he goes to sit with his girlfriend and puts his arm round her. I go to the Model Fish Bar with Dobber, tell her about my arse and drown my sorrows in chips, mushy peas and a pickled onion. Even that ran away from me and rolled down Broad Street. I couldn't afford another. Skint.

11.52 p.m.
Laser BEAM not Laser BREAM. He's not a real fish. He's just named after one for code reasons.

Sunday 28.1.90

11.25 p.m.
ROUND DOBBER'S HOUSE.
     Dave Bridges TOTAL TWONGO is currently ruining a girly night with small-cock-big-gob bollocks. He clearly fancies Dobber and thinks the way to her heart is taking

the piss out of me. Well it's not and she's well loved up
with Fig. So piss off you twat and yes I am fat. I could
lose weight though. You'll ALWAYS be the boy who
ADMITTED in the pub tonight that She-Ra Princess of
Power turned him on. At least the people I fantasise about
are not cartoons and crap *He-Man* spin-offs.

Monday 29.1.90

6.35 p.m.

TALKING IN THE COMMON ROOM today about
cartoon characters you fancy. I brought it up taking
the piss out of Dave Bridges but people understood what
he meant. And I get called weird! Mia reckons she's
fancied Captain Caveman for 'years'. He's just a mass of
hair! AND loads of girls fancy Fred from *Scooby-Doo*.
When I pointed out he was a total dick everyone went
mental. But it's true. Shaggy does all the work.

Tell you what diary – I am Velma in *Scooby-Doo*
amongst loads of Daphne Dolly birds. I've got the brain
but I'm in a shit orange jumper and everyone is looking
at Daphne's legs.

I love school. I can't imagine not being there. I'm
shitting it about leaving.

Tuesday 30.1.90

7.12 p.m.

I ALREADY HAVE THE LETTER for my procedure.
It's on the 12th February, a Monday, so I can't eat

all weekend. How the hell am I going to manage that?!

I know you're going to think I sound melodramatic but I can feel death all over me.

8.39 p.m.
OK reading that back that is the most melodramatic thing ever but I'm so worried.

If they do tell me there's something really wrong do I tell people? No – because I know what it's like when you tell people horrible shit, like with what happened. They just pity you. Would I want sympathy shag off anyone? No I don't. I want to be shagged senseless for me and the shape of my bum – not because of my death arse.

A Haddock sympathy shag. It's a shag off Haddock but it doesn't count.

Wednesday 31.1.90

9.12 p.m.
MY MOCK RESULTS SPELT UCCA again. Why won't they just let me drop History. It's because Theatre Arts is seen as a bit of a pathetic A level, like General Studies. Oh bugger it – it's an A level. Who cares? I might not be here next year and I'm worried about this nonsense?!

Thursday 1.2.90

11.47 p.m.

JUST HAD A GIRLIE PISS-UP with Dobber. Who is now unconscious on the floor.

I have been drunk.

I have sobered it up.

Bad thoughts back. Take them away.

Friday 2.2.90

11.45 p.m.

I FELT BAD TONIGHT. ALL this hospital stuff is really getting to me. Anyway, Battered Sausage took me down the pub and said 'What's up Razza?' so I said 'Look. They think there might be something wrong with me and I've got to go into hospital.' Battered Sausage looked at me for ages and said really seriously 'Is it your flange?'. I was ON THE FLOOR pissing myself. No, Battered Sausage, it's not my flange it's my other bits. My tummy. Then he just was really sweet and said 'Don't worry about it Rae. No fucker messes. We will sort it.' Then he bought me an ACTUAL DRINK. The tightest sod in the world bought me a pint of Sam Smiths!

I need to be ill more often!

No I don't. I don't want to be a sympathy merchant.

Saturday 3.2.90

11.01 p.m.
SOME WOMEN ARE . . . they are just – I can't compete.

Tonight, this girl kept disappearing into the Vaults pub garden with a couple of blokes. They all came back laughing. I kept asking what they were doing and they kept giggling 'nothing!' and looking really gormless. Eventually Battered Sausage went out with her and came back and told me she was doing public performance FANNY FARTS. She can make big loud noises with her vagina!

How can you do that?! I've been trying since I've got home. No noise.

WHY would you want to share it . . . NO! Because the boys were loving it and saying what a 'top bird' she was.

No, Haddock didn't go out and experience it. He is beyond that sort of attention seeking shit and he was arguing with his girlfriend then snogging her all night after that. I don't stare but I can see he holds her very bloody tight.

Fanny farts and rejection and cider indigestion. All shit.

Sunday 4.2.90

8.34 p.m.

BATTERED SAUSAGE.

Let me just give you the state of affairs. After conversations with Mort I have to admit the following to myself –

1) I genuinely do actually love him.
2) If he asked me to marry him tomorrow I'd probably say yes.

But the thing with Battered Sausage is, if he fancies a slice of floozy he will completely ignore you.

Monday 5.2.90

10.12 p.m.

UNBELIEVABLE!! NELSON MANDELA HAS BEEN freed from prison!! Winnie met him outside the gates – it was really emotional.

Nelson looks nothing like his T-shirt. He's lost loads of weight.

No – I don't want to be a political prisoner. I'd rather be fat than put up with racist South Africans. Also, I want a diet that works quicker than 21 years in captivity with shoes that are too small to fit your feet. Thanks Special AKA for the historic knowledge.

Tuesday 6.2.90

8.46 p.m.

IT'S WEIRD BUT EVER SINCE Bethany went I've
been spending more time with people who aren't cows!
Like Shellboss, Chelsea and Ronni. Life is like a sandwich
– if you fill it with bollocks there's less room for Brie and
grapes.

10.12 p.m.
That last bit sounded weird but I know what I mean.

Wednesday 7.2.90

10.35 p.m.
1) If I want to go to university I need to do some
   bloody work.
2) Brain threatened badly by stuff.
3) Amber is Battered Sausage's ideal married
   woman. Haddock told me this for – I don't know
   what is the bloody reason.
4) Humungous crush on Michael Ball.
5) Have a massive period.
6) I want to be a brunette stunner.
7) I do not want to be starving taking hospital-
   strength laxatives when everyone else is in
   Benetton.

Thursday 8.2.90

10.22 p.m.
THE CHARTS ARE TOTALLY DEPRESSING at the moment.

'Nothing Ever Happens' by Del Amitri – Great song but says it like it is. AKA everything is SHIT, we all have boring crap lives then die and the Post Office is always shut when you need it.

'Hangin' Tough' by New Kids on the Block – I bloody hate it when BOYS pretend to be hard. I have never wanted a band to be involved in a plane crash more.

'Instant Replay' by Yell! – Two floppy-haired tossers wanking over Dan Hartman. Well, not over him but his tune.

Feel bad about the plane crash thing. I don't wish the New Kids would die I wish they would just fuck off.

Friday 9.2.90

11.56 p.m.
I'VE JUST BEEN DOWN THE Vaults. BRILLIANT night except for:

1) Everybody asking why I am jibbing on the beers tomorrow. I don't want to tell people what's

happening and that I'm going to be not leaving the toilet. In the wrong hands I could be murdered with that.

2) Battered Sausage kept putting Phil Collins on the jukebox and singing 'Rae wishes it would rain down . . . down on her!' He was trying to be sweet but it was just pissing me off.

3) Haddock. I'd been avoiding him because all this makes me feel even bloody uglier than normal. He cornered me by the French doors in the Vaults. Conversation as follows –

HADDOCK: Why aren't you out tomorrow?
ME: I've . . . I just need to do some work.
HADDOCK: No, you haven't Rae.
ME: Well, my mum thinks I'm not doing enough so . . .
HADDOCK: If you're going to lie to me you can fuck off.
WHY DIDN'T I THINK OF A DECENT LIE?

I can't tell Haddock what's happening. I can't. If he's nice to me I might cry. And all this. He's got a girlfriend. He's got a life. I don't even want him to know me now. I don't want him to know THIS Rae. I don't like me – why the hell should he?

Saturday 10.2.90

8.24 p.m.

I'VE TAKEN THE MEDICINE. IT'S hell. I've – I don't want to write it.

I'm eating white rice. That's it. At least I'll lose weight this weekend but not 5 stone.

I'm listening to 'Shine On' by the House of Love. I'd love to be in a garden in the house of love. Not in a council house crapping my guts out.

Sunday 11.2.90

7.36 p.m.

THIS IS HORRIBLE. I JUST told Mum that I wanted to pretend it wasn't happening. She said 'I know duck but it is happening and you've got to get on with it.'

If there is one thing I am bloody sick of in my life it is getting on with it. Also, I am bored of my mum's suggestion that I should have a nice game of canasta. 1) I can't play canasta 2) I'M 18 – NOT EIGHTY.

They always make mental people play cards. When I had my breakdown she kept making me play gin rummy. Well I'm not mad at the moment I'm REALLY ILL.

Ignore me, diary. Mum is being lovely. I've just got a really sore arse.

Monday 12.2.90

2.35 p.m.
I HAD A BARIUM ENEMA this morning. Oh it hurt
like fuck. I'm pissed off medically and pissed off
completely. I asked the nurse doing it if she could see
anything but she said I had to see the doctor. They never
tell you anything.

Anyway I can eat now – so I have been doing. LIKE
YOU WOULD NOT BELIEVE. Chantrell's Lemon Curd Tart
– I LOVE YOU.

9.12 p.m.
There's a new couple in *Coronation Street*. She's skinny
and pretty.

SURPRISE SURPRISE!

Mum told me today that Mr Chantrell the baker hasn't
been to bed for 20 years. He sleeps by his ovens. I don't
know if it's true or not but he makes the best stuff in
history. My family have always abused his bread. My
brother used to get an entire loaf, scoop it out, fill it with
bacon and cheese and call it a Piggy Malone. Fuck knows
why.

Food is helping today. It's not been a good day.

Tuesday 13.2.90

7.36 p.m.

I'M STILL SORE. I'M STILL eating like a pig. I'm still watching shit on TV.

I'm glad I'm not at school tomorrow. I can't deal with roses and chocolates.

Wednesday 14.2.90

11.23 a.m.

JUST FOUND A CARRIER BAG pushed through the door. Inside there's a Beats International single and a little Valentine's Day ode scribbled on a bit of notepaper in Battered Sausage's mad handwriting. It's VERY sweet. It's not Haddock turning up and carrying me off like thingy in *An Officer and a Gentleman* but it will do!

I am very loved – it's just in the wrong way.

Thursday 15.2.90

9.01 p.m.

YES – SO ONE GIRL at school got her 2CV full of flowers and balloons by her boyfriend. Yes – another girl is going SKIING at EASTER with her boyfriend (you can't revise for your A level Chemistry exam on a chairlift love) BUT I got a handwritten ode and 'Dub Be Good To Me' and that's a special thing.

I also have an appointment to go and see the specialist next Tuesday. Humongous nerves now.

Friday 16.2.90

1.45 a.m.

I'VE JUST BEEN TO OLIVERS. Haddock walked me home. I AM SO SICK OF MOANING ABOUT SEX DESERT DROUGHT when a lust oasis grows legs and escorts me back through dark passages like a knight in really tight jeans.

I wish I could act like a cow rather than look like one.

Haddock is physical perfection. That is the least of it though. Regardless of what I or he believes, he has a totally brilliant personality. Protective and humorous . . .

Saturday 17.2.90

6.55 p.m.

SORRY, FELL ASLEEP. I'M ALWAYS doing that. I feel very bad at the moment. Home totally mixed up. When I write I feel better.

Chelsea has just been round. Nice attempt at superiority but not quite making it. I know her game. Typical, underhand comment – 'Oh, me and Haddock's girlfriend might go away together for a holiday.' She has TOTALLY got the Haddock knowledge and could actually destroy everything in my life.

TELL HER THEN!
My friend, impart then to win the battle,
And rub rhine into the graze
But know that sweet retribution falls onto those
Who dare to encourage the thick hand of fate
I'm not afraid your slate is not clean.
Your greenhouse is glass
Your secrets are stone
I have them in my hand
Kill my shed. I kill yours.

I didn't mean rhine I meant brine. Shakespeare always shoves it in. It's salty water shit.

I'm going down the Vaults.

Sunday 18.2.90

2.35 a.m.
I'VE GOT TO WRITE. IT'S late but I've got to write. The last couple of days have just been crazy. I've spent tons of time with Haddock and last night I ended up having this massive conversation with him about stuff. I wasn't going to tell him about him about medical things but when you sit down with him you just feel like you can tell him anything. It's weird. It's like being with a really nice woman who is also just the most horny man on the planet.

Anyway he told me off for not telling him and then he grabbed hold of my hand and said 'you'll be all right' and winked. I nearly died. I wanted to leap on top of him but instead I said 'fuck off you soppy twat' and punched him.

Sometimes I wish he'd just act like a knob to me because it would be bloody easier to deal with.

Monday 19.2.90

3.22 p.m.

I AM SO SICK OF not telling people what I feel. I'm sick of being fat. I'm sick of slapping Haddock instead of hugging him and I'm sick of hearing Rod Stewart on his downtown train shagging young blondes. Piss off and date someone your own age you gravelly old bastard. Uncle Disgusting. He should be knobbing Cher or Tina Turner.

Hospital tomorrow. Yes I'm scared.

Tuesday 20.2.90

1.12 p.m.

THERE'S NO EASY WAY TO say this. I have a benign tumour in my colon.

It's called a polyp. Some people get them in their nose. I've got one up my bum. I'm not going to die from it but they do need to take it out in the very near future.

It IS funny, diary. I laughed when the specialist told me. Mum looked really concerned but it's like God is having a laugh with my life. I'm huge and now I've got something else that means I will almost certainly die a virgin. In the past I've worried that I've had every illness under the sun from rabies to a brain haemorrhage and now I have a REAL bum growth. You could not make it up! It's my life and it's BONKERS as hell.

I'm telling some people but not everyone.

4.26 p.m.
No fuck it – I'm telling everyone. It's not my fault. Love me, love my polyp.

Wednesday 21.2.90

10.47 p.m.
I WAS MOPING AROUND TILL Mum said 'Rachel. You're not bloody dying. Go out with your friends!'. So I went ice skating with the Gads which was a total laugh until I fell over and someone shouted 'earthquake'.

Told Mum. She said ice skating was just a craze and would end up at the back of everyone's cupboard. That's not the point Mum and Torvill and Dean with their twenty gold medals for 'Bolero' would disagree.

Nearly a year since I had a snog. Total insignificance.

Thursday 22.2.90

7.10 p.m.
IT MUST BE SIGNIFICANT OR I wouldn't mention it.

Friday 23.2.90

10.57 p.m.

CHELSEA WAS WEIRD DOWN THE pub tonight. It's just the same as Bethany. I always end up with a pretty girl who looks down on me.

Dear Eleanor Roosevelt. You think no-one can make you feel inferior without your consent. Have you bloody met Chelsea?

Sometimes I think I might be the problem. Then I think 'No. I am sick of being the problem. The one that's nuts. The one in the ward. I can't be the problem in my problem life all the bloody time.'

Saturday 24.2.90

10.14 a.m.

'GOT TO HAVE YOUR LOVE' by Mantronix is not just ALL CLASSIC ACE, it's my Haddock tune right now.

No Mum. I'm not turning it down. I have a bowel polyp. I need MUSIC.

Sunday 25.2.90

2.13 a.m.

I'VE JUST RETURNED FROM A particularly brilliant Gad night. Battered Sausage's prime concern was slice and nothing else. I think he might have got off with Jasmine. I think he might be sexually frustrated. I hope it's temporary. I can't cope with this. The real Battered Sausage is worth his weight in gold. This one is a massive knob.

Haddock was not out. I might bomb where he works. With him not in work obviously!

Or anyone else. I don't want people to die for my love needs. I'm not the IRA.

Monday 26.2.90

8.31 p.m.

IT'S WEIRD HOW PEOPLE HAVE reacted to me being ill. Mum keeps saying I'm not ill which is an interesting way to view a REAL LIFE TUMOUR.

The thing is I'm not making a big deal of it. I'm just telling everyone I know when the time is right.

Tuesday 27.2.90

7.21 p.m.

WE WERE WETTING OURSELVES IN the common room today! Chelsea dumped her long-term boyfriend. BIG shock – but he bought her that shit Michael Bolton record for Valentine's Day and she said 'as soon as I saw the cover I knew it was over.' That is completely fair. You can't go out with a boy you don't respect musically. If Haddock liked Bros, New Kids or Shakin' Stevens (back in the charts – FUCK OFF

SHAKEY!) I would not . . . Yes I WOULD fancy him but I'd have to sort him out. HA HA HA! in many ways!!

Wednesday 28.2.90

6.24 p.m.
FEBRUARY, YOU'VE BEEN A SOD! New month new start!

Who IS Ben Liebrand?! He's remixing everything to shit.

Thursday 1.3.90

7.39 p.m.
BATTERED SAUSAGE WAS MEANT TO come round last night to take me for a drink. Well, I say he was meant to – unless he tells me otherwise he nearly always comes round on a Wednesday. It's like a tradition. Anyway last night he didn't. I sat at my desk listening to *Bummed* getting more and more pissed off. By 'Brain Dead' I knew he wasn't coming. So me and Shaun Ryder spent the evening together. The good thing about Shaun Ryder is he's not a complete TWAT that is only interested in pulling women and getting his todger out for a laugh in the Vaults beer garden.

Friday 2.3.90

5.48 p.m.

I THINK I'M BEING A bit unfair on Battered Sausage. He's not my husband. I can't expect him to stop wanting sex just because I'm a bit . . . needy. I AM needy, diary. This is because of SHIT! EVERYTHING!

11.35 p.m.

Haddock not out again tonight. According to his girlfriend, the night shift pays more and he is saving up to go away.

Oh don't go. Or take me with you. I'd probably be all right if I was with Haddock.

So Friday night was good but – BLOODY HELL I WISH MRS BARK WOULD CLOSE HER KITCHEN CURTAINS.

Saturday 3.3.90

1.10 p.m.

WELL, BATTERED SAUSAGE HAS JUST come over. 'Can I have my cardigan back? I can't stop. I'm going to Bedford. Might see you tonight but probably not.' Why do I love the cocky, womanising twat?! Why have I got a mate that's a cocky, womanising twat? Why do I get possessive? Why do I get worked up? WHY CAN'T I JUST BE MYSELF?

Sunday 4.3.90

8.02 a.m.

WHEN I WAS IN THE pub last night Battered
Sausage said hello and then I sort of ignored him
and he said something like 'Fine Rae.'

Then all night it was about other women. I give up on
men – they are either all over you, completely ignoring
you or earning £5 an hour stacking shelves.

Monday 5.3.90

6.35 p.m.

MUM IS ACTING EVEN WEIRDER than normal.
She keeps disappearing down the phone box all the
time. Now the rumour is that two women are running
some sort of helpline for lesbians from 63401. That might
just be a totally made-up rumour because Stamford is shit
BUT has my mum gone to work for them? She's not a
lesbian.

FUCK!

No. My mum is not a lesbian. My head is spiralling out
of control. Her second husband is gay but that does not
make her one. Now she is coming back. I can see her
charging up the road.

The thing is, nothing would surprise me anymore.

Tuesday 6.3.90

9.13 p.m.
I CORNERED MUM TONIGHT AND asked her if anything was going on. She said 'Rachel, I've got a few things to tell you. I'm trying to get Adnan over permanently so we can get married (I totally knew this already). Also I've had a tattoo of him done on my bottom.'

She then said 'Woo-hoo!' and pulled down her trousers slightly and yes there now is a drawing of a black bodybuilder in red pants on her buttock.

And I'm meant to go to school tomorrow and write an essay about Chaucer.

She said 'What do you think?'. I said truly and honestly that I thought it looked bloody awful. Then she said 'Oh it's a bit of fun.' No Mum – Alton Towers is a bit of fun. Permanently scarring your body with a six-inch picture of a bloke in tight pants ON YOUR ARSE is . . . WHAT IF I DID THAT?!

I'm sitting here listening to 'Closest Thing to Heaven' by The Kane Gang. It's beautiful and tender and gentle – it's everything a massive bum tattoo isn't.

Sometimes I feel like a mad rare flower in a field full of weeds and nutters.

No I'm a weed – but a good weird weed.

No Mum, I do not want a fucking Ovaltine. That does not make up for you acting like a child.

Wednesday 7.3.90

8.35 p.m.
I'm sitting here with a candle.

I had a huge debate at school today about tattoos. People actually think they want one. Mia has already planned a seahorse on her tummy. Yes she is gorgeous now but what about when she has a baby or something. I pointed out that my mum's tattoo probably wobbles like jelly when she walks.

I'm never having one. I don't like my body and I'm not buggering it up more with scribbles.

Thursday 8.3.90

10.35 p.m.
WHAT GETS TO ME IS I'm expected to be sensible even though Mum acts like she is actually 12. And she's been doing ridiculous stuff for years!

1) Went punk in about 1980. Blue hair, red hair, green hair. When we lived in Rutland Road! RUTLAND ROAD!! We were still going to church every week at this point.
2) Married a Latin teacher from a posh school. A LATIN TEACHER?!
3) We went to Izmir, Turkey for holidays because second husband went to teach English there. We ended up up a mountain with a Kurdish family slaughtering a goat.

4) I LIVE IN A COUNCIL ESTATE AND I WAS UP A
   MOUNTAIN HAVING SALADS AND ROASTED-
   OVER-A-SPIT GOAT WITH PEOPLE WHO LIVE
   IN CAVES. It's like David Attenborough not real
   life!
5) We went to Izmir zoo. A keeper was playing with
   a lion cub outside the cage. The lion cub attacked
   my ankle. My mum didn't help – SHE JUST TOOK
   A PHOTO. Yes it was just like a big kitten and
   playing but IT WOULDN'T LET GO.
6) THEN second husband moved to Casablanca and
   we went there.
7) He ran off with a man because he is GAY. Mum
   met a Moroccan champion bodybuilder and two
   minutes later they are going to get married.

HOW IS ANY OF THAT NORMAL?!

Then at other times she just sits in the chair looking as
miserable as sin and any noise I make is a DISASTER.

Friday 9.3.90

6.32 p.m.

WELL FACT-FANS, THE REASON WHY my mum
decided to tell me about the tattoo now is that one
of the people that looked after her in hospital described
her in a letter as a 'tattooed, obese woman'. She is angry
and wants me (as I am the 'educated one') to write a letter
complaining. She says though it's factually accurate that
she is obese, her tattoo has nothing to do with her 'ladies
reconstruction'.

52

I told her I was going down the pub. Which I am! Goodbye!

Saturday 10.3.90

1.04 a.m.

NO HADDOCK TONIGHT BUT HADDOCK TOMORROW apparently. Me and Dobber had a great night. Even though tonight she admitted that Rod Stewart 'had something'. Yes Dobber he has something – rickets and dentures. Snog him and you'll suck his teeth out. Battered Sausage loved this and said I was 'fucking funny Big Razza'. I am occasionally very funny but sadly also permanently fat as a house. The Elephant Man got more action.

Sunday 11.3.90

2.34 a.m.

I DON'T KNOW WHAT SHELF stacking does to a man or if it's just because I haven't seen him for yonks but Haddock – OH I WANT YOU TO SEE HIM. He is BEYOND IT ALL and he seemed genuinely pleased to see me. Battered Sausage had told him about my mum's tattoo. In fact when Battered Sausage picked me up tonight he asked to see my mum's tattoo. She didn't show him but I suppose it's only a matter of time. Perhaps she'll put a shot in the *Mercury*.

Anyway Haddock thinks tattoos are a waste of money.

I KNOW, he sounds very middle-aged doesn't he sometimes?! BUT he's not. He's just HIM – he doesn't really seem to give a fuck what other people think AT ALL. He's like me but with a knob and a six-pack.

He's not like me – I do give a fuck what people think ALL the time and whether they like me or not. I need Haddock 'don't give a shit' lessons.

I'm listening to The Beloved's 'The Sun Rising'. It's not. It's pitch black but it's just brilliant.

6.23 p.m.
I have written Mum's letter. I am particularly proud of 'The reference to my tattoo bears no relevance to my medical condition. The presence of a bodybuilder on my buttock would not affect my urinary tract.'

Mum can't decide whether to send it or not. I don't care – she's buying me a single as payment.

Oh Haddock. You're in my head a lot. Even when I'm writing letters about my mum's bladder.

Monday 12.3.90

6.13 p.m.
MUM HAD NO LUCK BUYING my single today from Woolworths. This was because she was asking for a single by Rogan Josh. Rogan Josh is a curry not a musician. I wanted 'Infinity' by GURU Josh. She's now given me £2 as it's too embarrassing for her to go back.

It's too embarrassing to go in Woolies but apparently fine that the whole of Lincolnshire knows she's got a permanent picture of a bodybuilder on her bum.

The fair is coming soon. Perhaps Mum can be the tattooed lady on a stall and make some money. It can't be any worse than Rhona the old girl who has a stand every year that is actually just a fat woman sitting in a sawdust pit with a load of terrified mice. HA HA HA!!

Tuesday 13.3.90

NAOMI FAILED HER DRIVING TEST again today. She stalled on St Peter's Hill AGAIN. She was in tears in the common room. I told her not to worry – she can always take the test in Peterborough! This didn't cheer her up much.

Some people need to count their blessings and be a bit less melodramatic. At least she has parents who can afford a car AND lessons. My mum is currently claiming that my Guru Josh record has left her 'short'.

Wednesday 14.3.90

5.38 p.m.
SHELLBOSS ATTACKED ME TODAY. NOT verbally but with a piece of stuffing from the chair in a comedy way! Then we had a MASSIVE cushion fight till Mr Mills reminded us we have A levels in 3 months. WE BLOODY KNOW. We need to let off some pressure, man!

Thursday 15.3.90

I'VE GOT A PERIOD COMING. I can tell this because a) I'm in AGONY b) Today I cried at 'Uptown, Uptempo

Woman' by Randy Edelman – which is actually just a
piece of soppy Yank shit.

Periods hurt but at least they prove the girl in me is
still alive and not killed by crisps.

Friday 16.3.90

7.32 p.m.

I CAN'T GO DOWN THE pub tonight. I can barely
move. I've got 2 hot water bottles and I'm sandwiched
between them.

Ponstan tablets are shit. Libra regular towels are shit.
Morrissey is not shit.

Please, please, please let me get what I want. I can tell
you what in living memory it WILL be the bloody first
time EVER.

Saturday 17.3.90

11.35 p.m.

P ERHAPS MY PERIOD IS MAKING me
hypersensitive but Battered Sausage was ALL OVER
Jasmine Bobbs tonight like a rash. Now I feel weird about
this because . . . I don't know. When Battered Sausage
gets a piece all he cares about is slice and I completely go
out the window. I don't need that right now. Dobber said
he is totally sharking round Jasmine and when we all
sang 'Sausage Techniques' to the Pearl and Dean theme
tune WHICH WE ALWAYS DO WHEN HE'S ON THE PULL
he looked angry. Which means it's serious.

I just know everyone is going to end up married and I am going to end up talking to the grannies table at the wedding doing the conga and pretending everything is OK when it is NOT.

Sunday 18.3.90

9.34 p.m.

RANG MORT AND TALKED FOR ages. She totally thinks Battered Sausage is after Jasmine. The thing is Jasmine is LOVELY. You can't hate women like this. She is beautiful but great to be with too. And she's always listening to David Bowie. She was the one that told me that on 'Starman' he doesn't sing 'picking my bum on Channel 2' but 'pick him up on Channel 2'. She knows LYRICS too – how can I compete?!

Monday 19.3.90

8.12 p.m.

I'M LISTENING TO DOLLAR. OH I don't bloody CARE. I love 'Hand Held in Black and White'. It's a great song.

Jasmine Bobbs in the common room today started going on about how funny Battered Sausage was. Oh yes HILARIOUS. Except when you've heard him ask for a bit of battered flange in Des's Superchip for the millionth time and then it's actually not funny AT ALL.

Ignore me I'm jealous. It's my Scorpio moon it makes me nuts.

Tuesday 20.3.90

11.22 p.m.

SOD OFF EVERYTHING BASICALLY.

Wednesday 21.3.90

10.32 p.m.

ME AND BATTERED SAUSAGE HAVE just been down the Vaults. Oh the big prick does make me laugh. I wish he didn't but he does. Tonight he was singing 'Love Shack' by The B-52's and shouting 'LOVE SHACK BABY' at me! I think you had to be there.

Thursday 22.3.90

5.13 p.m.

MRS BARK CAUGHT ME CHECKING the door again and again today. She muttered something so I said 'It has a habit of unlocking itself.' No it doesn't. I just have it in my head that I've left it open when I know I haven't.

I'm not taking any shit from a family called Bark who called their son Mark.

That's not fair. They are all right.

I'm having the heaviest period ever.

Friday 23.3.90

11.29 p.m.
OH HADDOCK, YOU MUST BE a multimillionaire by now the amount you are working. WILL YOU JUST COME OUT AND BE ALL FITNESS?! When his girlfriend tells me he's not coming out I try to look not bothered but I think I fail.

Saturday 24.3.90

11.56 p.m.
DEAR SATURDAY NIGHT. YOU WERE a bit of a twat.

1) Battered Sausage all over Jasmine Bobbs again.
2) Battered Sausage singing Candy Flip's 'Strawberry Fields Forever' as 'Strawberry Ice Cream Forever' was funny at 7.30 p.m. but NOT by 8 p.m. and CERTAINLY NOT by 10.30 p.m.
3) Ryan Bates kept putting 'Birdhouse In Your Soul' by They Might Be Giants on the jukebox and asking me what I thought of it. Not content with the answers 'utter shit', 'total bollocks' and 'twee indie shit' he asked me again and I snapped at him 'just fuck off.'
4) Then I felt bad and guilty but he'd left the pub so I couldn't apologise.
5) NO HADDOCK AGAIN.

6) Had 3 bags of beef and mustard crisps, 2 pints of cider (which according to Naomi at school are 'cream cakes in a glass') and then some chips. Can't stop eating. Don't want to stop. Empty and full all at the same time. Usual, usual. Never gets better.

7) Cleaned the heads of my cassette player with toilet paper. Got loads of gunk off it but then got a big bit of Andrex jammed in the machinery. I need to get some tweezers.

I'm going to see the fair being put up with Dobber tomorrow. It's something to do and she's lovely.

Sunday 25.3.90

10.28 a.m.

ASKED MUM FOR SOME TWEEZERS. She said 'Oh, are you doing your eyebrows?' I said 'No – I'm doing my cassette heads.' She looked a bit disappointed. She probably thought I was finally changing into a real woman.

I'm not.

7.48 p.m.

We went down the fair. Usual rides. Big Wheel, Noah's Ark, Tip Top, Mexican Hat, Hook-a-Duck and the women who runs the cake walk is STILL there. Me and Dobber agree – she must be over 80. Just RETIRE WOMAN! Anyway, Dobber and me are going again tomorrow.

I can't wait to retire. I know I haven't started work yet

but I just want no pressure, to live in Edmonds Close and walk in fields.

Monday 26.3.90

9.36 p.m.

I NEARLY KILLED SOMEONE TONIGHT.

Dobber and me went to the fair. It was a laugh – it always is with her. We went on the usuals but then we went down Bath Row and on this new ride called the Zodiac. It's like this massive round disc with a seat all the way round it and it bounces you around. We went on it, they were playing 'Soul Finger' by The Bar-Kays and it went CRAZY. It was throwing people around everywhere and it threw me on to this middle-aged beardy bloke. He took it really well but I think I broke his wrist. Imagine if I'd fallen on to a townie twat. Everyone was already laughing. Why do I do this SHIT? I had the same thing at Alton Towers. Situations where I stick out are not good situations. Theme parks and fairs, pubs, school – actually everywhere except my bedroom!

Sometimes I catch myself in shop windows and I take up so much space. I see my outline. It's not me. Wish I could take my fucking skin off. RIP IT OFF.

One good thing – Dobber won a goldfish on Hook-a-Duck. Yes she is 18. We don't care. We've called it Silk Cut!

Tuesday 27.3.90

8.55 p.m.

I RESENT YOU AT THE moment, diary. I didn't want
to write you.

Fate, once encouraged, can twist horribly and
vengefully. Now that does sound melodramatic but it's
true. Battered Sausage is going out with Jasmine
Bobbs.

You know FULL well how I feel.

The winner takes it sodding all.

Wednesday 28.3.90

8.25 p.m.

S ILK CUT DIED TODAY. FAIR fish never last long.
In fact my sugar dummy has lasted longer – which is
a bloody miracle.

I'm so pissed off.

Thursday 29.3.90

9.54 p.m.

I SHOULD BE AT A party. I'm ill. I can't get out the
house tonight. I'm saying it's a sore throat. It's not.

I want to sit down with Battered Sausage and talk to
him.

Dear Battered Sausage,
Forget all the bravado. All the lads, everything and just get in touch with what you actually FEEL! DO YOU ACTUALLY GIVE A SHIT?!

I feel numb in life. I want out of this town. I want out of my bad points. Angry, angry, angry, ANGRY and very paranoid. Feel my mental condition slip – No, I don't. Probably all this is normal A level syndrome.

No it's not. I'M A MESS.

Friday 30.3.90

Late.

WENT DOWN THE VAULTS. BATTERED Sausage and Jasmine all loved up. I feel like a spare part. Like the pantomime horse from *Rentaghost*.

Haddock won his girlfriend a cuddly poodle thing at the fair. Apparently he's good at throwing balls in buckets or something. They were taking the piss but it was sweet. It was funny. It was Haddock.

And then he disappears into the night. No, I'll walk my own way home thanks Haddock. Actually I'll go down the Meadows and listen to Kate Bush. 'Cloudbusting' in the dark. It works. Then I will come home to write this and eat CRAP.

Diary – I feel so lonely I could die.

Shit – now I sound like Elvis. He ate himself to death too. The difference is he'd had sex and a career before he did.

Saturday 31.3.90

4.35 p.m.

DOBBER IS DOING THE 24 hour famine for World Vision. Apparently a normal person can fast for a day safely. A NORMAL PERSON. What's one of those? She wanted to know if I thought Snakebite was included on the fast. Er . . . yes!

So we're not going out tonight.

On days like this 'Bedsitter' by Soft Cell IS my life. I am fooling myself I'm having fun a lot of the time but inside . . . I'm going. I can feel myself going.

Sunday 1.4.90

10.19 p.m.

IT'S KICKED OFF IN LONDON about the poll tax. Humungous riots – THATCHER, WE ARE NOT PAYING. I feel sorry for the police horses but that's the price you pay for having eyes on the side of your face. You are handy to the law.

I would love to go down and join them but I know I'd have a panic attack. St. John Ambulance probably have enough to cope with without me having a turn.

Monday 2.4.90

6.39 p.m.

I HATE THATCHER BUT AT the same time how do you get this confidence that she has? The confidence to always just do what the hell you like. She doesn't seem to care that everyone wants to blow her up. I'm worried about EVERYTHING. Who is the psycho? Is it me or her?

Mum says I could be prime minister if I wanted to be. Mum, I can't leave the house properly most days. Haven't you noticed? How could I nip abroad to sort things out with my head. 'Miss Earl – Mr Bush will see you now about the crisis!' 'Hang on – let me check the iron is off for the 36th time.' It wouldn't work would it?!

It is sweet she has faith in me though.

Tuesday 3.4.90

12.38 a.m.

'MY DEDICATION' HAS JUST BEEN on the radio. I can feel everything slipping away. Friends, school, the pub . . . it's all going.

Numb – that's how I feel. Bloody numb.

Revision.

> VOID
> Great big void
> Pray for its temporary stay
> I just need to be with you.

I remember the good times
I thought they were bad
Let me hold onto them
And you
And life

Wednesday 4.4.90

6.34 p.m.

MORT IS GETTING US A special yearbook printed – we've all got a load of questions to fill out with stuff like Pet Hates, Pet Likes, What Will You Miss Most About School, What Will You Miss Least About School and What is Your Greatest Achievement. As this yearbook will be around for eternity I am going to be bloody careful about what I write!

10.56 p.m.
It's taken me an hour to fill out my nickname section!

Thursday 5.4.90

4.56 p.m.

WHAT IS MY GREATEST ACHIEVEMENT? I asked this in the common room today. Mort said it is definitely getting sent to the deputy headmistress for answering the question 'What are guerrilla tactics?' with 'Throwing bananas'! YES!

What will I miss least about school? Honestly just the lasagne.

6.38 p.m.

Yes Mum, I am still filling in this yearbook. I know this is hard for you to understand but it's actually vitally important that I get this right.

Going to put the time I went into the lunch queue twice and had 4 fishcakes and loads of other stuff for a greatest achievement. It is legendary!

Friday 6.4.90

7.33 p.m.

HANDED MY YEARBOOK THING IN today. Mine was a bit long but now I'm wondering why I mentioned the fishcake thing. WHY? I don't want to be remembered as the fat jokey one. That's got to stop. I don't have to be that anymore. It can be OVER. I think that's the scary thing though. I don't know what else I can be.

Oh shut up Rae.

'My World' by Secret Affair. Impossible to feel bad listening to this though I'm giving it a good try.

Saturday 7.4.90

11.22 p.m.

HADDOCK ASKED ME TONIGHT IF I had mentioned him in my yearbook. WEIRD!

Er . . . He didn't mention me in his last year! What is my greatest achievement? Not jumping on top of Haddock every time I see him and licking him to death like an excited Alsatian.

No I didn't write that but it's true!

I have mentioned him but I'm not telling him that.

Sunday 8.4.90

9.24 p.m.

I HAD A TERRIBLE PANIC attack today. All this talk of yearbooks just reminds me it's nearly the end and I've got to go in hospital. I ended up in the field down the back listening to the *Good Morning, Vietnam* soundtrack feeling the white flashes in my head and my heart stopping and everything shutting down. Felt better after Louis Armstrong. It is a wonderful world but that's hard to remember sometimes.

Oh diary, I am a mess. I'm a mess in a mess. I know you're sick of the self-pitying crap but who else can I tell? No-one wants to know.

Monday 9.4.90

11.26 p.m.

S POKE TO MORT FOR AGES today. She totally understands. She's going to try to ring the printers to see if she can get it taken out. Mort gets it. Mort ALWAYS gets it.

Tuesday 10.4.90

10.15 p.m.

I JUST MADE THE GREATEST compilation tape
called *Dusk.*

'Love and Affection' – Joan Armatrading
'Stay With Me Till Dawn' – Judie Tzuke
'My Oh My' – Sad Café
'The Man With The Child In His Eyes' – Kate Bush
'Night Owl' – Gerry Rafferty

And loads of other great stuff. How do you get a job
putting records together? 'Now That's What I Call Music'
NEED ME! Mum always says it's who you know. How do
you meet people in the know? Not by sitting in your
bedroom on Edinburgh Road without a bloody home
phone.

Mort couldn't get hold of the printers.

Wednesday 11.4.90

4.58 p.m.

THE PRINTERS ARE COMMITTED. SO forever I will
be the fishcake girl.

Great.

Thursday 12.4.90

ASKED MY MUM TODAY IF I could have a year off. The answer is 'No'. A big loud 'No'. Apparently we can't afford it. We can afford tattoos but not the break I need after all the pandemonium (thank you Milton for something). Also, it's not so much the money but the fact I need to get away and start again. If I stay here it's bad for me. That's true – but no-one has noticed I can't actually travel anywhere.

Friday 13.4.90

3.29 p.m.

MUM DOESN'T WANT ME HERE so she can have a Moroccan love palace harem.
No. I don't want to write. I'm sick of writing it.

Saturday 14.4.90

11.38 p.m.

CONVERSATION BETWEEN ME AND HADDOCK tonight –

HADDOCK: Are you alright?
ME: Yes. Why?
HADDOCK: Because you don't seem yourself.
ME: You know. Stuff.

HADDOCK: It'll work out.

ME: Will it? You're sure of that are you?

HADDOCK: No. But why shouldn't it? You're funny. You know loads about stuff. You've been through all sorts of shit and come through it.

ME: You might be right.

I don't believe that for a second BUT this is why I love him.

All this whilst Battered Sausage was talking about 'muffs'.

Sunday 15.4.90

9.25 a.m.

I DREAMT ABOUT HADDOCK LAST night. Someone stroked my hair and I looked round and he was there. Smiling, eyebrow ten foot in the air.

His eyebrow wasn't detached from his face by the way. It was just high.

> Sorry if I seem cross and mardy
> I'm frustrated, I need tongue, too lardy.
> WHY CAN'T I BE NORMAL?!
> I'll write in blue ink
> All the things I wanted to say but couldn't
> The blue and the red
> The good I felt will be useless fuel
> I want to give in but I can't. I won't.

71

Monday 16.4.90

5.43 p.m.

I DON'T THINK I'VE EVER been so unhappy at home. My mum is a constant bitch. Totally oblivious to everything I am going through. It's so uncomfortable. I spend all my time upstairs. She is so selfish.

I've nothing or rather no-one to live for. There are shallower and nastier people than me. Why am I the one that is lonely?! All this shit – when will this end? I know I sound like a crappy sympathy merchant but how can I be when no-one will ever see this?!

I'm so fucking repulsive. Oh that's a load of rubbish as well. People are in immeasurably worse difficulties than me. I just feel so used all the time. Like the eternal agony aunt with just a desk and a cup of tea and NO BLOODY SEX. I must be worthless. I can't do anything and then I punch myself and hit myself. Why not? I deserve it.

I'm a mutant. I'm so ungrateful but I can't control it. I'm loud and funny but men always hate me before they like me. I'm a monster. I'm abnormal.

Look, how would you feel if all your friends, even your mum, had somebody to love. Always the fat gooseberry. I must be deficient. I should sleep.

Tuesday 17.4.90

9.12 p.m.

THAT LAST ENTRY DIDN'T MAKE me seem terribly well did it? Sometimes I'm not at the moment.

Wednesday 18.4.90

2.02 p.m.

I'M TRYING TO REVISE WHILST Paula Abdul is on TV flirting with a cartoon cat. More people trying to sleep with drawings! Try a real person! You might like it.

'Opposites Attract!' – No they don't Abdul.

Thursday 19.4.90

7.32 p.m.

MRS BARK IS ATTEMPTING TO remove a dead hedgehog from the patch of grass outside our house whilst I listen to 'All of My Heart' by ABC.

She's just called to her husband to get a shovel. Mrs Bark – you're ruining MY SONG!

Friday 20.4.90

11.45 p.m.

HADDOCK TOLD ME TONIGHT HE used to have trouble getting off with people unless he was pissed.

The thing is, a lot of people think Haddock is a right cold bastard. He's not. Actually people think that mainly because he's so fit – they assume he can't be lovely. It's like when people assume stuff about me. I get fat prejudice – he gets fit prejudice.

I can't feel sorry for him though. I'd kill to be him. No – I'd kill to be with him.

Saturday 21.4.90

1.12 a.m.

HADDOCK HAD BEEN CRYING TONIGHT. There's no hope if someone who looks and acts like him is miserable with the love thing too. He was sniffing with a snot bubble.

> MUCUS
> Red with pain
> You can have my tissues
> To mop up your issues
> Hanky no panky
> Forget your worst and terrible fears
> Don't care about your snot

If that's the worst you've got
Your mucus is not detriment to me.

Sunday 22.4.90

4.31 p.m.

HELLO DIARY, LAST BASTION OF sanity in a world gone completely stark raving mad.

Well, big event, I'm going in hospital on May 1st and they are going to put me to sleep.

The letter came yesterday but Mum hid it because she wanted me to have a lovely Saturday night after the revising. That was quite nice I suppose if slightly still treating me LIKE I AM BLOODY 7.

Major phobia about the anaesthetic. Mum is going to ring up and ask if I can just be sedated. Yes – that would be good. I'd rather be in pain than asleep.

No I can't cope but there's a party at Fig's tonight. The last big one before all the exams.

Monday 23.4.90

10.12 p.m.

USUAL. I AM ALWAYS DUMPED unceremoniously in the kitchen reading the *Daily Mail* eating choc ices. Still it was a good laugh. Had vodka and didn't give a shit much after that. Why can't they just give me some Smirnoff in hospital?

Tuesday 24.4.90

11.01 p.m.

HAVE TO HAVE ANAESTHETIC. NO way out.
Mum did try.

Weird evening, weird day but BRILLIANT.

The day was beautiful. Sunny – it makes such a
difference. We had a massive water fight at school with
all the classics. Then I went to ring up Mort but she was
engaged so I rang up Dobber. There were stupid cows at
63401 so I went down 62929. Rang up Mort, talked to her
for YONKS. Then I saw this bloke on a bike right outside
the box and I thought 'you rude berk sod' but it was
HADDOCK!! Come to see me! To deliver a note! HEART
STOPPAGE! He came to look for me. Mum told him where
I was.

THEN as soon as I got in the door Battered Sausage
knocked. He was in a really good mood.

School classic. Battered Sausage and Haddock
Classic. Why do I have A levels and a tumour up my
arse?

Wednesday 25.4.90

8.13 p.m.

MUM HAS BOUGHT ME SOME pyjamas from
Bewise. They are blue and white striped old man
pyjamas. It's better than a nightshirt with Betty Boop on it!

She's also bought me a washbag for the hospital. I

know she is just trying to be nice but I'm frightened to
death. I'd rather just forget it's happening.

Thursday 26.4.90

5.21 p.m.
DIARY, I AM GOING TO Olivers tonight because I
might be dead next week and I want to have some
more SHIMMIES!! Plus Haddock is coming out. I'm not
missing out on that!

   I might leave a note – if I do go into a coma just bring
Haddock's arse to the bed and I will recover.

Friday 27.4.90

2.48 a.m.
WHAT A NIGHT!
         Oh it was brilliant. Everyone was at Olivers. It
was WELL funny! Ronni was pissed and during Bizz
Nizz's 'Don't Miss The Party Line' she shouted 'Hey DJ –
WHERE'S THE BASS?' at COMPLETELY the wrong
moment. EVERYONE looked. Then Battered Sausage was
going mad to Snap's 'The Power' and making us all go on
the floor laughing. Haddock danced all night – even to
'Kingston Town' by UB40. NO-ONE can dance well to that
– HE CAN! He is 'Black Velvet' by Alannah Myles. He is
Elvis before the cheeseburgers. I am Elvis after.

Saturday 28.4.90

Midnight

MY LIFE IS LIKE A Carry On film at the moment.
Just not a funny one.

Hospital tomorrow. Shit. Today.

Sunday 29.4.90

9.32 p.m.

HERE I AM IN STAMFORD hospital.
I really don't think I can go through with this. I
am convinced I am going to die. It's agony. I just had
a look at my medical records at the end of my bed. I
am described by one doctor as a 'curious girl'. What
that's got to do with rectal problems I don't know.
Same with my mum's tattoo. Doctors have a God
complex.

I want to run away. Maybe I'll have a painful tummy
and bum but at least I won't be dead.

Monday 30.4.90

7.39 p.m.

I KNOW THIS IS WEIRD but I have had the most
amazing day. I've had to be weighed (don't ask – BAD
BAD BAD) BUT first Battered Sausage came to see me and
stayed and chatted for ages. THEN HADDOCK came to see

me with a plastic plant he had bought from the shop where he works. He said 'This crap will last longer than flowers.' Then he had to go again because he was working. Now all the REAL plants are being taken out but MY one stays because it can't produce carbon dioxide and it's PERFECT.

10.15 p.m.
Long entry – morbid in places but it's all there.
Rae Earl emotionally checking in.
Let's go through everyone shall we.

MUM
Sometimes I 'hate' her but all the time I love her. Never have I met someone with such force of character. You have fought through so much. Looked after me in times when I was unbearable. I trust you and I love you. Simple as that.

Dear Haddock,
Well my friend, time for some honesty. You are –

1) One gorgeous person
2) GORGEOUS looking. Honestly Haddock YOU ARE GORGEOUS. YOU ARE THE HORN.

Stop doubting yourself and listen. I think underneath it you and me were the same. Hypersensitive little sods. Anyway I bloody loved you. I would have never had told you when I was alive as I know you didn't feel the same way. You should STOP HIDING! Everyone who got to know the 'underneath you' would LOVE it. I mean you are handsome – PHYSICAL PERFECTION – but moreover inside you are very special. Remember that – good and pure.

Please get off your arse and listen to one of the few people who thinks that they knew you and saw through the grumpy bastard part of you. You are a massive bomb of potential. I can see your face tutting and your eyebrow going up in the air but I AM RIGHT!

Do you know what I was going to do? I was going to lose loads of weight. I wanted you to fall in love with me as well as 'loving' me as it were. Oh I don't know. I know that's the worst kind of selling out but I just ADORED you. I wanted to hold you but you sort of pushed me away.

No more else to say but I love you and I mean that and to have you as a friend was a great honour. Past all of the feelings of really, REALLY wanting to shag you – you were one of my best mates. I mean that. I love you Haddock. Love Rae XX

P.S.
I know more than you think I do so I'm in a position to say so. I think a hell of a lot of you and a hell of a lot for you.

MORT
Morty – you're a classic and I love you lots. No person on earth could have had a better best friend.
Love Rae XXX

P.S. Short message. You're well solid and don't need any of my daft advice. My records and smurfs are all yours mate.

Everyone is now snoring. It's hilarious! Actually I'm tired, I love this world and my mates.

Dear Battered Sausage,

When you are drunk you can be a knob end but I bloody loved you. Wherever I am I'll look out for you. I love you. RXX

Life ~~was~~ IS good. Must be positive.

Nil by mouth sign. Wish they could hang this over me all the time. Don't feed the Rae.

Tuesday 1.5.90

2.50 p.m.

WOOH!!!
Rae Earl is still here! She can take the beer! She can take the anaesthetics! What a stupid cow I was. JIBBER!

1) I've got half a brain.
2) For the first time in TWO YEARS I HAVE MY HEALTH!
3) I have brilliant mates!
4) AMEN!

PARTY!!!!!

9.35 p.m.

W ILD RAE'S DO AND THEY don't regret it!
Now I'm bloody worried about post-operative complications.

Typical.

> FROM MY HOSPITAL BED
> You came
> You sat.
> We talked.
> A smell of antiseptic. Nurses staring
> You made that sterile ward
> Come alive.
> Even old ladies admired.
> All their parts removed. They still felt for you.
> I love my plastic plant
> But I wish it would come alive
> Like our love
> And grow into a garden
> Packed full of passion
> Like our love.

10.35 p.m.
This is fatal, I'm sure something is going to go wrong. I feel like writing an erotic fantasy. HA HA! Yes I am going to. Shocking.

He comes in, undresses me. He puts me in his massive masculine bed. As I hide under the sheets he undresses. He says I am the wild mare that needs breaking in and he intends to do it. Then we make mad passionate SCREAMING love until I collapse in his arms.

I'm wearing gauze surgical underpants. I can't think of rude things.

Fuck it – I can do what I like with my head. It fucks me up enough.

Wednesday 2.5.90

3.12 p.m.

I'M HOME!!
I don't believe I wrote that last thing. But isn't it a turn-on? Talk about gorgeous situations.

I'm allowed to feel sexy things too!

Thursday 3.5.90

6.35 p.m.

BATTERED SAUSAGE JUST BROUGHT ME round a chilli con carne he'd made.

I have lovely friends.

9.35 p.m.
I can't stop crying. Mum says it's general anaesthetic. It might be but it's also the fact I've done BUGGER ALL revision for my A levels. TOTAL PANIC.

Friday 4.5.90

9.00 p.m.

I'M SO INADEQUATE. FRIGID. HOW wonderful it would be to hold him.

How can I be such a bitch? I mean I'd never do anything but . . . Haddock's girlfriend is going through a really hard time and I'm listening to everything she says and I love her to bits but . . .

How can I even write this?!

11.45 p.m.

When my inadequacy gets the best of me . . .

When everyone else attacks

When I'm scared.

The solution to what I'm feeling is easy.

I just put my head on the pillow and I pretend that it's him.

Arm around me stroking my hair.

Being a proper woman. Being safe. Feeling comfortable.

Why do guilt and reality exist?

Saturday 5.5.90

Late

EUROVISION HAS JUST BEEN WON by the most boring song there has ever been. Some Italian crap about Europe uniting. AWFUL. And the Italians made

'Ride on Time' and 'Numero Uno'. They should know better!

I can't stay in anymore. I've had enough rest. I'm missing out. I'm spiralling down.

Sunday 6.5.90

4.02 p.m.

MUM THINKS I'M MAD FOR going to the pub tonight but look at yesterday – without other stuff I start going off it again. I need other people.

Monday 7.5.90

12.30 a.m.

HERE'S HOW IT IS. HE looks beautiful from the side. And I look like a house.

Just been to Olivers. What a laugh! Haddock told the DJ it was my 19th birthday. We were VOGUEING! He kept hugging me! Even when he's striking a pose in a twat way he looks gorgeous.

He kept framing his face with his hands. Beautiful. But I beat down everything inside of me or I'd explode with it all.

Haddock. Vogue with me forever.

Tuesday 8.5.90

9.20 p.m.

IT'S BLOODY RIDICULOUS. I'VE HAD a major operation but all I can think of is my total inability as a person.

I'm frigid. I can't hug people. And I'm so lonely. The loneliness eats me up. There is no-one who gets up in the morning, gets a passing glimpse of me in their head and thinks 'You know I might see her today.' I have A levels in less than a month. I can't go to university. How can I move away? I love people who can't love me back. I love the most impossibly beautiful man on earth.

How many more times do I have to smash all the bad from my head and hit myself. I am so ungrateful but most of the time I HATE MYSELF. That's the cardinal sin. All the shrinks tell you to love yourself, if not you are completely useless. But HOW DO YOU LOVE YOURSELF? They don't tell you HOW.

HOW DO YOU LOVE THIS?????????

Wednesday 9.5.90

11.25 p.m.

I WISH I COULD BLOODY sleep. Did 3 hours revision last night. Feel better about school things at least.

Sod *Gulliver's Travels*. Sod those tiny shits!

Why?

Why is someone's beauty, strength, grace, intelligence and humour all spoiled by a person's unfounded and utterly destructive dislike of themselves?

I don't mean me. That makes more sense.

Thursday 10.5.90

10.35 p.m.

I DIDN'T TELL YOU ABOUT Ryan.

Well you know when you get those sorts of vibes from people? Well he's been hanging around me a lot and then tonight I said something and he said 'Rae, I fancied you till about 5 minutes ago.'

But he doesn't really. He just wants someone like we all want someone and he thinks I'm easy. I don't mean a slag. I mean he thinks I'm desperate. I'm not though. I'm hardly a gratuitous snogger. And he's lovely but I don't think I really fancy him.

Friday 11.5.90

9.35 p.m.

WE ALL WENT DOWN THE Meadows after school today and had a right laugh! Until this old biddy came along and started saying stuff like 'I'm an old girl – in my day you weren't even allowed to be seen eating in the street.' Old spinster cow – all we were doing was having a good time in a PUBLIC SPACE which we are entitled to do! A lack of sex really does turn people into horrible, miserable things. It's a lesson to us all. MORE SEX.

Actually she could have been having LOADS of sex for all I know. Certainly more than me! In fact I never jib on anyone's sex parade. The only place I moan is here!

Saturday 12.5.90

12.25 a.m.

HADDOCK WAS GORGEOUS TO ME tonight. He had his arm round me for a time. We can dream. I couldn't hug him back. He'd fallen off some steps at work packing tinsel away. I'm not joking, I love Haddock. I really do. This is not the prattling of a lovelorn teenager MUM!

Sunday 13.5.90

11.25 p.m.

HOME IS UNBEARABLE. SCHOOL IS unbearable. Work is unbearable. Nobody loves me. I'm deeply unattractive. I have A levels in 3 weeks. My stomach aches all day. I'm lonely. Tomorrow is Monday. I'm sure my friends actually don't like me. Bad horrid thoughts are back as are the dreams. Voices telling me I'm terrible.

I know. Tell the voices they are talking shit. But it's hard. It's hard.

Monday 14.5.90

9.01 p.m.

THE INSPIRAL CARPETS HAVE MADE a song called 'This Is How It Feels'. I think they have been in my house and listened to everything that has gone on and everything that has been said. That's all tonight.
BOLLOCKS.

Tuesday 15.5.90

5.12 p.m.

DOBBER HAS COME UP WITH a brilliant idea but it also scares me senseless. She wants to go for a holiday after the exams to Cornwall with Ronni and Fraggle. I want to but Cornwall is miles away. MILES. 7 hours away. It will cost about £150 plus petrol and spending money. I will get Mum to ask Dad. In a way I want him to say 'No' so I don't have to go. I can't tell my mates about my head. It's pathetic.

8.49 p.m.
Mum has been down the phone box. Dad has said 'yes'. I get yeses when I want no's and no's when I want yeses.

Wednesday 16.5.90

6.32 p.m.

UNBELIEVABLE!!
      WE ARE FRONT PAGE OF THE STAMFORD
EVENING TELEGRAPH TONIGHT!!!

It says 'RUMPUS OVER AMOROUS SCHOOLGIRLS –
They smoke, drink, kiss in public view'.

Apparently councillors are having urgent meetings
about us! An 'outraged' Tory says only one or two boys
from Stamford School seem to be involved! THEN WHO
ARE WE KISSING??!! I'M NOT KISSING ANYONE IN
PUBLIC OR PRIVATE. I do have a laugh on the Meadows
though – WE ALL DO. It's not Stalin's Russia is it??!! The
best thing is Miss Byron is quoted as saying that 'I would
defy anyone in 1990 to make sure that 18 year old girls
are perfectly behaved 24 hours a day.' YES!! Finally a
biddy that talks sense! We are allowed to be living loving
women AND wear a school uniform.

We are going to get ROYALLY DONE tomorrow
though! I'm glad I'm at the hospital having a check-up!!

Thursday 17.5.90

5.23 p.m.

WE DID NOT GET BOLLOCKED! Apparently the
      Lower 6th did – HA HA HA!!

My operation was a complete success. As they thought,
I haven't got cancer but this is something I will be prone

90

to for the rest of my life. I will have to be investigated every 5 years. Can't wait to tell any future husband that one!

Rae Earl – what a catch.

Friday 18.5.90

10.30 p.m.

WHAT A BLOODY CRAP DAY. Unbelievable. It's one of those days when you know it's going to be totally crap. First, I nearly got run over by a pissing navy blue Metro. Then my Theatre Arts teacher gives me a 40 foot lecture. My head is burning. And nobody knows this side of me. Nobody could possibly comprehend how utterly messed I am. Why am I so buggered up?!

I know partly because of stuff that happened.

I know the 'if onlys' are a dangerous thing but if I'd just had the sense to run. Get out before . . . I didn't fight. I can't understand. I was frozen to the spot. It wasn't even that serious. And I'm so numb about it. I feel nothing. I feel like slipping away. Going somewhere where no-one knows who I am or what I am. But I couldn't cope. I know that.

It wasn't that bad. Other people have had it far, far worse. I was bad before that. I've always been weird.

When I hit myself it hurts but it feels like a massive relief. A relief from all the anger and the guilt and being TERMINALLY PATRONISED.

At least I'm not under a Mini Metro. Look on the bright side.

Saturday 19.5.90

11.12 p.m.

I HAVE HAD TO LISTEN to both Haddock and Battered Sausage go on and on ALL NIGHT about how fit Kylie Minogue is. Battered Sausage put on 'Better The Devil You Know' on the Vaults jukebox about 7 times. I came home early – they were a right pair of lads tonight.

On the quiet, it's quite inspirational for us pretty-faces-but-fat types. Not that Kylie was ever LARDY but it proves that you can change. I just need a fit man for a sex transformation.

I think a problem with my life may be that I'm waiting for people to come along and sort things when actually they can't be arsed!

That's not fair. No-one can. If they could they would have done.

Haddock is growing bloody sideburns. Yes he still looks gorgeous.

Sunday 20.5.90

5.12 p.m.

TOMORROW IS THE LAST WEEK of school before . . . FOREVER.

Shit!

Monday 21.5.90

8.12 p.m.

WE HAVE OUR YEARBOOKS!!
They are great and everything but I'm slightly annoyed. In the 'What Will You Miss Least About School' section there are loads of things about me like –

Rae's annoying moods
Rae's being self righteous and lecturing me
Rae's tantrums
Rae's singing
Rae scrounging at break
Rae's gob

I'm also in the 'What Will You Miss Most About School' bit tons too BUT it's a bit harsh!

Tuesday 22.5.90

5.34 p.m.

IT'S PROBABLY GOOD THAT IT'S the last week at school because there is basically now CIVIL WAR over the yearbook. Natty Dawlish has written in the 'What Will You Miss Least About School' 'the false pretentious stuck up cows who one tends to find in the U6 common room' and then Ava Laird wrote in the 'What's Your Greatest Achievement' 'beating THEM at Rounders 91 to 85.' Apparently the THEM is US in the common room. I thought they were both OK till I read that. I tell you what, they both live in far better nicer houses than I do so don't call me a stuck-up cow!

BUT THEN that all faded into insignificance because Drew Walker had written in her Greatest Achievement bit 'fulfilling all my sexual fantasies.' EVERYONE was talking about it. She's quite quiet but at Olivers she did dance in a very odd way to 'Touch Me' by the 49ers. Bum wiggling ahoy and all over the place.

It all made my 4 fishcakes achievement look even crapper than I thought but never mind!

Wednesday 23.5.90

10.38 p.m.

YEARBOOK 1990 – WHAT WILL You Miss Most About School?

'The comforting sense of security that being so efficiently controlled has given me!'

ROSANNA – YOU ARE MY HERO! Her yearbook thing is brilliant. She's really clever and funny AND she's got a boyfriend. I should have asked her for tips!

Battered Sausage came round tonight. He took me for a drink. Haddock was waiting for us. Sideburns and all. Everything wonderful and perfect. And utterly beautiful. In a rugby shirt.

Can't wait till June 21st. PARTY TIME!!

Leavers' cheese and wine evening tomorrow at school. Sometimes it's so posh it hurts.

Thursday 24.5.90

10.12 p.m.

WELL THAT WAS BLOODY ANNOYING. Listen to this CRAP.

Mum thinks I shouldn't be annoyed but I bloody am.

Me and a few others were standing round tonight in the hall with wine (WINE IN SCHOOL – LEGALLY MAD!!) and a teacher came over. She started saying stuff to people 'I can see you doing very well at Cambridge' and 'you're a natural for law' and then she turned to me and said 'And Rachel you're just one of life's survivors.'

NOW WHAT DOES THAT MEAN?!

One of life's survivors?! When I think of a survivor I think of someone clinging to a bit of wreckage avoiding sharks with half a gob of salt water. Is that all I'm worth?! Sod being a survivor. I want to be brilliant. I want to rip up the sky.

Mum says she is saying that I'm tough. No. A survivor just survives. SOD SURVIVING.

Pissed off. And Camembert should be banned. It's like heroin. I was like Zammo from *Grange Hill* tonight for a piece.

Friday 25.5.90

7.35 p.m.

L AST PROPER DAY OF SCHOOL ever. We had
chips. It was a bit moving when we put our trays on
the conveyor belt for the last time. Normal life
disappearing through a hatch waiting to be washed up.

Saturday 26.5.90

11.35 p.m.

O H WHY DOES HE DO it? Why does he hug me and
stroke my hair. I push him away and joke it off
because I'm a twat but it kills me.

Once my A levels are over I'm going to stop dreaming
and start living.

Sunday 27.5.90

3.50 p.m.

T HE FUNDAMENTAL THINGS THAT ARE WRONG
WITH MY LIFE:

THE EASIER STUFF

1) A levels – ONLY DAYS AWAY!!
2) My mental condition. Confused.
3) People are very condescending to me because

they've had sex. But actually WHAT DO THEY KNOW? I feel like saying 'Oh yeah you may have had a boyfriend but what the hell do you actually KNOW?' SERIOUSLY??!! Bollocks. THEY KNOW NOTHING. ZILCH! People say to me 'Oh I bet you marry someone really nice!' SO PATRONISING. What if I JUST WANT TO MARRY A REALLY HORNY TOTAL BASTARD SEX MACHINE??!!

4) No-one really loves me. Nobody has given me a hug and said 'Rae – I really love you.' I mean I'm not loud and annoying ALL THE TIME! So why can't they? Have I just got really bad breath?

SPECIFIC PROBLEMS

1) HADDOCK.

Now this really is a sod of a problem.

I know it sounds immature when I write it. I can't say. Don't want to encourage fate to kick me up the arse.

I've GOT to change.

1) Lose weight.
2) Keep good bits.
3) Get rid of shit bits.

What a brilliant night down the pub. Atmosphere 400% on!

Haddock came in. He told me he'd had a dream about me. He'd bought a Harley-Davidson and I'd bust it. It's nice to be in his dreams even if I am breaking stuff.

I just take the piss out of him all the time. Blood is blue and it comes out red. Same thing.

Monday 28.5.90

2.36 p.m.

THAT LAST ENTRY SOUNDED SO monumentally pretentious.

I really need to start revising. Why can't I just be a pub landlady? Or Bez from the Happy Mondays.

Tuesday 29.5.90

11.23 p.m.

MUM HAS JUST TRIED TO show me she can moonwalk. She can't.

Her impression of Mick Jagger is also crap. Pursing your lips together and strutting on the lino doesn't make you the lead singer of the Rolling Stones. It makes you very annoying indeed especially when you're in the way of the bloody fridge.

Wednesday 30.5.90

3.47 p.m.

NOTHING IS GOING IN MY head. Nothing is sticking. I've just sung every word of 'Look of Love' by ABC though – even the bit where Martin Fry starts talking to himself. But can I remember the dates that Perkin Warbeck kicked off some shit? No. Don't care anyway. Like Mort says, he's got the same name as one of the Flumps so you can't take him seriously.

Thursday 31.5.90

5.12 p.m.

THE REASON WHY MUM IS so happy is that Adnan is coming back on Friday. That explains everything – the singing, the dancing, the way she actually dusted for the first time since I had to have the doctor out in the middle of the night. Adnan is returning. Can he help me with my A levels? No. Is he an expert in Elizabethan court politics? No. Will the dining room be turned into a gym IN THE MIDDLE OF MY A LEVELS? Yes. Will he eat an entire Morrisons swiss roll cake like the rest of us eat a Polo mint? Yes.

The selfishness of my mum beggars belief. Just go out with a normal man like other women!! I know marriages break down but why can't she marry someone with loads of money and a decent house. She's even trying to get preserved lemons from somewhere? PRESERVED LEMONS?! It's Stamford not Marrakesh. Tinned satsumas are exotic round here love!

WHY CAN'T WE JUST BE NORMAL?

Friday 1.6.90

11.12 a.m.

YES MUM, YOU CAN REVISE *The Tempest* and listen to 'Our Tune' on Radio 1 at the same time and 'Our Tune' is more entertaining. No Mum I don't care that you are going to the market to get some onions – WHY IS

THAT RELEVANT WHEN SOMEONE ON THE RADIO HAS
LOST THE LOVE OF THEIR LIFE HORRIFICALLY?! And
yes I will hoover. Does anyone exist in my mum's life
other than her?!

2.36 p.m.
Just hoovered in time to the theme tune from *Shaft*!
Think Mrs Maughn from across the road might have seen
me but I don't care. I do not fear people seeing my
funkiness. HA! HA! HA!

Oh I bloody do. If she tells my mum they'll think I'm
going funny again.

I do feel funny again but it's nothing to do with Isaac
Hayes or Otis Redding.

7.12 p.m.
Adnan has just arrived. There's a stinking olive tagine
orgy and kissing going on in the kitchen. I'm going down
the pub with Dobber where's there's just crisps and cider
and people under 20 who should be the only ones
snogging.

11.48 p.m.
I sat down the pub tonight telling Dobber about Adnan
and in the middle of it she went 'Ronnie Corbett.' I was
going on a bit and I know she's got her own stuff to
worry about but it was a bit harsh.

Do I go on, diary? Probably. But no-one else wants to
listen and compares me to the Two Ronnies.

Saturday 2.6.90

Dobber house. Late. Really late.

NO IT WAS NOT THE best idea preparing for your Shakespeare English A level by getting totally ratted and then hiding under an orange blanket whilst Battered Sausage ran around Dobber's front room with no clothes on pretending to be a male stripper and gyrating on the orange blanket to 'Hear the Drummer Get Wicked' by Chad Jackson. But that's what has just happened.

Sunday 3.6.90

4.15 p.m.

SOMEWHERE ALONG THE WAY I have gone drastically wrong. My being is so consumed with the most hateful anger. I want to scream and kick it all out of me. Punch it out till I bleed and others finally see it.

My home life is total bollocks at the moment. They have no idea what it does to me. There's no stability. Mum is either horrible or finding herself or making Adnan a massive non-pork sandwich. I'm staying round Dobber's. I want somewhere safe and secure. Vine Street is it.

Monday 4.6.90

5.45 p.m.

Ladies and gentlemen I am fucking up my A levels!

IT WENT ALRIGHT. IT'S ENGLISH. Let's start well and then spiral down like a massive crashing-on-fire plane disaster.

I can't think about Lockerbie. It proves you are not safe anywhere. Even at home. That night I wanted to sleep in the garden but Mum wouldn't let me because I was really ill then. And it was December and freezing.

Tuesday 5.6.90

7.23 p.m.

A LEVELS HAVE TURNED INTO a total fashion parade. You won't believe how many clothes some of my mates have. Some are coming with a different outfit to get changed into after the exam! Loads of white Laura Ashley shirts and riding ankle boots. And the make-up?! They look like Yasmin Le Bon. It must take them ages to get it plastered on. These are like proper women that juggle revision and sex. I juggle sandwiches and avoiding revision by watching the bloody Open University.

Perhaps I can just stay in Stamford and get a degree off the TV.

That'll cost though as our TV is still on a meter. Sorry I couldn't finish my essay professor, we ran out of fifty pence pieces.

Wednesday 6.6.90

6.34 p.m.

I NOW REALISE I AM the only woman in our school without a mini Liberty fabric frog. They are all bringing them in as mascots. I've just got an old Womble Uncle Bulgaria for luck.

Total depravity.

7.12 p.m.

Not depravity. Deprivation! Wish it was depravity. Massive Haddock-based depravity. Sometimes in the middle of exams he flashes in my brain like a sex storm.

Thursday 7.6.90

8.39 p.m.

E NGLISH HISTORY A LEVEL – I'd done no revision. None of the questions even made any sense. One of the questions was 'Explain the Advances in Elizabethan Culture and Music'. So I wrote this massive piss take about the popularity of 'New Kids on Ye Block' and Madonna being burned as a heretic because she was plainly too Catholic in all of her songs. When I told Mort she thought it was genius but I have a feeling it will not impress the massively virgin boring examiner who is looking for some shit standard answer. What sort of person decides to mark exam papers? People with no life who don't have sex.

Oh God don't let me become an A level examiner.

I've noticed sometimes when I have massive real stress then I worry less that I'm Satan or that I've got peritonitis. Perhaps I need to stay at school forever. No Rae you look stupid in a 38 inch waist kilt now – let alone at 31 or something ancient.

10.12 p.m.

ITV are going to show a miniseries called *War and Remembrance* about World War 2. They always show Nazis in Summer. Mum is taping it for me but I'm going to watch it on my portable too. John Gielgud and Jane Seymour are Jews and it's obvious they are going to survive because they are famous. Which will piss me off because the Nazis were total bastards and killed everyone, Jewish or gay or Gypsy or people who just told them they were knobs.

Why am I even revising the Hapsburg tossers when the Nazis were killing everyone less than fifty years ago?! All other history is pointless. Seriously Charles V can piss off. WHO CARES?!

Friday 8.6.90

5.23 p.m.

WHAT A DAY!
Mum called up and said 'Your mate is in the back of the paper.' Didn't think much of it but it was HADDOCK! She said 'He's a good-looking boy isn't he?' Oh – I cannot tell you how much this is the understatement of the century. It is FRIGHTENING the

104

level of horniness. He is crouching down with his team in shorts. THE THIGHS!! THE THIGHS!! You have never seen thighs like them. They are rock and silk in one. They are like a sculpture. When Mum went to make Adnan something halal I ripped it out. It's just – LOOK AT IT! Tell me you wouldn't. He could make nuns doubt themselves. Haddock – ruiner of nuns. Habits drop at the thought of him. I don't mean biting nails or anything, I mean what nuns wear.

8.12 p.m.
Mum just burst in to tell me off for ripping the paper. Oh yes because she's really interested in the local over 60s bowls league! ANY chance to have a go at me.

No-one is going out because of A levels. Annoying but if I was down the Vaults I couldn't stare at Haddock's legs for as long as I am without questions being asked – especially by his girlfriend HA HA HA!!

Listening to *Hup* by The Wonder Stuff. 'Golden Green' is brilliant. They are talking about somebody so brilliant even crap things they do still shine – who does that sound like?

Saturday 9.6.90

9.12 p.m.
BAKED BEANS ARE HALAL. THAT has been established today. Baked beans with pork sausages are not halal. That has been established by STATING THE TOTALLY OBVIOUS.

Sometimes I think my mum just asks me stupid

questions to check that I am still here. Or she wants to include me in family life. I don't want to be part of it. I want to be EXCLUDED.

A levels, no-one down the pub, World Cup football and religious diets. What a nightmare combination.

> CUTTING
> You're a crumpled piece of paper
> A black and white bit of stuff
> A cutting from my local
> A tabloid bit of rough
> But you're more than just a photo
> You're the reason I tell lies,
> You're hope, you're beauty, you're kindness
> With a magnificent pair of thighs.

I should be revising not writing poems.

I just don't care about what's going to happen.

Sunday 10.6.90

10.12 p.m.
THEY ARE SHOWING SOME HORRIBLE stuff on *War and Remembrance*. Makes A levels seem like totally pointless shit. In fact it's making everything seem like totally pointless shit. Including all the stuff I worry about but that won't stop me next time I'm having a panic attack. Or thinking that I'm dying. That's how weak I am.

Mum has just been up. Should I be watching this? She's worried I'll go loony again. If this didn't make you feel slightly loony though you'd probably be a Nazi.

I'd rather be mad than Hitler. He was mad. I mean my type of mad where I just seem to hurt myself and slightly annoy others rather than murder millions and invade countries because my moustache is a bit itchy. Wanker.

Monday 11.6.90

5.49 p.m.
EUROPEAN HISTORY. I COULDN'T EVEN write anything funny after last night and Catherine de' Medici apparently had sex with everyone and everything including horses. That's funny but I don't feel funny. I feel just lost and empty and worried and . . . just gone.

Tuesday 12.6.90

8.12 p.m.
I'M REVISING FOR MY POLITICS exam. At least understanding how the House of Lords works has some relevance to life. Mum is in one of her funny moods. Just sat in the chair staring into space. Working on the checkouts at Morrisons obviously brings with it enormous pressures. American Tan tights or normal tan? No wonder she's a woman on the edge. Meanwhile upstairs I'm revising the role of the monarchy in a country with an unwritten constitution whilst trying to stop myself thinking that in my bowel another massive cancer is growing. Whose life would you prefer to have?!

Keep peeking at the thighs. I think when I next see Haddock I might think of a reason to press them.

Wednesday 13.6.90

9.28 p.m.

JUST BEEN DOWN THE VAULTS with Battered Sausage. I could not revise politics anymore. You have to think about Mrs Thatcher too much. It drives you to cider. Though I only had soda and black because I can't face an A level hungover.

Mum came home, smelt my breath and gave me a lecture. Apparently drinking blackcurrant will now lead to a dead end job and a life of misery. Ribena will also make you a teenage mother and condemn you to a life of poverty. If I hear the line 'You don't want to end up like me' one more time I may explode. Even Adnan – ADNAN!! – told her to stop going on at me. Well he said 'Stop!' At least my mother's bodybuilding Moroccan boyfriend understands how hard exams are.

Actually the pub was boring. Hearing about Battered Sausage and women is nearly as dull as hearing about Nigel Lawson, Geoffrey Howe and other old tosser Tories who all went to Cambridge and have no idea what it is like to be fat on a council estate. Bet no-one gets called Jabba in Westminster.

Thursday 14.6.90

9.23 p.m.
>5 MORE MINUTES
>5 more minutes
>I KNOW the time
>11.15
>Halfway through my final essay
>Pens down
>UP YOURS!!
>UP YOURS!!!!
>Exams are so unfair
>Designed not for the clever
>But for the Swots
>Swots end up in good Jobs
>The clever cast aside
>Injustice has many forms
>Those like me who are bright but not bothered
>Get the cruellest cut of all
>No steak just gristle.

Friday 15.6.90

9.34 p.m.
THE LIGHT IS SLIGHTLY VISIBLE! THE END IS NEAR! Theatre Arts, U.S. Politics and English set texts and THEN I AM DONE!!

Loads of people going out tomorrow night so obviously I am too. I'm not missing out.

Saturday 16.6.90

5.12 p.m.

MUM JUST ASKED IF I am going out tonight. When I said 'yes' she said 'Rachel – you've got 3 exams coming up. You can't stay here all your life. You need to get out and travel. See the world. Get a good job.' What she really means is I can't stay here and upset her exotic love nest. Well I'm not – I'm going down the Vaults. BYE!

Sunday 17.6.90

9.45 a.m.

GREAT LAUGH DOWN THE VAULTS last night. CLASSIC but annoying! Battered Sausage put on 'World in Motion' about 6 times on the jukebox and when it got to the bit where John Barnes says 'get round the back' a load of the lads were laughing and shouting it. I didn't know why and Battered Sausage wouldn't tell me. He kept saying stuff like 'Keep innocent Rae . . . keep innocent!' Anyway eventually he told me. Apparently a girl from a couple of years above us has ANAL SEX with her boyfriend and he told everyone. ANAL SEX! Now fair enough gay men doing that – that makes total sense – but girls?! Diary, am I a prude or is that actually slightly disgusting? I mean do what you want in your spare time but having it up the bum? Isn't that just pleasing a man for a man's sake? Perhaps this is where I am going wrong.

I'm not prepared to be in pain just to make a bloke happy. Sod off! I've had barium enemas – they are not sexy. This is where I can't make it work – I don't want to wear flowery dresses, have big red lips, laugh at shit jokes and then go home and have anal sex. THIS is why I'm single – I'm fat, I'm funny and I won't take it up the bum. Well the fat part I want to change but the other things are staying.

And no, Haddock wasn't there so I couldn't look at his thighs or make up some excuse to touch them.

Monday 18.6.90

4.12 p.m.

ME, MORT AND SHELLBOSS MADE a pact today. We are NEVER mentioning Restoration comedy ever again. It can honestly fuck off.

Tuesday 19.6.90

3.39 p.m.

I SHOULD BE REVISING CAUCUSES and primaries, instead I'm wondering what women do in bed that I don't know about and I should know about. And even if I do know about it would I do it?

Wednesday 20.6.90

9.13 p.m.

I THINK I MADE WHAT I know fit the question. That's the point of the entire exam system – bullshitting. Which is an essential skill for life. A level Politics exam asks you about the role of the vice president? Bullshit about Dan Quayle and his vice presidential cock-ups.

Going or feeling mad? Bullshit and say you are not. Totally in love with a man that treats you like his sister – bullshit and pretend you're just mates. When people ask are you OK? Bullshit and say fine. Make a joke.

Thursday 21.6.90

11.12 p.m.

WHY DID I WATCH ENGLAND v. Egypt in the World Cup? I don't even like football.

You're allowed to take the books in with you tomorrow so I can't really do anything now. I will quite miss Doctor Faustus. 'This is hell – nor am I out of it'. Best quote ever to describe feeling that your head is messed up. I could be a multimillionaire, lying on a beach, in a size 10 bikini with Haddock by my side and I'd still feel nuts.

No – if I was in a size 10 bikini with Haddock in Blackpool my life would actually be perfect.

Friday 22.6.90

1.23 p.m.

FINISHED!!!!!!!!!! A LEVELS HAVE ENDED!!!
    Got home – FIRST thing Mum said 'Good! Are you getting a job this summer?'

WHAT I SAID – 'I'll try!'

WHAT I'M REALLY DOING – Going down the pub and down the Meadows for the best summer there has ever been.

Pub tonight. Haddock is bound to be out.

Saturday 23.6.90

10.23 a.m.

SORRY I DIDN'T WRITE LAST night. I was very pissed and a bit emotional.

Got down the Vaults at about 8 and everyone was there. The atmosphere was just ON! The garden was packed. Bar the people who do foreign languages, most people have finished. Anyway I was just chatting to Dobber about shagging (I was actually digging for more info on sex things that I might not know about) and Haddock walked in WEARING BLOODY SHORTS. Yes it was hot but – in a way it should not be allowed as even his calves are amazing. Anyway he came to sit with us and then – oh – bloody hell. We ended up having this semi-pissed conversation and then he dropped a Hiroshima bombshell.

HADDOCK: What you are you going to do now?
ME: Doss. Avoid getting a job. Wait for my results.
What about you?
HADDOCK: I'm going Interrailing all summer. I go
next week.

Now he did say last year he was going to South Africa for
6 months but when he kept on working I just thought
he'd given up on the travelling thing. But no. He hasn't.
He's off. Anyway I said . . .

ME: Oh really?! That's brilliant (no – it's not. It's
shit. Haddock it's so shit you have no idea because
frankly without you around everything is grey and
flat and hopeless).
HADDOCK: You should do it too! Do you good. Get
out of this place.
ME: Nah mate. I'm skint. And I'm going to Cornwall
for a week aren't I? (which I am shitting myself
about)
HADDOCK: Well I'll come and see you before I go
and I'll send you postcards.

And that was it. What did I want to say? God, I would
love to come with you because you're fit as hell, you make
me laugh like a drain and you just make my brain and
heart leap ten foot in the air you dry-as-a-bone, genuine,
real bloke who listens to me and is totally not a cock AND
is the most fantastic example of a man that I would
probably consider doing all sorts of sex things with.

But I can't get to Peterborough without feeling mad so
Greece on a train is out of the question so I said:

'Have a great time mate.'

Have a great time mate. Everything I feel for Haddock gets diluted down into the sort of thing I would say to our bloody postman.

I am officially shit.

Sunday 24.6.90

10.12 a.m.

*Y*OU MAGAZINE IS FULL OF stupid thin actresses and the paper is full of famine. IT'S SICK IN THE HEAD.

Seething masses
Formless cameras
Flashes kill the player
While in one click
A fat bellied baby snuffs it
And the tattered queen sucks up the good stuff.
Perhaps they should get together
Former Hollywood society belle
And emaciated bag of Ugandan bones
No more milk for the child
You must starve
They milk her Queen, Tattered beauty queen
Shrivelled breasts are out in this studio and in Africa
    too.

Monday 25.6.90

6.12 p.m.

IS THAT POEM BRILLIANT OR bollocks? I can't decide.

Mum said to me today 'You seem a bit down Rach. Adnan noticed too.'

If Adnan didn't sing so badly, snore like a rhino, eat everything in sight and use everything heavy as a toning opportunity he'd be OK really.

I am down because everything is changing, I have no idea where I'm going and Haddock is going away. I can't speak to anyone because they will either think I'm pathetic/mad/going mad/totally and completely intent on nicking their boyfriend, and they would be right.

Tuesday 26.6.90

11.22 p.m.

WE BEAT BELGIUM IN THE World Cup.
Haddock is probably going to travel through Belgium. Hope he doesn't get attacked for being English. Though he could probably beat the crap out of anyone Flemish if he needed to.

What am I going to do this summer? My head is already starting to . . . I'm fighting for stability. I can feel it.

And I'm listening to Dire Straits' 'So Far Away'. DIRE STRAITS! Old people in sweatbands from my brother's record collection but that song says it now. Everything I love isn't here or isn't about to be here.

Dire Straits though. That's bad. Tell a psychiatrist that I'm listening to them and I'd be straight back in the ward.

Wednesday 27.6.90

'WORLD IN MOTION' HAS BEEN ruined for me. Every time I hear it all I think of is anal sex.

Thursday 28.6.90

9.34 p.m.

I WAS IN MY BEDROOM with Shellboss this afternoon and I heard car doors and then a voice. I've been hallucinating Haddock everywhere so I just thought it was me being barking. But he'd come to say goodbye. I told him to take care and then he went to hug me. I ended up headbutting his chest in a sort of hug. And then he went.

I spoke to his girlfriend for ages the other night. She's so pretty and lovely and funny – you can't not like her! Haddock wrote her a letter. Listen to this. He wrote her a letter saying he said a prayer for her every night. BIT IRONIC! There's me saying one for him every night and he's praying for someone else.

Mind you, I also pray that I don't go to hell, that God won't let me catch rabies, that God won't kill the people I love, that I'll pass my A levels and that The Smiths will re-form . . . so he's part of a long list.

117

Shellboss said to me 'You like Haddock don't you?'.
When I said 'yes' she said 'No Rae – I mean you really
like him.'

Shellboss can see it but she has known for me for ages
and she can see through loads of crap other people can't.
Other people can't see it. He can't.

I looked at some photos today and I am honestly
totally disgusting.

Friday 29.6.90

6.20 a.m.

I'VE BEEN UP SINCE 3.30 a.m. I can't sleep. Last day
of school after 7 years. I shall miss my mates
immensely. Still what can you do? I shall hopefully keep
in touch with the people I can keep in touch with.

My thoughts – a mixture of sadness and fondness.

No – my thoughts are just SHITTING IT.

9.12 p.m.

So that was it. We had made a massive spider to levitate
over the headmistress's head when she was doing the
usual Bible reading in the final assembly but Mrs C
caught us and said she didn't think it would be a good
idea. She's lovely and we didn't want to get her in trouble
so that was abandoned. We did sing 'Angelo' by
Brotherhood of Man though and the rest of the school
went mad and clapped.

And that's that.

But how the hell am I going to manage? That place . . .
it kept me OK and now it's gone. Seeing my mates

everyday has gone. Food at the same time everyday has gone. Escape has gone. The common room has gone. Wellington Fudge pudding has gone. I feel like someone has pulled the carpet from underneath my feet and I've fallen over but, like a massive fat beetle, I can't right myself. I'm on my back legs kicking in the air and it looks funny but it's not.

Saturday 30.6.90

9.34 p.m.
S O I'VE LEFT SCHOOL AND I don't really know where the hell I am going. I can only party while I wait and watch *War and Remembrance.*

> To life and love I say cheers.
> Close all the curtains
> The doors – slam them it hurts less
> I bloody loved school.

Sunday 1.7.90

2.20 a.m.
S UMMER '90!!
    Welcome. I hope you can be as good as '89. You've got one hell of a lot to live up to.

11.35 a.m.
Got in bloody late last night after Olivers.

11.45 p.m.

Good Gad night down the pub. John D is a bit of an epic slice and a total classic.

It's good to know other men exist when the one man who you DO want around is on a train God knows where.

Battered Sausage was lovely. He took his shirt off in the pouring rain to lend it to me so I didn't get soaked. It was totally useless but fine.

Monday 2.7.90

2.11 a.m.

JUST COME BACK FROM OLIVERS. I've got gross Olivers ear. All I can hear is beeeeeeepppssss but you HAVE TO PLAY MUSIC LOUD.

I have got the most humungous crush on Paul Gascoigne. We won 3-2 against Cameroon. I'm not usually very patriotic at all but this World Cup I'm really enjoying and the football.

5.57 p.m.

I went round Fig's house with Dobber this afternoon. He's a right laugh and such a love. Dobber was talking about the trip to Cornwall. I should be looking forward to it but I'm scared. I'm scared of dying, of leaving here, of being stuck somewhere in Cornwall that's not near a hospital, of my friends' seeing what I really am – weak and nuts and like an 11 year old. I'm scared of people seeing my mad head and my panic. If they see that I'd have no mates left.

<u>Essential holiday list of things to take</u>
Rennie
Colofac
Gaviscon
Paracetamol
Travel sickness tablets
Clothes
Purse
Sheet
Pillow
Batteries
Camera
Walkman
Walkman tapes

8.12 p.m.
Even medicines are coming before music in my lists. The
hypochondria has started. You can see it. I'm not good.

Tuesday 3.7.90

9.45 p.m.
I'M STAYING AT MORT'S. TOLD her about the
holiday and how frightened I am about going. I can tell
her everything – even some of the really, REALLY mental
bits. She says I just need to take it one hour at a time and
when I feel myself going downhill I've got to do
something else. It's brilliant advice but I know my head.
When it says that I'm dying, I'm dying. When it says I've
eaten a Death Cap mushroom, I've eaten one and I've got
delayed symptoms of poisoning. I can't stop it. I can't

121

stop the voices. The tablets didn't stop it either. I saw a programme once about a bloke who'd had a lobotomy because he couldn't stop ripping clothes. Perhaps I need one of those. Perhaps I should just bang my head hard with a tea tray like the bloke used to do 'mule train' on *Tiswas* and see if that works.

That was a joke. I'm not going to attempt amateur brain surgery.

Wednesday 4.7.90

Late. Who cares! PISSED off.

TONIGHT WAS JUST ONE OF the biggest most gutting nights of my life and I mean that. I've just watched England v. Germany in the World Cup Semi-Final. It was a draw for ages and then Paul Gascoigne got a second yellow card, realised he couldn't play in the final if we got there and started to cry! Like PROPERLY cry and Gary Lineker had to go and give him a cuddle (footballers cuddle – why can't I?). Then it went to extra time, then it went to penalties and the sodding Germans won. Honestly the tension made me feel sick. It was more tense than Eurovision 1988 when Scott Fitzgerald nearly won. In fact I think the Germans buggered up that for us too.

Poor Paul Gascoigne. Then Chris Waddle and Stuart Pearce missed the penalties and that was it. Out!

The one good thing was they showed a brilliant *Naked Gun* advert for Red Rock cider directly after we lost. Which cheered us up a bit.

Why can't one thing just work out?

I have to get A levels into perspective. It's not like missing a goal and messing up the entire dreams of a nation. I haven't liked Chris Waddle since that 'Diamond Lights' crap he did. Perhaps he should have practised penalties a bit more than singing love songs with Glen Hoddle. I've never had as shit a haircut as him either, unless you count the time Chloe put my hair up like a Mel & Kim pineapple look in 1987, told me it looked good and then pissed herself laughing at me in Ironmonger Street.

I am very unforgiving and I'm not the Saint and Greavsie either. Shut up Rae.

Thursday 5.7.90

5.36 p.m.

EVERYONE IN ENGLAND IS PISSED off today. I'm back from Mort's. I wish I could just go and live there. No tension. No arguments. No Mum talking pidgin English. No kissing in the kitchen. No weightlifting equipment that you would like to get out of your way but it's actually too heavy to move.

Friday 6.7.90

6.12 p.m.

LACK OF ACTIVITY HAS CAUSED chronic hypochondria to return combined with this blind panic of WHAT THE HELL DO I DO NEXT?!

It's all an anticlimax. End of school. End of everything. I'm just waiting for stuff to happen.

NEW ACTION PLAN

But before this let us look at the successes of the last action plan, mid-year, and see what has been achieved/ rectified/ resolved:

1) *Get A levels and get away!*
   Not yet
2) *Have a bloody good time.*
   Sometimes
3) *Keep cool and calm.*
   Hardly ever
4) *Maintain spiritual stability.*
   That actually means not go mad. Trying.
5) *Try to have some remnants of a decent relationship with a real man that exists as a breathing thing.*
   No.
6) *Become a bit of a sex bitch.*
   No.

Well it's not an overriding success is it? Still here goes this one –

ACTION PLAN

1) Whatever A level results I get utilise them in a positive way.
2) Make peace with my head.
3) Body overhaul.
4) Mind overhaul.

Saturday 7.7.90

11.47 p.m.

I DIDN'T GO OUT TONIGHT because my head is . . . it's not well. So I watched *War and Remembrance*. This was not a good decision. It was the most horrible thing I have ever seen. Basically they were at Auschwitz and they showed the Nazis gassing people. It was . . . kids and everything. They didn't give a shit. And they killed John Gielgud's character – which was brilliant in a way because they just didn't care. It was evil. Horrific. People screaming to get out the gas chamber.

Now I can't get it out of my head. I know it happened. I know about it but . . . oh God it was terrible. Now in my head – I'm convinced if I don't do stuff it'll happen again. And I've said the Lord's Prayer about 15 times and hit myself for the thoughts that all this has made me think but I can still see kids screaming and I can't fix it. I can't make it go away. I can't take my mind off it with music because that seems like being disrespectful and the bad stuff WILL happen. And what if a government like that gets in power in Britain one day and takes the people I love away? This is when I just want to cut into myself just for the relief. The distraction. The relief. I just want to be in control of everything but I can't even be in control of my head. It's a mess and it's getting messier. Wish I had exams again or something. Might start learning the *British Book of Hit Singles* again.

Sunday 8.7.90

2.15 a.m.

JUST WOKE MUM UP BECAUSE I needed to talk
about Auschwitz. She was cross at first because it
reminded her of the time I woke her up at 4 in the
morning to tell her Indira Gandhi was dead. Her reaction
then was 'Indira Gandhi will still be dead when I bloody
get up.' I told her I couldn't get it out of my head. She
said 'Look Rachel – it was the worst thing. A bloody
terrible thing but you just have to make sure, in your life,
you stand up to any nonsense and if you see people
getting picked on you say something. And you do. You
use your big mouth to good effect most of the time. You
can't change what happened but you can change things
now. Now can I go back to sleep as I'm on for 9 hours on
fresh produce tomorrow.'

My mum gets it sometimes. I'm listening to All About
Eve and trying to sleep.

Monday 9.7.90

3.45 a.m.

CAN'T SLEEP. HORRIBLE FEELING. IT'S like a
huge numbness. It's partly thinking about the Holocaust
and partly thinking about whether I can cope with going to
Cornwall. YES! I know how pathetic and appalling that
sounds but if I can't tell you I can't tell anyone.

126

Tuesday 10.7.90

10.36 p.m.

I CAN SEE HYPOCHONDRIA, ANXIETY and me just being mad buggering up this holiday. I've just been down the meadows for a piss up with Dobber and Battered Sausage. My heart was just thumping like crazy all the time. It could have been the drink but I've even got chest pains. That could be my bra though. It's tight and the boning is coming out. I can't go to casualty with crap underwear but I don't want to die either.

I'm losing it again. I can feel it going.

Wednesday 11.7.90

9.21 a.m.

I LOVE *SMASH HITS*. I can't imagine life without it but this week Craig McLachlan is on the cover. It actually says 'You're the goat from *Neighbours*'! Am I even getting too old for *Smash Hits*? I already have *Q* every month. Perhaps I should give it up? The truth is I don't need a free Candy Flip sticker anymore and Check 1-2 are . . . WHERE'S THE STONE ROSES?!

Thursday 12.7.90

10.21 p.m.

THE FACT IS I TOLD people at school that I wanted to be Kate Adie and report from war zones as a career. Or do a Michael Buerk and start a massive protest against famine and make Live Aid happen by going to Ethiopia. I'm having a panic attack about going to Cornwall. Unless the BBC need a foreign correspondent in Rutland I'm fucked.

Two days to go. Just calm down Rae. You can cope with this. It's still Britain!

Friday 13.7.90

6.26 p.m.

I WAS A TRAITOR TODAY. I went to the café where the owner was horrible to Mum. Mum had gone in with a teacher from the boys' school, who she ironed shirts for. The owner said 'I suppose you are going to tell us you're just good friends.' Mum shouted across the shop 'No – we're fantastic lovers!' This wasn't true but it shut the stupid nosey cow up! Anyway it was years ago but Mum sort of banned me from there but today I just fancied a jacket potato and they were the only ones selling them. It serves me right – it was horrible and had green bits. Now my guts are even more on fire and tomorrow I've got a 7-hour drive to Cornwall.

Well I'm just sat in the back but I'm in charge of music.

Which is hard because Fraggle likes a bit of Bros. Not in any vehicle I'm in love!

I'm so worried about going away. Normal people would be excited about going on holiday. I'm sat here necking Gaviscon and doing deep breathing in a bag. What am I? A mental virgin who is very unlikely to ever have sex or become a foreign correspondent.

Saturday 14.7.90

7.12 a.m.

JUST WAITING FOR DOBBER, FRAGGLE and Ronni to come and pick me up. I've made the most amazing compilation tape in history. Nervous though. Scared. It's miles away and if I lose it there then I'm not near Mum or Mort or most of my record collection. I can't take that all with me. I'd need a trailer. I need extra space for all my tablets as it is!

10.13 p.m.

We're here. It's a lovely flat. We've filled the fridge. For some reason Ronni brought one sausage with her. We've nicknamed it 'Gazza's Sausage' and we are NEVER eating it! It's the pork product holiday mascot!

Sunday 15.7.90

2.35 a.m.

THE SEA IS BLOODY LOUD. It's not relaxing. It just reminds me of drowning.

Tummy hurts. Head hurts. And I can't do what I need to do to keep spiritual stability in case people notice or hear.

Heart thumping. I'm not dying though. Can't be.

6.29 a.m.
Just looked in the tourist brochure thing in the flat. The nearest emergency department is 59 miles away. That's further than Stamford to Peterborough.

Listening to Soup Dragons' 'I'm Free'. I'm not. Wherever I go there's THIS HEAD. God is out to get me.

Then Glenn Medeiros comes on the radio. I'm blaming him if I go off it again.

7.12 p.m.
A day on the beach. Joy.

Spent a fiver on an inflatable tyre for the sea only for this massive tanned Australian lifeguard to come and tell me that 'inflatables are banned as they pose a safety risk.' Yes Bruce, I have seen the public information films – this is St Ives not Bondi! On the beach all the others looked amazing in bikinis. I had a Daffy Duck T-shirt covering everything and men's shorts from John Justin. I dragged the inflatable out of the water. I got stares. The wrong ones but I'm used to that. One hilarious boy said 'Do you really need another spare tyre?'. I said 'Bet your mouth isn't as big as your cock.' I meant to say 'I bet your cock isn't as big as your mouth.' My mum taught me that one. I got it wrong.

Now we are going out for dinner. Daffy Duck covers lots of things. He can hide more chips.

Monday 16.7.90

8.12 p.m.

I'M PRETENDING TO SMILE BUT . . . head is gone. I had it sorted last year but now SHE is coming back. We went to a nightclub last night. Boys danced round the others. You get the message. You act the tit. My heart was bursting out of my chest. No interest from Cornish men. So at least I know my lack of sex appeal is worldwide and can't be blamed on Lincolnshire. Tonga is good for fat people apparently but as I can't pass Clay Cross services without getting palpitations, somewhere in the Pacific is probably a bit far to go to get laid.

Or is it? I'm mental everywhere.

Gazza's Sausage is going off.

I keep checking my pulse. I'm getting on everyone's nerves. Everyone's.

Think I do need a doctor just to be on the safe side. If I die here it will ruin their holiday even more.

Dobber looks like a lobster she is that red. She never bothers with sun tan lotion. She's heard if you cover yourself in Flora margarine you get a better tan. Men still fancy her though. Even with third degree burns. You can see it.

Why can men see through peeling skin but not through fat?

Tuesday 17.7.90

2.39 p.m.

FRAGGLE JUST RANG THE DOCTOR for me. I feel really, really bad.

6.34 p.m.

Doctor came out. I've got hypertension. He said is there a history of it in the family? Probably. There's a history of everything except malaria and dengue fever. He said my weight wouldn't be helping and to see my GP when I got home.

Told everyone I'm going home tomorrow. To be honest they didn't protest too much. I think it's a relief. Who wants a nutter? I don't want this nutter. Nutters ruin meals, mess up nightclubs and gooseberry your pulling action.

I hope I've got enough money to get me home. I may have overstretched things financially by buying an inflatable tyre that I couldn't even bloody use.

Wednesday 18.7.90

11.34 p.m.

NIGHTMARE DAY – I AM in so much shit.
 Basically got to St Erth station and I only had enough money to get me to either London or Birmingham. So I opted for London. It took ages to get to Paddington then I had to lie to the Underground staff that

someone had stolen my purse and I had run out of money. For some reason I put on an Irish accent because I thought they'd feel more sorry for me. It worked. I even said 'May the Virgin Mary bless you.' I have no idea why. Got to King's Cross. Told the bloke there I had no money for a ticket home. He rang my brother, who went round to my mother and she went down to Stamford station and paid for the ticket. When I finally got home she was LIVID. 'What's the bloody matter?!' and 'There's nothing bloody wrong with you' and 'You've got to get over all this.' Adnan had to stop her having a go at me. I told her I was in pain and she threw a distalgesic at me.

Adnan – a bodybuilder who can barely speak English – has more understanding of me than my own mother. Perhaps Muslims get anxiety and OCD more than SO-CALLED CHRISTIANS!

No. That's not fair. Mrs Kirby the welfare assistant at school is religious and she totally got my panic attacks. She was cross at everyone else and blamed everything on period pains but she was lovely to me.

I think I would test the patience of Jesus with my head. And I just pretended to a member of British Rail that I was Irish and Catholic. I'm going to hell. I'm in hell.

Thursday 19.7.90

9.09 p.m.

NO-ONE OUT. WATCHING TV AND avoiding Mum.

I'm pleased for Elton John that he's got his first solo number one but it's a right pile of drippy poo. 'The Bitch is Back' CRAPS on it. So does 'Rocket Man', 'Goodbye Yellow Brick Road', 'I'm Still Standing' – EVERYTHING ELTON JOHN has EVER done is better than 'Sacrifice'. Same thing with Stevie Wonder. 'Master Blaster' was number two. 'I JUST CALLED TO SAY I VOMITED' was bloody NUMBER ONE!!

The world has no fairness. Mandela is out. The Guildford Four are out but the same old injustice reigns.

And people are cross at me because I can't travel? I'm not a lying, corrupt copper who puts people in prison because they are Irish or someone who buys shit singles to give to boyfriends who probably think they would rather have a gift-wrapped turd than a drippy pile of bollocks.

Wonder what happened to Gazza's Sausage.

Friday 20.7.90

9.12 p.m.

I'M NOW NERVOUS ABOUT SEEING my friends tomorrow. They were . . . I can't blame them. I don't understand it. How can others? If I say God is after me and will kill me if I don't close the door 36 times . . . If someone said that to me I'd be scared. The psychiatric ward. The woman with the itchy skirt going off her head. I wanted to run from that. I've kept it all together with school and socialising but if that goes then what? And the tablets do nothing. They just tingle my head and make me dozy. They don't stop the thoughts, they don't stop being molested, they don't stop God coming after me. They stop nothing.

Oh look, ignore me. I'm lost. I'm lost and I shouldn't even write this down. What's the point? Tell people what happened and they say 'Well that's why you feel this way' like it's magic. No. I was gone way before that. That just sealed it. The icing on the bollocks. The straw that didn't just break the camel's back but totally mashed up its hump. It was confirmation that you can't trust anyone. It wasn't even that much. It was just . . . and then coming upstairs and saying 'Are you crying because of your parents divorcing?'. Trying to twist it. Why am I even going over it? Raking it over. Sod it. Sod it. Just one man. There are lovely men everywhere. My brothers and my dad are lovely. They would kill the wanker. And there's loads of other men in my life. One in particular is too far away and I so want him to be here. NO – I will be BOLLOCKED if some paedophile twat is going to put me off men. No. NO. Even though being touched is . . . it was always difficult. It will be difficult.

Ignore me I'm a self pity merchant. Being felt up has got nothing to do with me being nuts. That started – I can't remember when it wasn't there.

Thank GOD for Kit Kats and Sinead O'Connor.

Saturday 21.7.90

9.12 p.m.
I WENT DOWN THE VAULTS. Everyone a bit shitty with me. I did ruin their holiday. They wanted funny, life-and-soul-of-the-party Rae and they got the mess. They weren't horrible. I just said to one of them 'Are you in a mood with me?' and they said 'Look – it was just all

a big drama that's all.' When I said I can't help being ill they said 'But you're always ill.'

And that's the truth.

Came home. Cried.

Now feel totally isolated from Stammy Gads.

Sunday 22.7.90

7.54 p.m.

BLOODY TORTOISES ARE NUMBER ONE!
Not tortoises. Turtles.

What is happening to the charts?! Teenage Mutant Ninja Turtles?! Where's Johnny Marr? Where's the great pop? It's all shit with shells.

Monday 23.7.90

4.12 p.m.

MUM JUST CAME INTO THE room 'Oh – this came for you whilst you were away. Just found it behind the gas bill.'

POSTCARD FROM HADDOCK!!

It had a photo of a Greek statue on it with an enormous erect cock. Haddock had written:

Dear Rae,

Look at the size of this bloke's doner meat. He must be exaggerating. The beer is cold and the weather is hot. See you soon. Love Haddock XX

Oh you're funny. You're handsome. You get it. You arrive just at the right time even when you're shoved behind a gas bill. I'll put the postcard with all the other stuff I've got of you and wish.

Wonder if anyone else has got one? I'm going down to see Dobber tomorrow. I'll ask her in a secret way.

Tuesday 24.7.90

10.35 p.m.

BIG REVELATIONS TODAY.

1) Dobber tapes *Wacaday* EVERYDAY. She says she likes Timmy Mallett and Mallett's mallet.
2) She hasn't had a postcard from Haddock.
3) She doesn't think Haddock's GIRLFRIEND has had a postcard from Haddock!!
4) No-one has had a postcard from Haddock!
5) Does he just feel sorry for me though? He knows I'm a bit weird.
6) No. He sent me a postcard. He at least thinks of me. He thinks of me when he sees massive Greek erections too which can't be a bad thing.

Wednesday 25.7.90

3.56 p.m.

MUM SAT ME DOWN TODAY and said 'What happened in Cornwall? Do you need to see someone again?'

I told her genuinely no and I thought it was the green jacket potato that I ate on the Friday that made me ill.

She said 'How can a vegetable give you anxiety Rachel? And I told you, you shouldn't go in that café anyway.'

No I don't want to see someone again. Drawing pictures of gardens. According to the psychiatrist, that's my dad the uninterested gardener, that's my mum the unsupportive trellis – what a load of bullshit. Let's talk about what happened. Let's talk about why you feel like this. No. Let's NOT because it doesn't bloody work. I still eat. I still hate myself. I still can't go anywhere. I still check the gas hob a million times. I still have voices.

The ONLY thing that works is friends, music, pretending I'm in a pop video and pretending I am doing Haddock senseless on a regular basis in fields.

Thank you Mr Shrink – now piss off.

I don't want to go to university. I can't. That's the truth.

Thursday 26.7.90

10.34 a.m.
EMERGENCY!! PHILLIP SCHOFIELD IS AT the Radio 1 Roadshow tomorrow in SKEGNESS. Even I can do Skegness for the day for Schofield. I know if I can get on Bits and Pieces I will win NO PROBLEM. I get ten out of ten everyday on the radio and it's PHILLIP SCHOFIELD!!! WE HAVE TO GO!!!

5.35 p.m.

Dobber is working and can't skive as she's had loads of
time off already with the St Ives holiday. Getting there by
train will be a nightmare so YET AGAIN I miss out
because I'm the only person who does not have a car. No
Mum I cannot bike there on my shopper. IT'S SKEGNESS
NOT UFFINGTON!

Friday 27.7.90

2.34 p.m.

A DNAN TRIED TO ASK ME why I was pissed off.
How do you explain the concept of the Radio 1
Roadshow to a Moroccan when you only have
conversational French about buying food in cafes?

'La Radio Une rue est tres bon' is the best I could do.
He just looked confused.

Going to Mort's on Saturday. I'm going to take her the
Haddock postcard so we can have a full analysis.

Saturday 28.7.90

2.59 p.m.

I THINK I'VE MANAGED TO get a high-paying gig at
Stamford Music Shop in Peterborough if I need a year
off (PLEASE LET ME HAVE ONE!). The bloke in there
seemed to like me. I just went in there on the off-chance
of a job. I know shedloads about records and I can learn
about instruments. He said it was really refreshing to see
someone come in off their own back and show such

enthusiasm. I think I could manage Peterborough everyday. I think.

Sunday 29.7.90

12.52 a.m.

WELL IT'S LATE AND BY all accounts I should be extremely knackered. Stayed at Mort's last night. Watched *Dick Tracy* at the pictures which was TOTAL CRAP.

Home is crap. I know I don't make it any better. I hate it but I don't want to leave it. I can't go anywhere for fear of dying. I can't breathe. It's why I had to come back from St Ives really. Mum's right. It wasn't the potato.

Mort and me discussed the postcard at length. Mort said, 'Haddock must think about you loads to send you a postcard. He's on holiday having a great time and you're in his head.' I know. It is weird but then he'll come back and there'll be nothing so you just have to have your dreams. Unless he comes back and things are different and he's had a revelation.

Not unless he's been to Lourdes. I need a miracle. A TOTAL miracle.

Monday 30.7.90

10.34 p.m.

TOLD MUM ABOUT THE RECORD shop job sort-of offer. She said, 'Rachel – you can't have a year off.'

140

BUT IF I'M PAYING MY WAY AND PAYING BOARD then what's the problem?!

Apparently I'm too good to work in a record shop. WHY??!! Here is why – screw my happiness, Mum wants to boast that SHE has a daughter at university. And apparently 'with a brain like mine' (??) I will always have to keep myself busy and distracted. I CAN DO THAT IN HMV MUM!! I could even start my own record shop up. In fact I even have the name already – 'I Know It's Only Rock and Roll But I Like It' Records! IT'S BRILLIANT and everyone is ALWAYS going to need music. But let's not do what I want – let's listen to a checkout woman from Morrisons.

GETTING PISSED TOMORROW WITH DOBBER.

Tuesday 31.7.90

11.45 p.m.

BEEN FOR A DOBBER SESSION. I'm a bit drunk. I hate this life. I despise it. I'm so numb. Sometimes I can't even feel anything anymore.

1) 'Home'
I use that word in its loosest term. No-one wants me here and funnily enough I don't want to be here! A levels and LIFE in general are not helped by Moroccan bodybuilders singing Michael Jackson records AT FULL BLAST. I'm just a gooseberry. I live in my room with White the cat.

2) Mad
I can't tell anyone what I think. I'm not ending up back in a psychiatric ward again.

141

At least that was the first decent piss up of the summer. July was proper crap.

I want to be a woman. A proper woman. Not this mess.

I am so drunk it's phenomenal. I've only had 3 pints of cider. Full of shit la la la.

Wednesday 1.8.90

9.24 p.m.

LET'S HOPE BLOODY AUGUST CAN be better than July which was bollocks.

Fraggle's mum apparently thinks I have a nervous problem. I think I hide things well. I clearly don't. These people notice but they don't actually offer to help.

Oh what can they do? Nothing. No-one can. Professionals couldn't help. People with degrees that can see through all your shit.

Jasmine made Battered Sausage grovel. It's amazing to see the power pretty women have over men. They dissolve.

> DISPRIN
> Sexiness is like a water
> Men are like a disprin
> Watch them fall to bits
> And settle at the bottom
> Bitter and beaten
> I long to be the pill

In fact I long to take the pill for sex reasons as opposed to messed up hormones reasons.

Thursday 2.8.90

8.09 p.m.

I CAME HOME FROM A massive walk to Tollbooth to find Mum and Adnan watching a video of him winning a bodybuilding competition. So I watched *EastEnders* on my black and white portable. This is the WORST REASON EVER for not seeing Grant Mitchell and Simon Wicks in colour. The soap I have watched since 1985 replaced by idiots covered in oil pulling stupid poses. IS THIS HAPPENING?!

Friday 3.8.90

11.24 p.m.

I RAQ HAS INVADED KUWAIT. IF this was two years ago I would be currently running to the Orkney islands with some baked beans. Thank GOD the Russians are sort of not nutters anymore.

Saturday 4.8.90

8.24 a.m.

I JUST HAD A TERRIBLE thought. I hope Haddock is not near Kuwait.

No. That is me just being mental.

Looked at the atlas. Greece is a bit near but I don't think an Interrail ticket covers Iraq.

Could I get over panic attacks to save Haddock from Saddam Hussein? HA HA HA! I'd give it a go. I'd get as far as Heathrow then let the SAS take over.

Sunday 5.8.90

UNBELIEVABLE.
Mum just told me that her and Adnan are getting married on Wednesday!

I said 'Well, don't expect me to be bloody bridesmaid. In fact I'm not coming.' Mum looked upset but come on – I went to the last one! How many others are there going to be?! LIZ TAYLOR OF STAMFORD! She'll have to teach Adnan to say 'I do'. He's having trouble with 'Hello!' at the moment.

That was horrible. Adnan is all right really and his English is a lot better.

Oh no it's not. It's all ridiculous! You know you CAN be single Mum! It is allowed in law for a woman to not actually be with a man. Does she realise this? You don't have to crash from one relationship to another. AND why can't it be a normal Stamford bloke?! It's either a gay Latin teacher or a Moroccan bodybuilder! Why not a butcher or a businessman or someone NORMAL?!! Someone who doesn't need protein booster shakes would be nice!

Monday 6.8.90

12.53 a.m.

JUST BACK IN FROM OLIVERS. Convinced the burger I just ate tasted like bleach. Domestos can't be good for your spleen. Can it burst your spleen? Do you need a spleen?

Head mad again. You're bored with it diary? TRY HAVING IT!

Tuesday 7.8.90

7.24 p.m.

DESIRE TO BE THIN GROWS bigger and bigger. As does my appetite.

HA HA HA!

All my jokes are faintly tragic really.

Mum just showed me her wedding outfit. It's red. It's lovely actually. Her witnesses are her friend and her old psychologist from when she went through a 'strange patch'. Has that ended? When? I'd like to know.

Wednesday 8.8.90

2.56 p.m.

I SHOULD HAVE GONE TO the wedding. Mum may get on my tits like no-one else ever on earth but I could tell her I'd murdered someone and she would look after me.

5.32 p.m.
Mum and Adnan have just got back from their wedding. I ripped up the *Daily Mirror* for confetti. They loved that. Then Mum nipped to Woolies and bought me *Now Dance 902* for being 'so understanding'. Feel like a massive cow. I'm going down Dobber's tonight. Having a honeymoon on Edinburgh Road is bad enough without me being here.

9.36 p.m.
Dobber just admitted she liked Roxette. I may have to go home.

Thursday 9.8.90

8.32 p.m.
DON'T ASK ME WHY I'M writing this. I'm just narked off. To think they know our A level results NOW and they are not telling us! Why must they keep us waiting?! JUST TELL US!!

Friday 10.8.90

10.36 a.m.
HADDOCK POSTCARD 2!!

Dear Rae,
    You'd like it here. Beer is warm though. Keep your boots on. Love Haddock XX

The writing is all over the place. Clearly pissed but WHO CARES!!

Can't work out where it is either. I don't think it's Kuwait or Iraq so I don't care!

11.40 p.m.
Just look at this diary. It reflects total boredom, apathy and basic misery. This summer has to be the biggest non-event of the century. I crash and burn whatever I do. I make the wrong decisions.

I feel as though this is one massive dream sequence. Everything is so hazy. I can't explain. I feel like a ghost haunting my own life. And a ghost that people are actually shit scared of and freak when they see it.

Saturday 11.8.90

11.37 p.m.

MY LIFE IS SO EMPTY without the thrill of Haddock. I go down the pub and it's just NOT the same. I wait for the letterbox just in case he writes again. This is bad though. I should be thrilling myself not relying on a man I've never actually snogged to thrill me, but my life is EMPTY without him. I wish I could take comfort in the mutuality of that emotion but there is little indication as to the depth of his feelings. A postcard with a big Greek penis on it does not mean marriage.

147

Sunday 12.8.90

9.20 a.m.

SO WEIRD DOWN THE PUB last night. George Betchum and Ryan Bates came to see me looking very proud of themselves. They have started to write their own comic book called *237 Ways to Kill Rae Earl with a Cheese Grater*. They think it's hilarious and not at all offensive. And the odd thing was it was quite sweet in a mad way. They said it was a 'tribute' to my weirdness. George had also bought me a badge that said 'Too ugly to live, too weird to die'.

I like it. Fuck it. I'm wearing it.

Monday 13.8.90

12.09 a.m.

PISSED. REALLY PISSED. DOING A Joan Collins. No. A Jackie. DOING A JACKIE.

PROLOGUE

The girl seated uncomfortably in her white iron chair heard him come in. Though quite clinically ugly the boy had a charm of the gods, a wicked animal magnetism that inevitably meant that his life was littered with a string of passionate relationships. Though the label round his neck screamed 'Fatherless person', women flocked to him like flies to a ~~particularly~~ rotting piece of meat that was still attractive even in the most disgusting state. Sweet and irresistible yet guaranteed to leave you with fatal food poisoning. The man was an icon to his male counterparts and had at least grudging respect from the female population.

But the girl, seated upon a throne of the purest iron, could see straight through it. It was not him that thrilled her but the Prince that lagged beside him. Quieter, more assured but as prickly as a cactus that rarely flowered but when it did flowered with pungency. The girl knew when she looked at him that one day she would turn into the Queen. Into a fuck off Cinderella that doesn't quaff diet Coke but champagne.

10.23 a.m.
I think that was meant to be part of a book but I read it back and it's SHIT. Snakebite does not make you write well. I can't see Jackie Collins or Jilly Cooper with Snakebite.

A level results. I am not going to a place I don't want to go to. What was I thinking?! Exeter is too far away. Who cares if Battered Sausage is going there?! Prediction: C for English, D for Politics, E for Theatre Arts and definitely U for History. Unless they give me marks for imagination. Which they won't.

Tuesday 14.8.90

11.13 p.m.
JUST BEEN FOR A CHAT with Shellboss. We went to the Lord Burghley. Then we went to the total classic bar where Nibbles café used to be. Shellboss is

brill. You can tell her anything and we have a right laugh.

Bad thoughts returned with a vengeance. Stress. Anxiety. Worry. I can feel it.

Massive numbness. It's HADDOCK! He gives me my spark! He makes me feel funny and pretty. He's like a lucky mascot and he's probably shagging some impossibly skinny Italian woman. I just love him. I LOVE HIM! This is love I can totally feel. He is totally gorgeous and amazing.

When I look in the mirror I can't write this because I feel I shouldn't because I'm fat and I will never get him. I wonder how he's doing? What's he doing now? Please don't be shagging Cicciolina the porn star. I love the Pop Will Eat Itself song but don't shag her. You're fit enough, you're in her league but don't do it.

Wednesday 15.8.90

4.56 p.m.

ADNAN HAS TO GO BACK to Morocco! Apparently being married isn't enough! The Home Office have to come and investigate to see if the marriage is legitimate! They think Adnan has just married Mum to get a visa. Yes – because you'd really leave Morocco, a bodybuilding career and constant sunny weather to live in Edinburgh Road and watch Mrs Bark peg her washing out with a fag hanging out her gob for a British visa. You HAVE to be in MAJOR LOVE to do that! It PROVES it.

I told Mum I thought it was a load of racist Tory crap and she had to agree. She voted Conservative in the early 80s though. One time at Peterborough station the striking

miners were collecting and they said 'Support the miners!'
and Mum said 'Yes I will – the working ones!' I was
horrified. The miner swore at her. I agreed with him!
What goes around comes around. That's what Nan used to
say. Thatcher closed all the mines and she's now closing
down marriages and love. I hate to say it but it sort of
does serve Mum right in a way.

Really, this is just Thatcher biting Mum on the
marriage bum.

Perhaps Mum voted Tory at the same time that she was
seeing the psychologist! HA HA HA!

I am trying to be Ben Elton. I am not.

Thursday 16.8.90

12.03 a.m.

HERE WE FINALLY ARE! A level Day is here with
a vengeance. The culmination of two years' work.
Well the bit of work I have actually done.

The grades I need for the University of Exeter – ABC.

I hope TO GOD I don't get them. I desperately want to
go up North (I KNOW this was meant to be. I KNOW it).

Can it really be a year since A level Day last year? I
wish Haddock was here. If I do really well it would be a
bloody good excuse for reapplying and more importantly
A MASSIVE HADDOCK hug. I'll get drunk before so I can
actually enjoy the cuddle.

I'm sick of having no-one to hold me at times like this.
Times when everything is up in the air and nothing is
working in my head. I'm scared. Terrified.

11.14 p.m.
BCD!
B in English
C in Politics
D in Theatre Arts
U in History

Full of shit – la la la! Crashed and burned. Not bad but not good. Future is getting weird with it. What the hell?!

Mort did brilliantly and Shellboss got BBB! JAMMY! She has done NO work for two years but I love her so it's totally deserved.

The totally worst thing about the whole day was that Haddock's girlfriend said to me 'I looked in Chelsea's scrapbook of her school years. She has a photo of Haddock – now that is NOT on!' FUCK! I have currently about 10 photos, 3 cuttings from the *Stamford Mercury*, 2 postcards and a crap plastic plant that I won't let go of!

I haven't got a scrapbook. I've got a HADDOCK-BASED MUSEUM.

And I am not letting go of it. I'll hide it but it's MINE.

Friday 17.8.90

9.23 a.m.

MUM WAS ACTUALLY QUITE NICE about my A level results. She said 'If you've done your best you can do no more.'

Er . . . I haven't but when you've got a tumour in the bum a month before your exams and you were in a psychiatric ward just before your A levels started you're hardly going to be swanning into Oxford are you?!

Now she's asking me what I am going to do next. Well Mum, because we don't have a home phone and arranging your entire future from a phone box is difficult when you have A) limited 10p pieces B) women are shouting at you to hurry up as they need to speak to the DHSS or C) people are chanting 'Jabba' or 'Fat Bitch' at you. I'm going to see if I can go over the road and use Mrs Armitage's home phone. I need Exeter to reject me and then I need Essex to tell me to bugger off too then I CAN have a year off.

3.45 p.m.
EXETER HAVE REJECTED ME!! YES!! Sorry, they said, I needed to meet my exact grades! No problem posh lady. Thank you for being nice but that's actually just what I wanted thank you! Just did a victory dance round my bedroom to MC Hammer but pretended to Mum I was gutted and ate two packets of crisps to make it look really authentically pissed off.

Oh I ate the crisps anyway because I wanted to but it helped the general effect.

Saturday 18.8.90

11.01 p.m.
I MIGHT BE READING TOO much into this but when I told Battered Sausage I wasn't going to Exeter he looked a bit narked off. Oh live with it. He blows hot and

cold and takes the mickey all the time. I'm not being donkey to his racehorse.

And another thing – yes – Dobber looks like Betty Boo. She is gorgeous and undeniably looks like Betty sodding Boo. And yes Battered Sausage, I look like Pavarotti without the beard. Well Betty Boo 'Doin' The Do' only got to about number eight in the charts and 'Nessun Dorma' got to number two so looks aren't actually everything are they? No!

Yes. YES. YES. Of course I'd rather look like Betty Boo. It's called looking on the bright side apparently. Psychiatrists tell you to do it but most of them don't look like sweaty Italian opera singers.

Sunday 19.8.90

11.23 p.m.

WATCHING A PROGRAMME CALLED *FALLING on your Feet* – it's a show for jobless teenagers. It might come in useful.

I will have to go over to Mrs Armitage's again tomorrow to use her phone. Just reject me Essex! PLEASE!

Monday 20.8.90

7.13 p.m.

WHEN WILL I BE A proper woman? My tits grew way before anyone else's. I was in Harwayes getting bras when other girls were still in vests. Yet now

154

they snog, have relationships and I'm still the fat cow
making everyone laugh and then pissing off home for
ten chocolate digestives and a *Prisoner Cell Block H*
session.

I suppose university could be the chance to start again.
Be who I want – not what I am.

Tuesday 21.8.90

5.09 p.m.

I GOT INTO THE UNIVERSITY of Essex. Bastards. I
feigned happiness on the phone when they told me.

Mum is thrilled. Of course she is. A clever daughter not
mad in the loony bin – somewhere else being clever
doing clever things.

Mort has given me a pink dinosaur teapot as a well
done present. It's lovely. I'll keep it forever but – Essex.
Why the HELL did I put Essex?! I've never been there!

I have to go. I can't stay here but I'm terrified.

Wednesday 22.8.90

10.39 p.m.

A PPARENTLY HADDOCK'S GIRLFRIEND GOT
OFF with someone. She's finished with Haddock in
his absence. It's all a storm in a teacup. I've seen it all
before.

Mum has a phrase – she says some people will always
fancy a rough bit of scrag end even when they have steak
at home. I know what that means now. Haddock is fillet

steak. The finest. And yet his girlfriend has just snogged scrag end.

Fig said to me tonight 'You're back on form Rae. You've been a bit weird.' Yes Fig I've gone mental but nobody has noticed. I didn't say that of course. I never say what I'm thinking.

Thursday 23.8.90

11.35 p.m.
IT'S WEIRD BEING NUTS. BEING on holiday proved it really. Had I got meningitis or brain or bum cancer everyone would have been lovely and turned up with grapes, magazines and plastic plants. When I'm mad people either move away from me or offer me the emotional equivalent of the shit sandwich.

And bugger off Timmy Mallett – *Wacaday* was bad enough but making records is bang out of order.

Friday 24.8.90

10.47 a.m.
I SWEAR I WILL BURST.
Haddock is back from holiday. He just turned up on my doorstep this morning. I can't even express the level of gorgeousness. He HAS A TAN. Never have I been so aware of my inadequacy, my fuck ugliness and my weight. How much does it kill me? It won't stop.

He told me they had finished. I want them to get back together. At least she is lovely. What if he ended up with a bitch? His girlfriend said to me 'Rae, will you talk to him because he listens to you' so I tell him the truth – she loves him and she's lovely. I don't tell him the other part of the truth which is 'Haddock. I love you. I genuinely think we are meant to be together and what will it take to make you like me in a sex way?!'

Haddock's girlfriend calls me her marriage guidance counsellor. I feel like a double agent.

And Haddock looked lost. A person totally lost and it kills me because I think he's lovely. He IS lovely.

11.58 p.m.
It's all sorted!

What did I tell you?!

Bugger this all. Stop all this noise because it's me who is left at the end. Stranded.

Saturday 25.8.90

9.23 a.m.
NEXT TIME SOMEONE ASKS ME my advice on anything or for help or anything I am going to point them in the direction of the following people – Irma Kurtz in *Cosmopolitan*, Clare Rayner on *TV-AM*, Marje Proops in the *Daily Mirror* and Miriam Stoppard wherever she is. I can't sort out my problems let alone yours. In fact I might write to them all. Irma Kurtz is a bit harsh though. She'd probably tell me to pull my crap together. She'd be right.

Clare Rayner is nice. I'd like her to be my mum. Dear Clare. Please be my mum as mine is marrying bodybuilders and having tattoos on her arse. P.S. Can I come and live at yours during my year off please?

Sunday 26.8.90

1.32 a.m.

BLOODY HELL! WHAT THE HELL IS GOING ON! THIS IS BAD!!

Dobber couldn't get into Olivers for some very strange reason. The bouncer wanker completely thinks she's someone else that he had to carry out once. She is not. I've had to prop her up sometimes but never carry her out. This is bad. Olivers is the place where we all go. We need to SHIMMY!!

Battered Sausage's amazing and totally BOLLOCKS theory is that maybe Betty Boo has been to Stamford, got bladdered and had to be carried out of Olivers. Naturally they think Dobber IS Betty Boo and that they won't let her in again.

4.12 p.m.

I have spent most of the day trying to convince Battered Sausage that Betty Boo has never been to Stamford. There is no mention of it in any *Smash Hits* (I keep them all) AND it would have made the *News of the World*. It has NOT. Plus Olivers would love Betty Boo to come to their nightclub. No celebrities have ever come to Stamford.

No – the following celebrities have come to Stamford.

1) Harry Secombe doing *Highway*. Sang a hymn on the Meadows. VERY unlikely to have visited any nightclub.

2) Michael York – actor bloke in *Logan's Run* – smiled at Mum. I have heard this story a billion times.
3) Gary Wilmot. Opened a jewellery store down Stamford Walk.
4) Bill Oddie came to our school to talk about the rainforest. He looks nothing like Dobber by the way.
5) Una Stubbs dressed as Aunt Sally from *Worzel Gummidge*. She came to open the Bradford and Bingley building society when I was about 9. Dad refused to wait with me for an autograph as he wanted to go to the pub. If I told Mum that fact even 9 years on she would go mad.
6) The Queen and Princess Anne. I can't see the Queen dancing to 'Naked in the Rain' by Blue Pearl but I'm sure in Battered Sausage's head it's possible.

Monday 27.8.90

9.34 p.m.
I'M TRYING NOT TO THINK of Essex. I'm trying to think of other more important stuff like 1) getting Dobber back into Olivers 2) convincing Battered Sausage that Betty Boo is very unlikely to visit Stamford and even less likely to sleep with him if she does 3) trying to get Haddock out just so I can see him before we move to opposite ends of the world.

Tuesday 28.8.90

9.35 p.m.

TODAY DOBBER ADMITTED TO ME that she likes, no, LOVES 'Itsy Bitsy Teeny Weeny Yellow Polka Dot Bikini' by Bombalurina.

I have told her she should not be allowed in any nightclub ever.

Wednesday 29.8.90

4.56 p.m.

JUST WHEN MY LIFE COULDN'T get any weirder, today I was watching *Tell the Truth* with Fred Dineage and Mrs Crane our teacher from school was on it!! I COULD NOT BELIEVE IT. I managed to quickly tape most of it! Anyway I've not told anyone WHY but everyone is coming round tomorrow to watch it!

9.12 p.m.

Mum was cross when I told her everyone was coming round tomorrow (the house is a bit of a tip) BUT when I showed her the video she totally understood. She said 'And people think I'm eccentric.' To be fair being on *Tell the Truth* isn't half as loony as having a bodybuilder tattooed on your arse but I wasn't going to argue.

Thursday 30.8.90

6.32 p.m.

EVERYONE THOUGHT THE VIDEO WAS EPIC. In fact the words 'I'm Mrs Crane and I'm the school teacher' have become a national catchphrase. Well a Stamford one anyway! Ronni thinks we should get T-shirts printed with it on!

I'm going to miss all this. There's always someone up for a gig and a laugh. Even about stuff featuring Fred Dineage.

Friday 31.8.90

11.58 p.m.

HADDOCK OUT BUT TONIGHT HE was a bit of a git. He was with these two amazing looking women (where did they come from – Europe?) and he winked at me and said, 'Don't get the wrong impression Rae – seeing as you're my girlfriend's friend.'

What is that actually meant to mean? I'm not your friend anymore?

And Battered Sausage singing 'Itsy Bitsy Teeny Weeny Yellow Polka Dot WILLY' full blast in the Vaults is not funny – it's tedious. Especially after the 405th time.

Saturday 1.9.90

5.39 p.m.

YET ANOTHER ARGUMENT WITH MY mother. She started this one by calling me a 'little shit of an 18 year old'. I said 'Better a little shit of an 18 year old than a massive shit of a 48 year old.' That was it. The killer line. I beat the teacher at her own game.

Sunday 2.9.90

2.46 a.m.

DO YOU KNOW THAT IS just the way it goes. You think Saturday is going to be a total load of crap and then you get a great night down the Vaults. Firstly I got pissed with Mort down the Meadows. What a classic love she is. Then, I can't believe it, without any pre-planning I had a massive in-depth session with HADDOCK.

I can't live with what a total and utter epic person that man is. He says he's 'sorted himself out' (I'm beginning to wonder if I'll ever be). He told me about things. He's had some quite hard times in his life. Why isn't he addicted to fucking chocolate and crisps?

Anyway some things I said
1. I wish you were my brother (NO I DON'T – I
    WISH WE WERE BLOODY MARRIED YOU
    HANDSOME, FUNNY AS HELL, BRILLIANT SOD)

2. You are in my top 5 best friends.

<u>Things he said to me</u>
1. Stop undervaluing yourself.
2. I'm sure you'll find a bloke at Essex.
3. I know you're lonely but there's no need to be. You're brilliant.
4. If you lost weight you'd be doubly attractive. (NOTICE – 'doubly attractive' – in other words I'm at least a bit attractive to start with)

Dear Dr Haddock,
    You could cure my loneliness.
    Please write me a prescription for your love and frankly a totally hardcore full-on session of DO.
    Love from Patient Earl (PATIENT in many ways too. Too bloody patient)

Monday 3.9.90

2.13 p.m.
KEEP THINKING ABOUT SOME THINGS Haddock said. His girlfriend must talk about me. That's weird. I don't want people to get this impression that I'm this fat, ugly, unapproachable pitiful figure.
    Even if I am.

163

Tuesday 4.9.90

4.23 p.m.

TOMORROW I'M GOING TO HULL with Aristotle. I love Aristotle (that's another Mort codename) – we have a real laugh. He's Battered Sausage's mate and he's going to Hull to sort out his accommodation for next year or something because he's going to university there. I'm in charge of music because his crappy car doesn't have a radio or cassette player (his parents are loaded – this makes NO sense). He's just got a mini ghetto blaster at the back. He loves The Wonder Stuff and it will be good for me to go somewhere different. I took some of Mum's funny tablets just in case I have a 'do'.

Wednesday 5.9.90

THIS IS A WEIRD ENTRY because I will sound mad. I think I'm meant to go to Hull. I can't explain it. We just went all round the city and this instinct, this voice in my head said 'Come here'. It felt RIGHT. Now every time I have ignored that voice (and it's different to the panic voices) something bad has happened. Like when – when you know what happened. I had a funny feeling about that man but I told myself it was just me being stupid and then look what happened. He got me on my own and ... Anyway this voice was shouting 'Come here ... Come here!' Even though there was nothing special about it. In fact one of the last things we saw was

164

this really dodgy sex shop! But it didn't matter. It all felt like it was meant to be.

And it's near Leeds. One train journey away. Just one.

Aristotle's music was great too – 'Charlton Heston' by Stump. LOVED it!!!

I feel like I've . . . found somewhere. It had white phone boxes. It was all odd but odd in an 'I'm Hull – deal with it' sort of way.

But I'm going to Colchester. Where the phone boxes are red and we are nearer to France than Leeds probably.

Thursday 6.9.90

10.54 a.m.

> My personality eats up my gender
> The femininity is denied
> It doesn't hurt me till I see him.
> Then I feel like a boy monster
> I've got tits but they're hidden
> Underneath this uncomfortable gob.

No. Why should I stop being funny? THAT'S ME.

The one I want doesn't even want me to stop being funny either.

Just went mad in my bedroom to 'Groove Is In The Heart' by Deee-Lite. I could just dance some days till I died. Or was nearly sick, like then.

Friday 7.9.90

11.01 p.m.

WHAT A PALAVER! MAJOR PROBLEMS. Haddock's girlfriend in tears. I love him but he is acting like a bit of a git. She stayed at mine last night. I had to hide the Haddock museum of photos and artefacts so far under my mattress. She has no idea. I can tell. She honestly believes I just like him.

Saturday 8.9.90

7.09 p.m.

BLACK BEAUTY IS BACK ON TV! It's got the same theme tune and everything! It's set in New Zealand though but who cares?! I LOVE *BLACK BEAUTY*!! Might gallop down to the Vaults with that on my L–N compilation tape. Thank you London String Chorale.

11.08 p.m.
No Haddock. Dobber still can't get in Olivers. *Black Beauty* was the highlight of the entire day.

Sunday 9.9.90

8.23 p.m.

SAT HERE LOOKING OUT MY window, listening to 'Wishing on a Star' by Rose Royce. It's the most beautiful song. It's about when you've lost someone and you just want them back. I wish on everything. On stars, on rainbows, on the mangy black cat from 3 doors away that sprays on Mum's passion fruit plant and drives her loony. I wish on it all that the bad stuff all goes away and only he'll be left. He is the prize for getting rid of all the fat on my body and the mad stuff in my head. But even I know it's going to take more than wishes.

If I know that, why do I have to swipe myself 6 times and say the Lord's Prayer 10 times perfectly to stop my mum dying.

'Groovy Train' by The Farm is brilliant.

Monday 10.9.90

4.35 p.m.

I'VE BEEN TRYING TO SORT out my grant today. I get £790 A TERM!!! THAT'S A FORTUNE!! Mum says you'll have to make it last but £790!! AND apparently because you're a student the banks give you massive overdrafts too! HELLO HMV!! I can just get the textbooks from the library and MUSIC BINGE!! This may have been the greatest thing Thatcher has ever done!

Tuesday 11.9.90

11.01 a.m.

WOKE UP THIS MORNING TO find an envelope put through the letterbox. It had a chicken bone put through it and the message 'Put this in your nose and fuck off back to where you came from'.

Now I've had some fat abuse in my time but this does not make any sense at all.

1) I don't binge on chicken. Stamford doesn't even have a KFC. I occasionally eat too many spicy wings and stuff but not regularly.
2) I was born in Stamford Hospital. Go back to where I came from?! Do they mean Rutland Road where I first lived or Stamford High School?! Either way it's STUPID.
3) Putting the bone of anything through someone's letterbox is vile.
4) So now I get bullied not just in the street but in my own house too by thick twats who make no sense. WANKERS.
5) I wish I could get out of this place. Even though I'm scared to.

7.09 p.m.
I showed Mum the letter and the bone when she got back from work and told her I was sick to death with being bullied. Mum said 'Rachel – things aren't always about you and this isn't for you. It's for Adnan. It's saying he's a savage. Bone through the nose? Go back to where you came from?'

Oh she's right. That's BLOODY AWFUL. So now we basically live near Hitler and a load of fascists! I know I don't always like Adnan but that's not because he's black! It's because he sings badly, eats everything in sight and doesn't get fat and turns this place into a right gooseberry palace. He would do that if he was purple! Where do people get off being horrible to him because he's black. Why don't we just rename Stamford South Africa!! No – because even they've released Nelson Mandela.

I asked Mum what she was going to do about it. She said 'What can I do? Hide it from Adnan.' Then she told me people had been making ape noises behind his back too. 1) That's too horrible to even think about 2) That's suicidal! Adnan could kill them with his little finger. But he won't, that's the point, because he's a real gentle giant. So he just has to put up with it.

Just like me. We just have to put up with it. BUT WHY SHOULD WE?! I could lose weight and stop it. He can't change his colour. WHY SHOULD HE ANYWAY?! AND WHY SHOULD I LOSE WEIGHT? I never thought being black and being fat had anything in common but we both have a massive history of injustice.

9.05 p.m.
Can I just say I am not completely comparing the civil rights struggles of Martin Luther King and Malcolm X to me being obese. That's bloody ridiculous but it proves people get shit for just being different and it's always from the same idiots. Bet the Green Lane Twats are behind the note. I wish Adnan would kickbox them in the face but he won't. He's too nice.

He goes back on Friday too. Which will make them think that they've won.

I might put an advert in the *Stamford Mercury* that says 'To whoever sent the anonymous note and bone. You are a thick, spineless twat that needs a good kicking'. I don't think they'll put that in the announcement sections

though with the 'Congratulations on the birth of your
beautiful boy'. There should be a COCK NOTICES section
though. I'd pay.

Wednesday 12.9.90

11.48 a.m.
I WALKED INTO TOWN THIS morning and every
person I saw I thought, 'are you the phantom bone
sender?' It just makes you doubt everybody. Who secretly
underneath it all is a total racist who would happily be a
member of the National Front? And what is going to
come through the letterbox next? A bomb? A dog poo?

9.09 p.m.
Just rang Mort. Jasmine was telling her that Battered
Sausage is hypersensitive and spends loads of his time
asking her if 'Rae really meant what she said'.

HA! Isn't it good to know that men suffer too AND that
I can make them suffer!

Thursday 13.9.90

11.02 a.m.
N OTHING CAME THROUGH THE LETTERBOX
this morning except some kind of bill. Wonder if
Mum would prefer a bone and some racist balls. At least
it's not demanding money!

No she wouldn't by the way. That was a joke. If Mum
finds out who sent the bone she will be scary. She's not

violent. She will just destroy them mentally. I've seen her do it.

Good. They deserve it. I hope they end up in Ward 4 of Edith Cavell doing exercises with beanbags and I hope all the psychiatrists are Asian, Chinese and really, totally black.

8.32 p.m.
I just watched *Top of the Pops*. The KLF's 'What Time Is Love?' is a MONSTROUSLY good piece of music. It was all slightly buggered by Sonia singing some utter balls but you can't have everything.

Friday 14.9.90

10.12 p.m.
ADNAN HAS LEFT. HE HAS to for Home Office immigration purposes. I said goodbye to him this time. He's a nice bloke and doesn't deserve to become the Steve Biko of Stamford. Now Mum has to go through this massive process to prove that her marriage is legitimate. It's probably because he's not white. This country is racist. Sinead O'Connor is right in her song 'Black Boys On Mopeds'. She's spot on.

11.23 p.m.
Thinking about it, it's probably more to do with the fact that Adnan is 20 years her junior, he can't speak English very well, she'd known him for about 5 minutes before they got together and she'd only just divorced her 2nd homosexual Latin teacher husband BUT still – Britain is racist. FIGHT THE POWER!

Saturday 15.9.90

10.45 a.m.

L IFE IS A GIFT BUT this present keeps repeatedly
 kicking me up the arse.

I'm getting hammered tonight.

Sunday 16.9.90

9.23 p.m.

D EAREST, DEAREST HADDOCK,
     Where do I start?

You're never going to see this so I don't think it
matters where I start does it?

I think you'll never talk to me again after last night. I
know I was pissed but that's no excuse is it?

Look at me Haddock. I can't explain it to you but I'm
so fuck ugly, fat and have enough hang-ups to keep the
psychiatrists in business for years. And you. You are
bloody everything. What I feel for you cripples me. I've
had it for so bloody long. In fact since exactly 23.7.89.
That brought it down to an immature level. I don't want it
to. This isn't a school crush. It's something deeper.

Oh God – it all comes out wrong. That sounded bloody
laughable. That's what I am. Oh I am not going to get
self-pitying. I'm worth more than that.

Last night I can't remember what you said. I remember
crying and you taking me out of the Vaults and you kept
hugging me and holding my hand and basically being a

172

total love. Saying all these lovely things. You told me you loved me. But I know you said that because I was so upset and I told you I wanted to die. Half truth. I don't, I just can't find a way to like living.

Then you force-fed me some pizza and then I farted in front of you. OH, TRAGIC AREN'T I? God I've broken all the rules of etiquette. Not only being drunk in front of the man I love but farting in front of him too!

I hate myself sometimes (you're not meant to put yourself down either).

I know I sound like a prattling schoolgirl. I just think I've found someone and something beautiful and I want to be part of its life. Please let's never lose touch.

I am a floundering pissed up twat but I do love you.

Monday 17.9.90

STILL FEEL TOTALLY EMBARRASSED.

Tuesday 18.9.90

11.30 a.m.

A TYPICAL DAY.
Wake up at 7.00 a.m.
Feel happy for 1 second then think of Haddock.
9.00 a.m. Watch *The Odd Couple*.
9.35 a.m. Go back to bed.
12.00 p.m. Get some dinner.
12.35 p.m. Go back to bed.

Eat. Eat. Eat. Eat. Eat.
Try to forget.

Wednesday 19.9.90

9.45 p.m.

ONE HALF OF ME SAYS you have every reason to
be terminally depressed –

I am fat, not beautiful, character faults galore, a family
that try to help me but can't because they don't really
know me, I'm a total hypochondriac, an image problem,
I'm a cheap laugh to many people, frigid, more chips on
my shoulder than the Brittania takeaway etc etc etc etc.
INSECURE!!

But then again –

I have half a brain and nice hair.

Thursday 20.9.90

8.45 p.m.

TODAY HAS BEEN A BARREL of laughs! Mum,
since she got home from work, has sat in the
armchair staring into space. IT'S HER BIRTHDAY!! I know
Adnan has gone home but at least she has a relationship.
That's more than me! Then she started going on about
Winston Churchill. 'You know Rach – they say he was a
hero but we waited for hours for him and he didn't even
wave from his car. He didn't come and save me either.'
When I said 'Er Mum . . . he was a bit busy trying to save

the free world' she shouted 'But this was in the early 1950s!' I left her staring into space and went down the pub and had a birthday drink for her. I wish she'd cheer up a bit. I know she is down but I know her. She'll make it work. She always gets what she wants.

Friday 21.9.90

11.01 p.m.
'My biggest vice when I fall from the tightrope is to attack venomously the ones I love the most'.

Richard Burton.

Why O Why O Why O why am I such a bloody bitch to Haddock? I take the piss all night – NIGHT AFTER NIGHT. I make him laugh but that's all I do. Why can't I just tell him how I feel?! Soon it's going to be too late.

No I can't risk it – it's the wrong time. I need to be thinner and prettier with decent bras NOT from old lady shop Harwayes. THAT'S the time to make my move. When my knickers are small and my bra is frilly.

I did my numerology today. I need to change my name or I'll never be successful.

Haddock doesn't. He's set for life. I did his too. Actually if I take his surname I'm fine.

Now I sound completely obsessed. Only you know how bad this is diary. Well you and Mort and even she doesn't know just how deep it goes.

175

Saturday 22.9.90

8.09 p.m.

IF JEREMY BEADLE WAS A woman he wouldn't be on TV even though I could do his job a million times better than him.

I'm going down the pub. This country is a mess.

Sunday 23.9.90

11.37 p.m.

HADDOCK SAID TO ME TONIGHT, out of the blue, 'I'll come to see you in the week.'

So I said 'OK.'

Oh don't get your hopes up. It will be about me giving him something back that I've borrowed and forgotten about. What I want it to be is 'Let's not go to university, let's travel the world. Every time you have a panic attack I'll give you a paper bag and you can blow into it and then we will do it in every continent, even Antarctica, totally naked except for furs.'

But it will be about a jacket or something because that's my life. Jackets. Potatoes. Medicines. Panic attacks. Jive Bunny and the Mastermixers still making records that Mum plays full blast. 'Can Can you party?' In a word – No.

Monday 24.9.90

12.16 a.m.

IF I WASN'T SO TOTALLY knackered I could write mountains and acres.

Why do I think such bloody horrible things?! If I told people what was going on in my head I would be locked up forever. I want to be at peace not in a constant state of worry.

So bloody worried about uni. What if I hate it? What if they hate me? What if I can't do the work? I can't stay here but I don't feel I can go anywhere else.

Haddock told me last night he doesn't want to come out in Stamford again. He says he hates it. It's 'full of bad memories.' It is for me too but it's full of classic ones too. Doesn't he remember the great nights? There were lots of them.

I'm already talking about it all in the past tense.

It feels like it's gone already.

Tuesday 25.9.90

4.32 p.m.

NOW I KNOW WHAT DONNA Summer meant in 'MacArthur Park'. I always thought she was talking bollocks but now I know what she was trying to say. The recipe she had was the special time, the mix of people and you can't get that back. That's what I've had and now it'll only be there in holidays if it's there at all. It's gone. Bloody hell it's all gone.

Mess. Mess. Mess.

Wednesday 26.9.90

7.34 p.m.

HADDOCK CAME ROUND.
He didn't say 'Let's go travelling and do it in every continent known to man' but he did say 'Here's a good luck card and a crap present. It's all I could carry on my moped. See you Saturday.'

Then he went round to see his girlfriend.

The card says 'Dear Funky Chick. Have a good time. You will. Make sure this stays blue. Love Haddock X'

The present was a mood ring. It apparently changes colour with your mood. Blue means calm and relaxed.

I love him. I'm sick of writing it. You're sick of hearing it diary but he could just – but he's going. He's going.

Thursday 27.9.90

6.37 p.m.

MUM SAID TO ME 'HAVE you started packing for Essex yet?'

I told her yes. The truth is I've got 5 tins of beans, a box of sugar lumps, a pink dinosaur teapot and a mood ring.

Friday 28.9.90

9.24 p.m.
TODAY'S BIG REVELATION. DAD IS taking me to Essex because a) he knows where he is going b) It's near Ipswich where he lives. c) I can fit everything in the back of his Opel Manta d) According to my mum 'it's about time he did bloody something.'

Well it'll be nice to see him for the first time in yonks – even if he is taking me to doom.

Saturday 29.9.90

12.16 a.m.
THE END OF AN ERA.

Sunday 30.9.90

2.10 a.m.
THIS REALLY IS THE END.

I am dreading tomorrow. Will I get that awful thing when I feel that blind panic for home and I start to feel ill? I want to be all right. I'll fight this thing. It's not part of me. I've got to purge it out.

That was the last Saturday night. Haddock just gave me a hug, winked and went. And that was it. He's gone. Too late now. I've let the person who seemed to understand me the most run off without telling him a bloody thing.

7.10 p.m.
Well I'm here at the University of Essex. I'm on the tenth floor of Keynes Tower. My TV doesn't work and my room is a bit bare and made of breeze blocks. My window only opens a little way. I'm thinking that's to stop me jumping out of it.

Oh fuck off Rae – it's a university not a psychiatric ward.

The courses don't start till next week so this is totally for what they call Fresher's Week. Going to go down and watch the film they are putting on for us. It's in Spanish – *Women on the Verge of a Nervous Breakdown*. I think someone is trying to tell me something.

11.23 p.m.
Film was brilliant and I've met some lovely people from Tawney Tower! Aggi and Sarah. Told Sarah I had panic attacks and she said I could kip in her room on the floor on the first night which was dead sweet of her. There doesn't seem to be anyone on my floor of my tower yet except for mature students.

Monday 1.10.90

5.45 p.m.
I SPENT MOST OF THE day with the Tawney Tower lot. I kept talking about Stamford a lot till one of them said 'You go on about your mates all the time. I'm sure

they're nice guys and that but shouldn't you talk about something else?' They've got a fair point but I feel that . . . I don't feel well. I've had about 2 sugar lumps since I've been here. I can't eat. I dread going back to my room. It's then it all hits me. The fuck up. The massive fuck up.

9.35 p.m.
Told Aggi how I felt and she is letting me sleep in her room. We are watching *Killer Clowns From Outer Space* on video which is horrible but I don't want to be on my own. There was a 'Library Orientation' today. I don't like lifts anyway but these don't stop apparently. You have to jump out at just the right point. It's wrong. It all feels wrong. This place feels wrong. Tower blocks. Concrete ponds. Confused ducks. American Studies?! Why am I doing American Studies?! It involves a year in America?! I'm struggling in Colchester. I can't go anywhere. But I can't go home. That's finished. This is finished. Finished. Fucked. I don't know where to go.

Tuesday 2.10.90

8.12 p.m.
AGGI AND SARAH TOLD ME today that I can't keep sleeping in their rooms and I really had to go back to mine. They are right. Plus Sarah has already pulled. She shouldn't be giving me hot orange squash and managing my hyperventilating when she should be shagging. So I did go back. I met a bloke called Dave-O who was reading a book about Sodom and Gomorrah for

fun. We chatted for about half an hour ABOUT HIM and then he said 'this is quite a boring floor isn't it.' Yes Dave-O it is. Asking questions about other people might help you.

This isn't right. It's not just me being weak and mad. I'm not meant to be here. It's all wrong. I can't go home though. Mum will kill me. Actually that might solve a problem. No – she wouldn't stop me coming home but . . . oh I would let so many people down. I'm the first girl in a million generations to go to university. My great grandmother was in service scrubbing floors even though she was clever as hell, Mum had to gut fish rather than do exams. My grandmother was a bit thick but that's not the point. I'm messing up the opportunities they all wanted. Well let them have them because I can't cope with them. I want to go home. I want to be at home.

I realise most of them can't have the opportunities because they are dead. Mum could though! Let her come to university if she wants it so much. There's even younger men here for her to go out with!

That was nasty. I feel mad.

Wednesday 3.10.90

5.24 p.m.

MY HEAD GOT SO BAD today. I took 4 Co-codamol. I fainted by the student union laundrette. I ended up in the university clinic. I told the doctor what I'd taken. They didn't need to pump my stomach. 4 tablets is a piss poor amount of pills, I know, especially spaced out over 3 hours. I just didn't want to be conscious for a time. I don't want to be dead. I just don't want to be here. They let me lie down on one of their stretcher-beds for ages to think but thinking just went in circles and ripples and spirals and words. Bloody words that mean nothing. Explain nothing. I'm watered down to the same old crap. I can't cope. I have to go home till I can.

They've all been lovely but you can see in their eyes – 'weirdo'. I have to go and speak to one of the student counsellors.

I'm leaving. I'm going to ring Mort tonight and tell her.

9.06 p.m.
Mort got it. Mort always gets it. It's not right. I know. She knows it. I've now just got to tell my mum.

Thursday 4.10.90

2.10 p.m.
I'VE JUST BEEN TO SEE the student counsellor. She was really kind. She asked me to give her some background on my life and my family. I told her my mum had just divorced a gay Latin teacher, then married a Moroccan bodybuilder and had him tattooed on her bum. My dad was a big drinker and he'd never been that bothered and I had always suffered with anxiety. I also told her about the time I was molested by a weirdo. I told her I thought I controlled nearly everything through my thoughts and that I had a growth removed from my anus one month before my A levels.

There was more stuff I could have told her but we only had an hour.

She looked at me for ages and said she thought I would benefit from further counselling.

9.12 p.m.
I rang Mrs Armitage tonight and told her that I needed to speak to my mum. She went to get her and predictably she went mad. 'I never thought you were a quitter Rachel. I'm telling your dad not to come and get you. You've got to stick it out. You've got to give it a chance.' I've told her I'm not. I said 'Look it's like the song says "We want the same thing!" I do want to go to university – just not now.' She just shouted 'Rachel – you're not coming home' and put the phone down.

I have to make the decision tonight.

Friday 5.10.90

1.05 p.m.
WHERE DO I START? I was frightened of coming here. Petrified. Still feeling pressure from myself and others – 'You can't have a year off'. So I got here and it's WRONG. WRONG! WRONG! Not wrong will eventually be right wrong. I can tell the difference. I can't go against what I want. I don't want this. I don't want university now. I can't cope with it. I can't convince my mother that reapplication is right. Perhaps use a Belinda Carlisle song to explain it was a bad move, I don't know WHERE I can be happy but it's not here. My mum says there are no jobs and this is the easy way

out and I'm a quitter BUT NO. SHE'S WRONG THIS TIME.

Thank GOD for Mort and her family. They get me more than my own family do.

I hate myself. I feel like crawling underneath a stone and shrivelling up. I keep fucking up. How many more times do I need to scrape myself off the floor.

I'm such a horrible, weak, evil cow and I hate myself. Despise myself.

I wish I was somebody else. Anybody else. Even bloody Timmy Mallett. Saddam Hussein. A member of Roxette! ANYONE!

Sometimes it feels like dying is the only way out of this mess. I've never felt so much despair. But I don't want to die. I just don't know how to live without messing up.

I'm leaving. The Mortimers are coming to get me tomorrow. Without them I'd be in a total mess.

Saturday 6.10.90

7.01 p.m.

MORT AND HER DAD HELPED me pack. They thought it was a bloody depressing place too. As I was putting stuff in the back of the car one bloke said 'Going already?' I said 'Yeah – not for me.' He shouted 'Not given it much of a chance have you?' Er NO. No I haven't but some of us just KNOW when things are wrong toss face so bugger off and let me get on with my own life. I've noticed that people with Inspiral Carpets T-shirts think they can say what they like. They can't.

When I got home Mum was LIVID that I was there. She

shouted at me for ages about how I had to get down the Jobcentre first thing in the morning. The thing is it will be SHUT as it's a SUNDAY. Apparently I've also got to start paying for food and 'board' as that's what REAL adults do. I've been buying my own salt and vinegar Hula Hoops for years and hiding them so ZERO CHANGE THERE WOMAN!

Sunday 7.10.90

9.23 a.m.

AND NOW I'M NOT ALLOWED to read the Sunday papers because they cost money too!

I completely missed all the news last week. Germany is now officially reunified and massive again. It's probably a good thing that Nan is dead as she'd be currently preparing for another war. She never liked the Germans. To be fair they did try to kill her husband so she had a point. There is a time to move on though.

I can't say that – I still feel bitter about loads of things. Bethany nicking everyone I ever fancied last year, Haddock not fancying me, Maria McKee getting to number one with drippy smooch crap about having an orgasm, Happy Mondays not getting to number one BUT Sonia getting to number one. SONIA!!!

My Haddock mood ring is permanently black. This means I'm constantly depressed or it's broke. Both are right.

9.54 p.m.

I have to ring up school tomorrow to tell them I've
dropped out and to make an appointment about
reapplying. That means I have to go through the entire
Essex saga YET AGAIN. I might get a T-shirt done –
'Don't like tower blocks. Didn't want to go there in the
first place. I'm nuts. NOW FUCK OFF'.

Monday 8.10.90

8.34 p.m.

I RANG SCHOOL FROM MRS Armitage's. Mrs Crane
the teacher was totally brilliant and I'm going in
tomorrow. Feel bad now about taking the piss out of her
on that TV show she was on.

Also I went in the Jobcentre and The Body Shop in
Peterborough want temporary staff up to Christmas! Shelf
stacking in one of my favourite shops! I can do that –
PEASY! The Jobcentre rang them for me and I have an
interview on Thursday. UP YOURS MUM. I CAN COPE IN
THE SO-CALLED GROWN UP WORLD!

I've got to tell everyone I'm home. I'll write to Dobber
and Battered Sausage. I'd rather Haddock didn't know just
yet. Ever in fact.

Tuesday 9.10.90

12.55 p.m.

S O HERE WE ARE – reapplication! I'm currently in
Stamford High School's careers library. I'm REALLY

flavour of the month. I am totally embarrassed by my shitness but fuck it – come on – this won't be the first time you've slipped in shit and it certainly won't be the last Rae.

Still I'm a total crash and burn artist. Not knowing if I can survive. Am I weak? Do I need my head taken apart more? Am I insecure or a raving exhibitionist?

It's time to move on I suppose.

I have to convince the universities that my A level grades aren't a fair representation of my academic ability. Of course they aren't! I was having a tumour taken out of my bowel a month before and did hardly any work for two years.

Must go. Have to see Mr B later at 1.30.

4.12 p.m.
Thank GOD for Mr B – a teacher who actually respects my bloody intelligence and says he will write me a sod off reference. He's Sagittarian. He gets it.

Wednesday 10.10.90

9.30 p.m.
BODY SHOP INTERVIEW TOMORROW. I don't need to prepare. Passion fruit cleansing gel to me is a way of life. As are Japanese wash grains and patchouli oil. Some of my mates go in there before a night out and put their make-up on for free from the samples! They never get done! It's the best shop ever.

Ideally, life would be spent in bed with the curtains closed, black and white TV and you-know-who stark bollock naked (me in his pyjamas) with those big monstrous arms round me in a constant state of semi-awakeness and warmth.

1) What would we live on?
2) Probably soon get bored.
3) Why am I such a screwed up obsessive git?

Thursday 11.10.90

11.20 p.m.

B ODY SHOP 'INTERVIEW' WASN'T! I couldn't get a word in edgeways. Mum thinks they have all the people they need and they just have to go through the motions.

So much other stuff is going through my head.

1) Will I get to uni and stick at it?
2) Will I get to a good poly?
3) How will people react to a potential new sex Rae?
4) What do I actually feel for him? Merely lust or real love or both which is actual relationship perfection?
5) Will I ever be settled?
6) Will I ever be married?
7) Will I ever get rid of the psycho bits?
8) Should I go and see a counsellor as suggested by the student counsellor. I don't want to get locked up again.

Friday 12.10.90

11.01 p.m.

CRASHED AND BURNED! WENT TO school and handed UCCA form in. Then I went down the Meadows and I was sat by the big willow tree and I heard 'RAE!' I realised it was HADDOCK'S GIRLFRIEND. Bless her. She is funny and pretty and sweet – I should bloody hate her but I can't.

They aren't together amymore. Haddock is apparently having a whale of a time. Perhaps he has woken up to what the rest of us have known for ages. HE IS THE LIVING EMBODIMENT OF HORN.

Anyway I told her he'd come round. Honestly I don't know if he will or not. I miss him everyday but I've just learnt to live with it like I learnt to live with everything else. His mood ring is black and rusting but I keep it on.

Why must I pray and hit myself in order to reach that security? It's an awful killing feeling. Repeat and repeat like a washing machine on spin – around and around. It's the only way to obliterate the pain.

That's what I am. A really crap washing machine that doesn't get anything clean but just goes round and round making a fucking big noise.

Saturday 13.10.90

7.45 p.m.

THE TRUTH IS I'M WAITING for someone to save me. I'm waiting for someone to come along with this amazing big wand, wave it over my life and make me skinny and normal. I want a way out. AN ANSWER. Not therapy sessions or clay or painting or sodding group sessions. I WANT AN ANSWER. Why can't someone just save me from me?

And why can't someone save me from Saturday night television? Surely every animal ever has had every disease ever on *All Creatures Great and Small*?! Can't they get an interesting animal on like a tapir instead of a bloody poodle or a Friesian EVERY WEEK?!

Sunday 14.10.90

10.24 a.m.

SLEEPING UGLY
I've looked in the best mirror,
My hair is down, unrestrained
My skin is pure, angelic, untouched.
I'll just check the gas for the seventeenth time,
And switch off the discussion about the recession.
The front door shuts it all behind
I throw the key to the grass
And feel the fruit in my hand

My gown has attracted a thousand stares,
So misplaced amongst the Saturday shoppers,
I ignore the gasps, the glares,
I take a bite of my apple
And I lie down.
I can feel a thousand eyes over me
My hands are clasped to my chest
My eyes tightly closed
Don't try to push me into the recovery position
I have fainted, read my note
Until this piece of apple is removed from my fat
    throat,
By him
This pedestrian precinct will be my home
I will sleep here till he arrives
So walk around me
He will come to know
Just make sure he comes before the police arrest me
    for obstruction,
Or the psychiatrists take me for therapy
Or the hire company come for their dress back
Or his lover comes baying for my blood
I know he'll come
Because he bloody loves me.
He whispered that to me in jest
But I know he meant it.

Monday 15.10.90

9.02 a.m.

YES MUM, I WILL GO down the Jobcentre after *Kilroy.*

Do I want a job at Morrisons? Er. NO! American tan tights, zip up dresses and my mum watching my every move whilst people ask me where the Jif and Persil is ten times a day – NO THANK YOU!!

The Body Shop will be different because people actually want to be there and buy nice shampoo.

Tuesday 16.10.90

10.52 a.m.

POSTCARD FROM LEEDS

Dear Rae,

Colchester is just full of pissed Essex girls anyway.

Love Haddock X

And you wonder why I can't get him out of my head and why he'll probably be there FOREVER.

Wednesday 17.10.90

9.25 p.m.
I WISH I COULD BE that totally together happy person
I am sometimes ALL of the time. Then I could actually
be useful.

I've met hundreds of blokes and no-one sparks my soul
the way that he does. I know I've put him way too high.
He's only a man!

Thursday 18.10.90

10.35 a.m.
JUST GOT A LETTER – I HAVE THE BODY SHOP
JOB! I GOT THE FIRST JOB I WENT FOR! STICK THAT
UP YOURSELF MUM!

6.45 p.m.
Mum's reaction was 'Well done. You've got a job in
retail.'

Oh sod off!
I start in November. EVEN MORE TIME OFF!!

9.35 p.m.
Did all my applying today. So in the end it's unis –
Hull, Leeds, Leicester, Liverpool, Sheffield.

Polys – Manchester, Leicester, Nottingham, Sheffield.
Top of the Pops had the Happy Mondays on tonight
but it also had this bizarre woman in a kaftan and a hat

from Canada singing something that should be on Radio 2. There's no need for that shit Rita MacNeil – get back to feeding your beavers.

If Battered Sausage was here he would have a field day at me even mentioning the word beaver as he is mentally 12.

Friday 19.10.90

7.28 p.m.

1 CANDLE MAKES SUCH A difference to a room compared to a harsh light.

1 tape brings back memories of the person who made it and gave it to me. Every song is a memory. It's a time. It's us sitting there listening to 'Function at the Junction' by Shorty Long and throwing beer mats at each other.

I see so much bad in me. In the mirror I see a thing not cared for.

Equally sometimes, and I feel big headed even writing this, I see something that could be beautiful both inside and out. Something I could really grow to love.

I think that his love could cure this. But then I realise that he can't cure this. No other man could solve my loneliness either.

If I don't love myself nothing will cure my loneliness. So I have GOT to learn to love myself before I can enter anything.

BUT HOW? You go into Stamford Library – there are books on great orgasms, orchid growing, how to do the Rubik's cube (does anyone care anymore?! – just take the stickers off!!) THERE'S EVEN BOOKS ABOUT LULU! But there's nothing on HOW TO LOVE YOURSELF.

If somebody wrote a book called *How To Stop Being a Twat* it would sell a MILLION copies – especially to me.

But I'm sure to make it all add up I need someone to build me up a bit. The thought of him just chases all the bad away.

No Mum – this candle will not burn the house down and I am not 'navel gazing' again.

Saturday 20.10.90

8.34 p.m.
STATUS QUO – PLEASE FUCK off with your Anniversary Waltz. You should not be celebrating.

This is now a Saturday night in Stamford. Shouting at Quo. Perhaps leaving university was the wrong thing to do.

Sunday 21.10.90

9.45 p.m.
FEEL LONELY, LOST, CONFUSED AND disorientated.

I so desperately want to be reborn to get rid of all the compulsions, the obsessions and to love myself. I'd be better use to everyone if I could just sort myself out.

Mum has bought the Rita MacNeil record. Of course she has. It's about a 'Working Man'. Endangered species here love – Thatcher has killed all that.

Monday 22.10.90

11.29 p.m.

I WISH I COULD JUST hibernate through all this.
   Mum is certainly nicer to hedgehogs and blue tits than me.

Tuesday 23.10.90

8.34 p.m.

MUM PUTS OUT FATBALLS AND filled coconut shells for the birds. Yet when I eat anything these days she basically offers me the bill.
   Bloody hell, things are bad when you want to be a robin more than yourself.

Wednesday 24.10.90

11.05 p.m.

DO NOTHING ALL DAY THEN wonder why I can't sleep at night. Feel grotty tired yet can't sleep. Bad thoughts.

11.53 p.m.

I just coughed up blood. I've probably got TB or something terrible from cows. I spend more time with farm animals than with real people.

My chest is so tight. It could be the 3 cigarettes. Thank GOD for Tiger Balm which I have smeared all over my chest. I AM SO SEXY! I smell like Boots. Not the perfume section. The pharmacy.

Thursday 25.10.90

8.45 p.m.

WHAT REALLY WORRIES ME IS that music is ending or heading to some sort of crisis. Tonight's *Top of the Pops* – 'Unchained Melody' by The Righteous Brothers AGAIN. 'Take My Breath Away' by Berlin AGAIN. It's like people have run out of ideas. I saw this film once called The Seventh Sign with Demi Moore where it said that Jewish people believe that there is something called the Guf. All souls of people come from the Guf and when the Guf is empty the world will end. I think the pop Guf is nearly empty. Perhaps everything has been done and it's only backwards now. The Roses were the end. Now it'll just be Sonia destroying Motown.

I think I do need to go and see someone but it can't be prompted by Sonia.

Friday 26.10.90

8.45 p.m.

FIRST OF ALL, LET ME give you an example, diary, of my unique screwed up mess! I am convinced that I have killed someone today by looking at them. When I write it I know it sounds mental but I had to go and pray in the fucking toilets at Peterborough station to reverse my evil. I had to kneel in a cubicle. It was vile but felt I HAD to do it. How can I tell a psychiatrist that?!

Then I had soggy disinfectant knees from kneeling and praying.

Mum told me to stop wallowing in self pity today. She never tells me how though. How you can stop being mental? So I come to my bedroom and I write and I listen to music and I look out my window at people queuing at the chip van. Billy Bragg and 'Rainy Night in Georgia' by Brook Benton go well with people queuing up for kebabs.

Saturday 27.10.90

1.35 a.m.

THE JAMES WHALE RADIO SHOW proves that a man can be gobby and ugly and everyone loves them. When will I be sorted?

Sunday 28.10.90

10.25 p.m.

HADDOCK'S GIRLFRIEND HAS JUST BEEN round. God she's lovely and I'm actually the biggest bitch ever. In my head I have slept with her on/off boyfriend about 5 million times and not just in beds either – On fucking trains!! In fields!! EVERYWHERE! I have done it with Haddock in my head in every country in the world. Except in war zones or potential war zones like Kuwait. I have the time. Have the fantasy. Will travel.

But I've done nothing and wouldn't do anything anyway so I listen to her.

Actually, would doing it in a war zone make things even more erotic? Perhaps in a combat situation you think could be dead in the next hour so let's have really HOT WILD sex because we might as well?!

I have a feeling that's how my actual mum was produced in 1942. That was not a good thing. Not my mum being born. The circumstances. It was not good that when my Gran's husband came back from war after 2 years my mum was in the cot. My mum paid a terrible price for that.

Sex in Kuwait, even with Haddock, is officially OFF.

Monday 29.10.90

10.47 a.m.

I HAVE AN INTERVIEW IN Hull on Thursday!! I
CANNOT MESS THIS UP. This is the ONE place I just
think I could be OK at. I don't know why, I just have a
feeling that it's RIGHT. I feel like it's meant to be. The
Housemartins were from Hull. I LOVE the Housemartins.
The Beautiful South are from Hull. I LOVE them too.
There was NEVER a famous band from Colchester.
NEVER. It's not a music city. That's why the University of
Essex was never going to work. Nothing musically good
will ever come from Colchester except from a military
marching band thing that my dad will love.

Tuesday 30.10.90

9.35 p.m.

I TOLD MUM ABOUT THE Hull interview as I need
some money to actually get there on the train. I told
her I thought that Hull was my destiny. She wet herself
and said that she thought that was the first time she'd
ever heard anyone say that.

Wednesday 31.10.90

6.02 a.m.

I THINK THAT THE BASIC problem I have, on top of being mad, is that fundamentally I am a lazy bitch. I wish somebody would pay me to lie in a field and listen to 'The Boy with the Thorn in his Side' and dream of Haddock. My CV for that is PERFECT.

University of Hull tomorrow. Rituals mad today. Please, please don't let me mess it up.

Thursday 1.11.90

10.36 p.m.

I HAVE HAD THE MOST MAD day in history. I think I've been offered a place at the University of Hull. It was as simple as that even with my grades. I think but I'm not sure because it all went like a dream and I had to meet different people. And weird stuff happened – I'll write tomorrow. Mum has made me Super Noodles.

Friday 2.11.90

9.23 p.m.

I NEEDED SLEEP. I WAS gone last night. No energy these days for anything. Here's what really happened . . .

I got to Hull (panic attack at railway station but got through it by breathing and listening to ABC's 'Look of Love'). Firstly met up with this professor bloke who said there's no way you can get in here with those grades. I said 'My teacher has written a letter – I was ill before my A levels.' He said he'd go and see if the special admissions officer was in. She was, by TOTAL luck (I TOLD YOU, DESTINY!) She's called Patsy Stoneman and we just got on brilliantly. I saw *Ulysses* by James Joyce on her bookshelf and I said 'I've read that.' Actually I've just read the back of it and a bit of it but we talked about that and Orwell. It was AMAZING, we talked about books for TWO hours. I told her about my life. I didn't tell her about the psychiatric ward. There was only really Reader's Digest books in there – it wasn't exactly relevant. She was lovely and at the end I'm sure she said 'I think we can offer you a place here despite your grades.' I'm sure she said that.

Now I'm thinking that she didn't but not even I could have misheard that?!

Could I? I had nothing to eat all day and things only made a bit of sense after the Super Noodles.

I think I've done it. A fuck up out-of-the bag epic.

Saturday 3.11.90

12.32 p.m.

NO HULL OFFER YET BUT even if she'd posted it first class it probably still wouldn't get here today.

Sunday 4.11.90

10.13 a.m.

NO HULL OFFER!

11.01 a.m.

Mum has reminded me it's Sunday. Lazy post office bastards – some of us are on tenterhooks here. It can't be that hard to pedal round on a bike with letters!

Monday 5.11.90

8.59 a.m.

NO HULL OFFER AGAIN. PERHAPS somebody who had read bloody *Ulysses* all the way through came in after me and my place has gone to them.

I've just got to get on with it now. I can't wait by the letterbox everyday – it will send me mental again. And it's freezing because Mum won't put the heating on. A homemade draft excluder in the shape of a sausage dog made from old tights is NOT ENOUGH to stop us freezing to death!

Tuesday 6.11.90

11.10 p.m.

IT'S IMPOSSIBLE TO KNOW WHERE to start. There is nothing yet everything to write. I've gone over it 1000 times in my mind but as usual when it comes to writing it down I seem to have forgotten what I want to write.

I'll start from where it ALL must start from.

Self love is the absolute core. YOU MUST LOVE YOURSELF.

This is not a suicidal entry. I am 'down'. I am 'sad' but I feel, above all the confusion, curiously positive. There is a bit to love – just at the moment there is more to detest.

1) I hate myself for the betrayal of my sex. There seem to be 3 genders – male, female and RAE. I have to be at the centre of things. I have to cause a stir. I know I'll never be a wallflower but it's overpowering. I'm too much. Like a massive stinking bright flower. I HATE writing it but I'm not a girl and I want to be. I have this vision – she's not perfection but she's Rae and she's a girl too! And she's strong and if you fancy me GOOD but if you don't – bollocks!

2) I hate myself for my weak screwed-up-ness. Sometimes I think it's major enough to warrant more help. The terrible thoughts. I bash myself to pieces in order that the physical pain will replace the nasty voices in my head. But I'm cut and

bruised. It's not right. The compulsions –
checking the gas, checking the tins so nobody has
tampered with them. It's ridiculous I KNOW! The
hypochondria. I shouldn't know so much about
botulism. The hypochondria, the worrier, the
neurotic. All these things partly inherited. Can I
blame anyone though? Anyway, it's there.
Messing up good days and making bloody bad
days shitter.

3) I hate the way I look. It's an ugly thing. Uncared
   for, grossly fat and I'm NOT happy with it. I binge
   ALL the time. I'm out of control. I hate the fact I
   couldn't get into a bed naked and say 'Look, this
   is me mate and I LIKE IT!', which brings me
   conveniently on to sex . . .

4) Sex. I hate myself because I'm frigid. When really
   in my head I do it several times an hour! I
   haven't snogged anyone for nearly 2 years. That's
   NOT NORMAL. And the one person I did snog felt
   sorry for me. Well sod that! FUCK YOU DEAR!

I feel as though a lot of things have messed me up. The
event when I was 12 is just a part of it. The psychiatrists
always go to that but I was mad before that. I've always
felt wrong. Perhaps I'm a man in a girl's body. I'm a total
bloody gay if I am. I think I would be a better gay man
than a girl. I liked my mum's homosexual second
husband's wardrobe more than my own for a start!

My mum is mad but she's had a life of TOTAL shit and
now she's getting reborn. Just her adolescence is crashing
head on into mine. She's not a raver. She doesn't go out
and never drinks but men love her. And she swings from

total neuroticness to pompous extreme self confidence. She's either Freddie Mercury or that woman from the psychiatric ward with an itchy skirt. It's all fucked.

Wednesday 7.11.90

4.23 p.m.
I HAD AN APPOINTMENT AT the hospital today. My ovaries are still a mess but the doctor was really sweet and from Sri Lanka. He said 'I am not saying you are terribly fat (I am) but I think losing weight would really help your condition.'

I'm getting Christmas over – then I'm losing weight. If I do get into Hull I'm not far away from you know who. Chocolate Brazils or . . . there's no contest! Plus if I CAN lose weight I think it will slightly piss off Mum because she can't!

Thursday 8.11.90

9.34 p.m.
THE POP GUF IS NOT empty! EMF are BLOODY AMAZING – in fact they are UNBELIEVABLE!! HA HA HA! What a song!

Paul Gascoigne, however, really needs to stick to football and crying because 'Fog on the Tyne' is UTTER shit.

Friday 9.11.90

7.12 p.m.

I START WORK ON MONDAY. I'm totally wound up about it but it could be a laugh. It IS The Body Shop. Anita Roddick is always cool on TV – it's probably going to be a doss.

The rumour is Battered Sausage is out tomorrow. I feel nervous about going out but I'm doing it.

Saturday 10.11.90

11.25 p.m.

I WENT TO THE VAULTS. I saw the familiar back in an Aran cardigan (WHY does he wear those?). Battered Sausage was back and I had a blind panic but I ignored it. Then he dragged me into the bogs because he needed a serious chat. This ended up being about his problems with women and his weight gain. He said 'Rae – how do I lose weight?' WHY IS HE ASKING ME?! Do I look like I'm a slim success?!

Then he's back to Exeter again. Everyone's spread out. Gone. Me still here. Trapped totally by my own crapness and choice.

Sunday 11.11.90

7.58 p.m.

I JUST HAD A MASSIVE argument with Mum. She said 'Good luck for tomorrow.' I shouted 'I don't need your bloody sarcasm thank you!' Apparently SHE says she wasn't being sarcastic. Balls. Yes she was. She thinks I won't be able to do it but I bloody will. In fact I could end up managing a Body Shop and doing my degree at the same time. It would be nice if someone in my family actually had some FAITH in me. Whatever I do I'll just be the nuts one. I could become prime minister and Stamford would still say 'She went a bit funny when she was a teenager you know.' OH SOD OFF – I'm RUNNING THE COUNTRY AND STOPPING WARS.

Well I'm not – I'm just stacking shelves with patchouli oil but that's not the point.

Monday 12.11.90

9.45 p.m.

THAT WAS HARD. LIKE REALLY HARD. I think I must have burned a million calories today. Easily. Thank GOD The Body Shop is next to McDonalds. I had 9 Chicken McNuggets at lunch, milkshake, large fries and an apple pie. I NEEDED IT!

Basically my job involves going up 2 massive flights of stairs, getting the stock and putting it on the shelves.

People really have got to stop buying camomile shampoo.
I fetched it about 10 times! The shop is busy all day.
Everyone seems nice enough but you NEVER stop and it's
a bit boring. OK, Mum was right. It's TOTALLY boring.
And customers are snappy to you and treat you like shit.
Dear woman whose life apparently depends on her getting
cruelty free mascara – I've got 3 A levels! You don't need
to explain things to me like I'M STUPID. I'm glad rabbits
haven't been hurt in the cosmetic process either but what
about cruelty to humans – The Body Shop need a lift! I
bet rabbits would find it easier hopping up the flights of
stairs to the stock.

I seriously think I've damaged my back.

Tuesday 13.11.90

10.12 p.m.

T HERE WAS A KIWI FRUIT lip balm crisis today.
Me and Maria who I work with got kind of told off
for not 'replenishing quickly' enough BUT the Mama Toto
range was running very low and there were pregnant
women everywhere. We decided stretch marks came first.

Mum just asked me how it's going. I told her 'Great!' I
lied. It's doing my head in. No-one actually needs lip
balm. JUST BLOODY LICK THEM! It doesn't taste of fruit
but it moisturises them.

Apparently Geoffrey Howe has made some bizarre
speech about cricket which basically was saying Thatcher
is a dictator bitch who doesn't listen to anyone. How
thick is he that he has just realised that?

I'd like to see how long Maggie lasts dealing with the

Peterborough public's cosmetic needs. I smell constantly of Fuzzy Peach. I had McDonalds again – mainly to get over smelling of fruit.

Wednesday 14.11.90

7.40 a.m.

O H NIGHTMARE IT'S WORK.
    I never thought I'd ever hate passion fruit cleansing gel but now I do.

11.01 p.m.

> Someone plays with us.
> Everything I wished he'd said to me
> He has said to her with such accuracy
> It's almost spiteful
> I don't mean heavy sighs of I love you
> Things more intimate, exclusive.

Don't ask. I'm too tired or pissed off to explain. And I smell of Dewberry.

Thursday 15.11.90

10.32 p.m.

I THINK I'M GOING TO hand my notice in tomorrow. There have to be better jobs than this.

I'm on a complete downer. I have no desire to do or be anything really. I just can't face putting out anymore novelty soaps of blue whales.

By siding with Haddock's girlfriend I've totally lost him as a friend forever.

Jive Bunny and the Mastermixers on *Top of the Pops* tonight finished me off. It was like a sign. You're beaten Rae. 'Let's Swing Again'. When will it ever end?! I think cosmetic experiments should be done on Jive Bunny. I'd shop there. I'd buy everything.

Friday 16.11.90

10.35 p.m.
I HANDED MY NOTICE IN. The manager was really lovely and said 'But Rae you're a lovely person to have around.' I told her I'd found a better job meat packing (lie!) and it was a shame as I'd really enjoyed working there (lie!) and now what the HELL do I tell my mum.

Saturday 17.11.90

10.50 a.m.
WHERE THE HELL AM I?
    I've got an interview at the University of Sheffield. I better go. I still haven't heard from Hull.

7.23 p.m.
Told Mum tonight I had handed my notice in as I thought I could get a better job. She didn't say anything. She just started whistling. That means she's so angry she can't form words.

Oh sod off. Bet I can get a better job.

Sunday 18.11.90

9.03 p.m.

SO EVERYONE IN STAMFORD KNOWS I left The Body Shop. Too much hard work for not enough dosh after 16 goes on train fares. Plus 2 flights of stairs 30 times a day could give me an injury that could last for life!

People stand judgemental on me. What the HELL has this got to do with them?! Unless they pay for my food, AKA my mother.

Monday 19.11.90

6.37 p.m.

I COULDN'T SEE ANY BETTER jobs at the Jobcentre today.

QUOTE OF THE BLOODY DAY
'Rae – you don't understand I need a cuddle.'
OF COURSE I UNDERSTAND.

All my friends think I am a weak cow that can't stick at anything.

They are a bit right.

All my friends think I don't need love and hugs and sex.

They ARE SO TOTALLY WRONG it actually scares me.

I used to love my Body Shop Japanese wash grains.
Now they are a gritty sink reminder of failure.

Tuesday 20.11.90

9.12 p.m.

Dear Haddock,
I wish I was you. Actually nice and good looking and you just don't think that you are. You stick at crap jobs. You travel. You sort yourself out.

Don't change. I know I've buggered things up but wherever you end up don't change. What you've got inside perhaps needs an untangle but don't destroy it or cover it up with man crap because you're special and different. Don't bugger it up mate because you're just gold underneath it all. You're fantastic at rugby but don't become a lad. Please don't get into anal chugging. Your arse is too magnificent to spoil.

Yet another letter I will never send. More emotional shoved in here. Closed. Under a mattress.

Wednesday 21.11.90

10.58 p.m.

JUST WHEN I THOUGHT THINGS could not descend any further into the depths of doom and misery TODAY happened!

1) I now have convinced myself that I have spray painted intimate secrets of people all over the

214

Meadows. This is because I just SAW spray paint in Wilkos. NOT BECAUSE I own some or would ever do that it's just that my wanker brain saw some and decided to torture me because the cocking thing can.

2) Ronni slightly lectured me about not being able to keep a job or stay anywhere. She's right. I'd like her to have my head for a day though.

3) Battered Sausage is coming back this weekend. Actually that's a good thing. If university is so good why does he keep coming back?

Thursday 22.11.90

10.43 a.m.

BLOODY HELL MRS THATCHER HAS RESIGNED. THATCHER HAS GONE! I ran down the phone box to ring Mort (she's working at her dad's factory). I think this was why I gave up the Body Shop job so I could watch Thatcher go. SHE'S GONE! She was totally stabbed in the back by the people who were meant to be her friends. Geoffrey Howe may make shit speeches about cricket but he batted her straight over the head. GONE!

I can't get over it – Thatcher GONE! It's like she's always been there.

4.13 p.m.

Still can't get over Thatcher resigning. She's resigning though to a lovely house and now she can just travel and play golf and do whatever old prime ministers do.

Wish I could resign like Thatcher.

It must be hard though – she had all that power. She could ring world leaders when she liked. Now she can only ring for a pizza and when people realise it's her they will probably spit in it.

WHY AM I FEELING SORRY FOR THATCHER?! SHE MESSED UP EVERYTHING AND NEVER GAVE A TOSS. And in *Smash Hits* she said she LIKED Cliff Richard. Sympathy for that woman. I need my head sorting. I do need some more tablets.

Friday 23.11.90

12.50 a.m.

LET ME WRITE IT HERE because you don't give a fuck.

I think because I haven't prayed enough I have told random people about how much I love Haddock because someone mentioned Haddock and my brain shouted something but I KNOW my mouth didn't.

I'm totally fucked & disturbed. I don't want to be like this. I want to be normal.

I know! WHAT IS NORMAL?! Well it isn't this. And neither is Anthea Turner presenting *Top of the Pops*! Yet more evidence that the pop Guf is emptying.

Saturday 24.11.90

BATTERED SAUSAGE IS TELLING WOMEN he is a virgin. Apparently people LIKE virgins. Hello? HELLO??!! MASSIVE VIRGIN HERE WILLING and ABLE!!

Sunday 25.11.90

3.07 a.m.

I HAVE HAD A TOTALLY crap day. I bloody roared
last night. If one more person asks me what happened
at Essex I'll swing for them I swear it. I'm fed up with this
town thinking that my business is theirs – WHEN IT
ISN'T.

5.13 p.m.
University of Sheffield interview tomorrow. I honestly
don't care but I'll have to show my face. I only partly
picked it because of The Human League and ABC.

Monday 26.11.90

9.23 p.m.

T HE BLOKE I MET AT the University of Sheffield
today looked like the sort of man who presents very
old Open University programmes. He was wearing SOCKS
AND JESUS CREEPERS. I couldn't take my eyes off them
so the interview did not go well. He asked me what I
thought about Yeats. I said I thought he was good. WHY
DIDN'T I JUST ADMIT I DIDN'T KNOW HIM?! He asked me
which specific poems I liked I said 'I prefer John Donne.' I
don't think I'll be getting an offer but I don't think I want
one either. Plus I hated that last song The Human League
did – 'Human' – with that drippy speaky bit in the middle.

On the way back I sat on the train with a soldier who

was really interesting. I told him I kept leaving stuff. He said everything in life was shit to start with. Everything. You just have to get over the shit. He nearly left the army. When I asked him why he didn't he said 'because things always get better and when they don't – that's when you go.' Then he got off at Nottingham. I didn't have a chance to add in the fact I was nuts but perhaps it was meant to be. Perhaps I need to stick at stuff more. He bought me a cup of hot chocolate too. No – he was not on the pull. He was kind and I told him I was skint. I couldn't marry a squaddie. I have to do stuff 36 times and worry when people I love go to the shops – let alone a FUCKING WAR.

Tuesday 27.11.90

11.23 p.m.
I WENT DOWN THE BAR tonight where Tegs works. It got really busy so she asked me if I wanted to help out. I LOVED it. I could do it too and I was BLOODY GOOD at it. My maths is good too! Piss off GCSE – I knew fractions and long division were pointless. Anyway she's asked me if I want to work tomorrow too. Answer – YES!!

Wednesday 28.11.90

5.45 p.m.
JUST TOLD MUM I WAS working in a bar tonight. This apparently makes me 'just like your father.' Thanks for the encouragement. Well Mum – here's the

deal. You like Moroccan bodybuilders and having them tattooed on your bum. I like socialising in bars and watching MTV. WHAT IS MORE NORMAL?!

Thursday 29.11.90

5.34 p.m.
I HAD A LETTER FROM Dobber yesterday. I live for letters from lovely friends who actually have lives.

But at least I have the bar job now on and off and I LOVE it. It's good fun and it pisses off Mum. The thing is I think I'd be a brilliant landlady. Like Bet Lynch but without the leopard skin. Actually no, why not WITH leopard skin and a miniskirt? WHY NOT? I'M A WOMAN.

But do I actually want to be that sort of woman? I look stupid even in earrings.

Friday 30.11.90

12.20 a.m.
IT'S LESS THAN 2 WEEKS till my birthday. I can't believe it.

10.56 a.m.
I haven't heard from Haddock for ages. I can't analyse this too much. It's depressing.

3.05 p.m.
　　　1000 pieces of pretentious crap,
　　　Litter all the scrawny books

In secret I embarrass his name
And misunderstand his sympathetic looks.
He used to think I was just a bitch
Slowly that began to amend
And then one of the exclusive
But like a sister. His bloke-like friend.
But bloody hell don't act like my brother
I want to be your everything and your lover.

Saturday 1.12.12

12.22 a.m.

AND DIDN'T NOVEMBER END AS craply as it started!

Work at the bar was fine until a piece of posh-public-schoolboy-shit kept calling me fat over and over. Kept saying 'Watch that belly!' and 'How do you fit behind there?' and 'Wouldn't you be better in a wider bar?' WHAT A NASTY COCK. What a complete BASTARD. He doesn't even deserve to be mentioned in this diary and HE was an ugly shit. International WANKERTHON!

1.12 a.m.

Yes he does. I HOPE YOU NEVER GET A STIFFY AND YOUR KNOB DROPS OFF. I hope you are bullied. Really bullied till you get home and cry and shove matches in your arm but people like him never do. They LOVE themselves. That's why I hope he gets a gangrene knob. I don't even know if that exists but . . . he's damaged one of the few places I felt USEFUL and WANTED.

5.50 p.m.
I'm listening to George Harrison. He calms me down.

That git last night. If I wasn't such a strong person (!!) I would think he had given me a complex . . . If I didn't have one already.

This is a weird bit of psychology. Sometimes when someone has shared a hard time with you and you've been their shoulder to cry on they don't seem to want to know you when they are better. It's like they are embarrassed by what you know about them. It's like YOU are living testament of THEIR bad time. The person then becomes resentful. There's almost dislike. I think this is what happened with Haddock.

So next time someone tells me their problems and confides in me I'm going to tell them to SHUT UP especially if they are FIT AS HELL. HA HA HA!

I'm joking but it's not funny to have lost the one person that can make you feel better. Feel something. Feel ANYTHING.

7.52 p.m.
I'm supposed to be down Dobber's for 8 but I feel so down I can't be bothered. I want to go to the pub later.

Haddock.

Don't know why I just wrote that. Bet his ears are burning. He even has nice ears.

Oh Rae fuck off – he's just a bloke NOT GOD.

Sunday 2.12.90

1.04 a.m.

WENT DOWN THE BAR. FRAGGLE'S boyfriend was there playing up so me and Dobber chatted all night. She is lovely and I miss her. I did a bit of work behind the bar. Haddock's girlfriend got off with someone because Haddock had apparently got off with someone in Leeds. I hate who she got off with – he's a right wet pretty boy. Josh Wyledon also fancies Haddock's girlfriend. So that's YET ANOTHER MAN in love with Haddock's girlfriend that I'd like to be in love with me.

Rae = fat cow = Joke
Rae = Joke.

I can do the maths that really matters.

Monday 3.12.90

5.25 p.m.

I WENT DOWN THE JOBCENTRE to sign back on. I told them that after all the travel expenses to get to Peterborough it made the job pointless. They accepted this and let me sign on again! I wouldn't have done that. Perhaps I've been more affected by Thatcher than I thought. My parents have both worked since they were 14!! I'm entitled to benefits that they've earned on my behalf.

Tuesday 4.12.90

5.32 p.m.

I'VE WRITTEN TO HEREWARD RADIO to ask for a job. Mum thinks this is ridiculous. No Mum – it's what I want to do. OR I want to be a three day eventer but since my equine experience stretches to the donkeys at Skegness I think I've got more chance with radio don't you?!

Wednesday 5.12.90

8.34 p.m.

MY LIFE AT THE MOMENT is –

a) Watching the postman belt it up Edinburgh Road and trying to see if he slows down outside my door. When he does it's never for me.
b) Singing to the British Gas jingle 'Shag – Shag – Shag – Shagability – that's the beauty of Haddock.'

It doesn't scan but it makes me happy. I mustn't sing it in public though.

Thursday 6.12.90

5.32 p.m.

THE POSTMAN FINALLY ARRIVED FOR ME today and the University of Sheffield rejected me.

Good!

Finally a rejection that I actually want – I just wish I'd got in first! That's a life lesson.

Friday 7.12.90

6.32 p.m.

TODAY I WENT INTO WOOLWORTHS and hid every copy of New Kids on the Block's 'This One's for the Children' behind 'All Together Now' by The Farm. Children need to be shielded from shit. It's pop activism not terrorism and it's completely legal. I would do an IRA Bobby Sands hunger strike against the shit but it's nearly Christmas.

Saturday 8.12.90

11-SOMETHING – MY WATCH HAS stopped! Brilliant down the bar tonight! For a piss take I re-enacted the 'Justify My Love' video with the aid of the beams! Everybody laughed and it was a piss take but I'm also a very sexual being and I think people I know may understand that. People are calling Madonna a slag but

sod it – if she wants to go to a Paris hotel and do it with
Arthur AND Martha let her! If a bloke did it no-one
would bat an eyelid. Her lips look stupid though and she
could pick fitter blokes. She is bloody Madonna! She
could have whoever she wanted!

Sunday 9.12.90

11.34 p.m.

MASSIVE DEBATE DOWN THE BAR tonight about three things.

1) What is an IRA coded warning? How do the
   police know what is a real IRA code and what is
   just some nutter making a fake bomb threat?
   Dobber suggested that the IRA sent the police a
   Christmas card every year saying 'This is next
   year's list of REAL bomb code words'. We all wet
   ourselves but hang on – is that what happens?
   Does Gerry Adams ring them on the IRA's behalf?
   Does Gerry Adams nip round for a sherry? WHY
   DON'T THE BBC TELL US?
2) Is Mrs Thatcher having a better Christmas now
   she has less pressure? Hopefully not. I hope she is
   sat there watching programmes for schools every
   morning thinking about HOW SHE RUINED
   BRITAIN.
3) This was the big one. I said I liked 'Mull of
   Kintyre' by Wings more than 'A Day in the Life'
   by The Beatles. Everybody went mad at me but
   they are just trying to be cool and I don't bloody

care. I am not saying that 'A Day in the Life' is
NOT a better song. I'm saying at this time of year
in particular I just want Christmassy and not
John Lennon being arty. 'Mull of Kintyre'
reminds me of brilliant 70s Christmases – Sindy
Doll Wardrobes, and *The Generation Game* with
Larry Grayson. 'A Day in the Life' is about A
BLOODY CAR CRASH. HAPPY CHRISTMAS
RINGO! Come on!!

Where's Haddock? That wasn't debated but that's what
I'm thinking ALL THE TIME. He'd agree with me about
'Mull of Kintyre'. He never gives a toss what people think.
He'd tell the world he liked 'The Frog Chorus'. Oh – he's
BLOODY AMAZING.

Monday 10.12.90

10.24 a.m.

MUM JUST SAID TO ME 'What do you want for
your birthday, duck? By the way, Adnan is back
tomorrow for Christmas.'

1) Happy Gooseberry Rae!
2) I'd like World Peace please Mum!
3) And Haddock so we didn't have to have sex in a
   rush because a war was starting.
4) And an offer from Hull. Or a rejection. Just
   SOMETHING. Why don't I just ring? Because a)
   I'll have to bother Mrs Armitage AGAIN b)
   Perhaps they haven't decided yet and me

bothering them will send them over the edge and
they will reject me c) My head says if I do ring
them it will stop it.

So I asked Mum if she could just give me some money.
Money means I get to be in the pub more and the house
less.

Tuesday 11.12.90

5.12 p.m.

WELCOME BACK ADNAN. MUM IS of course
totally delighted. He did bring me a silver leather
shoe keyring which is more than Mum has ever bought
me and I have to say his version of 'Ice Ice Baby' by
Vanilla Ice may be one of the funniest things I have ever
seen.

Wednesday 12.12.90

11.59 p.m.

I'M LYING ABOUT THE TIME. I'll get all these 18
year old neuroses written down now!

Well, look at my 18th year. It started in the last golden
days of 1989. Good days. What a Christmas and a New
Year that promised so, SO much – but like Cardinal
Wolsey's foreign policy it has delivered fuck all.

Have to use A level knowledge for SOMETHING
because so far it's been useful for NOTHING.

It seems difficult now to try to go back. People who seemed so important then are now irrelevant. Things that happened that seemed THE EARTH are nothing. My need for love did not diminish. I did A levels, I crashed and burned, I left Essex and packed in the one job I got. Leaving Essex was the right decision. Leaving The Body Shop was me just being a lazy fat cow.

I still love Haddock.

My head is still a mess.

So I start my 19th year, no job, no higher education place, I have annoyed my friends and family, the one person I could rely upon in the weird boy way I needed doesn't even speak to me much anymore.

But STILL I hold on to him.

I should make this year the year I change. The year I get motivated. I could sort myself out.

I'm very frightened. I'm scared. I'm worried. I'm tired.

Thursday 13.12.90

10.30 a.m.

TOTALLY OUT OF THE BLUE, Battered Sausage turns up!! Considering he lives in St Albans now when he's not at university this is a totally gorgeous thing to do. He got a lift with his mum just so we could go out for my birthday. He's a massive tosser but a lovely one. We are going down the pub!

No idea of time

I will write tomorrow as my roof is spinning. Even considering a tactical chunder. I hate being sick though and Mum will realise I am so drunk I'm probably dying.

Friday 14.12.90

9.28 a.m.

I SUPPOSE YOU WANT TO know about my birthday. It was a real laugh. We went down the pub. Then we went to Olivers. Then I fell over. Too much drink. I feel like death this morning. TOTAL DEATH. I can't even face toast. That's how bad it is.

No Haddock last night. Stamford just isn't that important to him. Or me. FACE IT RAE.

No, Adnan. Please don't start doing your Arabic singing thing to 'Saviour's Day' by Cliff. I might go and tell him that it's about Jesus being not a minor prophet (Islam) but THE prophet (Christianity). How do Muslims feel about Cliff Richard? Probably like the rest of us do – HA HA HA!!

Saturday 15.12.90

11.34 p.m.

S TILL NO HADDOCK OUT TONIGHT.
Talking of Haddock – I forgot to tell you I spoke to his girlfriend on my birthday. He now wants to marry her and go out with her again. However he has got off with 5 other women including one who sent his

girlfriend a Purple Ronnie card with 'Friends!' on it. Haddock's girlfriend ripped this into four pieces and sent it back with 'BITCH' written on it.

Which is BRILLIANT. She is BLOODY funny.

Sunday 16.12.90

I HAVEN'T SEEN HADDOCK FOR WEEKS now. He meant the world to me. He still MEANS it. Perhaps he always will. He'll be like my lazy eye. Cured but comes back when I'm pissed or tired.

But I was thinking today . . . What am I missing out on whilst I wait for him? What the hell am I expecting? It all to change overnight? It's not going to. And what do I expect him to do? Haddock and his therapy-cock magically makes everything better? Would it? Would it really Rae? Or would you just spend your entire time thinking a) What is the FUCK he doing with me and b) Touching things and praying so he never goes and so he loves me forever. I mean READ that back? THAT IS PATHETIC. I'm nuts but even I know that's not going to work.

But then I think – he GETS it. He's beautiful inside and out. He'd be a start. A way in to sort the shit out.

Monday 17.12.90

10.55 p.m.

H ADDOCK'S THERAPY COCK IS THE greatest name for a band ever. You'd never get on *Top of the*

Pops though. Especially now it's sometimes hosted by *Blue Peter* presenters.

Mum is panicking about Christmas dinner AS PER NORMAL. Everything is a drama. Just RELAX woman! None of us will die if there is no bread sauce.

11.02 p.m.
Actually we will – that's the best bit!

Tuesday 18.12.90

9.34 p.m.
LEEDS REJECTED ME TODAY. THIS is probably a good thing as I can't be in the same city as a Haddock that is a sex machine that is not sex machining near me.

Wednesday 19.12.90

11.22 a.m.
'FAIRYTALE OF NEW YORK' BY The Pogues and Kirsty MacColl makes me feel really weird. Be honest Rae – it makes me cry because it's lovely but it reminds me of having a breakdown. There are some songs that do.

'Run To You' – Bryan Adams
Tried to distract myself by playing 'OutRun' on the computer and listening to this at the same time. Failed.

'Rush Hour' – Jane Wiedlin
Played all the time on the radio when I was really off it.
Love it though. Brilliant pop where the video featured her
riding dolphins – a lovely image destroyed forever.

'Don't Worry, Be Happy' – Bobby McFerrin
Mum bought this for me. Bless her – she was trying to
help. She didn't realise how ill I was I don't think. To this
day if I hear that song I want to kill everyone involved in
it.

'Happy Ever After' – Julia Fordham
Another great song buggered by the thought of tablets in
trolleys and . . . Oh why am I even going here. TOO MUCH
TIME TO THINK. I'M GOING FOR A WALK.

Thursday 20.12.90

11.22 p.m.

DOBBER AND ME JUST SHARED a bottle of
Baileys down the Meadows. You can have too much
of a good thing. That was a mistake. As she pointed out
though, it was naturally chilled. YES IT WAS BLOODY
FREEZING. Thanks to the random boys who pointed out
my nipples were erect. Twats – but it made a change from
Jabba so look on the bright side.

On that note, there is a new name for ugly women like
me apparently – 'Moose'. I've already had it a few times.
Who makes this crap up? Bored men with tiny willies. I've
noticed I'm getting more and more aggressive. It's a lack
of sex. A good passionate session of DOING IT would cure

it. Dr Haddock and his therapy-cock cures all again. Shut up Rae – just learn to deal with the fact some men have big mouths and tiny pricks. I've noticed that penis size is one way you can really hurt a man. Tell him you heard he had a tiny one. It's evil – but all is fair in love and war and when someone calls you Moose.

But it still kills me. I hate being the ugly fat bitch. Please don't think I don't.

Friday 21.12.90

11.23 p.m.
IS CLIFF RICHARD GOING TO do this every Christmas now? Release a single? I never thought I'd say this but bring back Shakin' Stevens.

I'm sitting here listening to the most beautiful song – 'Keeping the Dream Alive' by Freiheit. It's Germans with terrible hair but it's saying everything I feel. Perhaps I do want too much but I can't let it go and why should I let it go? I'm fat. I'm not right in the head but Vincent Van Gogh was nuts too and his paintings sell for millions. He was thin though. I've seen his self portraits.

Mrs Bark has put tinsel round her sink. You have to love her for that.

I CAN'T HELP BUT LOOK – IT'S RED AND IT GLITTERS!!

Saturday 22.12.90

1.08 p.m.

I'VE JUST SEEN DOBBER OUT in town. Apparently Haddock is out TONIGHT!! FUCK!! Why aren't I nine stone yet? Or even ten stone? That will do. Why has the bloody crisp eating continued?! I'm still the bloody caterpillar. FUCK IT!! I NEED to see him. It's like a dose of something good. I NEED him.

Sunday 23.12.90

3.25 a.m.

WENT DOWN THE PUB. I was dreading seeing Haddock. Excited but dreading it. His girlfriend was with him. He ignored me. I had a drink and just felt so LET DOWN and PISSED OFF. So I went down the Meadows. I needed my willow tree and some peace. Sometimes in crowds it gets too much anyway. Then I see this total twat pretending to swim towards me. It's HADDOCK! Gives me a big hug, says sorry for not speaking to me as he 'was arguing with his Mrs' and wants to know everything that's been going on. I told him I had fucked up everywhere. He said 'Bet you'll be all right though.' I'm glad he has faith in me. I haven't. We talked for ages and then went back to the Vaults. He asked me to stay out longer but Mum has insisted that I have to get up early tomorrow to go and fetch the prawns for Christmas with her from Morrisons. So beautiful time with the man I want to be my eventual husband is now getting affected by seafood. Fucking hell. SOD PRAWN COCKTAIL – WHAT ABOUT COCK?

Monday 24.12.90

7.01 a.m.
YES MUM. I AM UP. Yes Mum I am coming to get the bloody prawns. Yes I will put them in the fridge as soon as I get home. Yes I won't start on the Quality Street till tomorrow (cross fingers behind my back – I'm having one the moment I get home. It's my reward.)

11.45 a.m.
BLOODY HELL!!
UNIVERSITY OF HULL UNCONDITIONAL OFFER!!!

It was here when I got home after getting the prawns!
   In the words of the Edwin Hawkins Singers, 'OH HAPPY DAY!!!!!'

WHAT A RESULT!! WHAT A CHRISTMAS PRESENT!!

That makes me think IT IS MEANT TO BE. Come on that is WAY TOO SPOOKY. That is INSANE. ON CHRISTMAS EVE!! I was right. I have to listen to ME more. I talk myself out of stuff all the time but perhaps I'm right. Perhaps I have this mad instinct that is – just – IT KNOWS SHIT. And I should follow it whatever it says. But then it gets mixed up with the other stuff, like you can speak to God and stop him doing stuff. If I can just separate them I could make stuff work. I could . . . I could. I just COULD.

This feels like a start. Of something. Perhaps just of not being a TOTAL twat.

Tuesday 25.12.90

8.30 a.m.

THE DAY OF CHRIMBLE!
As you may have guessed, I got into Hull. I rang up Mort. She wet herself. I LOVE THAT GIRL. She's there in times of shit and in moments of sugar.

Last night was the weirdest Christmas Eve I have ever had. The pubs were horrendously crowded but empty of decent people. People were moaning about how crap Stamford was. The top bar of the Vaults was NOT open (INSANE!!). Aristotle was a total love when I told him I'd got into Hull and looked genuinely pleased. Haddock came in and gave me a hug. Dobber and me (by now well pissed) went down the Meadows. Then I saw Haddock and his girlfriend screaming at each other. They were in MY spot. I just lost it and said 'Any chance you two can have a normal fucking relationship?!' Haddock said to me 'Bollocks – you of all people should get it.' Dear Haddock – in case you haven't noticed I don't get it because I'M NOT IN A RELATIONSHIP. Anyway they buggered off to rip each other apart elsewhere whilst I got plastered with Dobber.

'I should get it!' Oh fuck off Haddock. You could make everything better but you just piss me off. We could have the best laugh ever and the best thing ever but you just

236

opt for the same old, SAME BLOODY OLD.

You know what? Next time they are arguing I am going to scream at the top of my voice 'I can sort this out. No you shouldn't be together. Haddock's girlfriend, you have loads of blokes who want to be with you and I really want your man so there. Totally sorted sodding out!'

6.20 p.m.
They just showed *E.T.* on TV for the first time! This was brilliant as I've only seen it on pirate video before and at the end EVEN Mum cried! HA!! Adnan did not cry but he did try to do an impression of E.T. phoning home which was the worst and funniest thing I have ever seen. Imagine a six foot bodybuilder on his knees sticking his finger in the air saying 'Hone Hone!'

8.25 p.m.
Yes Mum, I am upstairs because I don't want to watch the bloody *Birds of a Feather* Christmas special.

Wednesday 26.12.90

10.11 p.m.
I REALLY FEEL LIKE THE fat old aunty who is there when there are problems then rejected when life gets good again. I'm taking up bloody knitting and getting into Cliff.

No I'm not getting into Cliff. No-one is getting into Cliff! HA HA HA!!

I think me and Cliff Richard have more in common than me and Madonna and Kylie. Especially now Kylie is sexy as hell and Madonna is taking over French hotels with orgy parties. Meanwhile me and Cliff are eating a box of Roses and watching *Noel's Christmas Presents* – which was the loveliest thing ever.

Thursday 27.12.90

11.10 p.m.

I'VE SENT MY UCCA THING in to accept my offer at Hull. I am now absolutely neurotic that I have ticked the 'You reject the offer' box BUT I haven't. I checked it at least 1000 times and got stuck by the main post office letterboxes. An old man said to me 'Just send it love.' It's all right for him to say, he hasn't got a fucked mind.

That's bad. That old man was probably in the war and never got a chance to doss at uni. He's probably got a B.A. in killing Germans and still has nightmares about their dead faces. My great granddad did. War is shit. I don't know why we still do it.

Friday 28.12.90

11.47 p.m.

I'M FEELING SO MAD TONIGHT. I'm trying to make sense of it.

Part of it is still leaving school.

Things were so different there. It was such security and such a laugh. It was friendship – it was just brilliant. Sometimes I think I had too much fun – it makes it harder. I've just spent the night with a load of my old school mates. It reminds you what you had everyday. I just took it all for granted.

And then there's the really mad stuff. When I'm with NORMAL people, when I'm sitting with them I wonder what they do in secret.

How many of them, how many people of my age, IN FACT ANY AGE beat themselves up in order to stop God punishing them or to stop bad stuff happening.

I'm worried that I might really hurt myself and then people might think, when I've had a stroke or something, that someone else has beaten me up. But they haven't. If you're reading this and I'm dead know I've hit myself for years. It's my fault I've had a brain haemorrhage or a stroke.

How many people check food for being poisoned, wash their hands 100 times, think their thoughts can hurt people, think their lack of prayer causes misery, are so paranoid that they think that everyone is scheming to get them.

Is all this shit just me? Or do I just hide it the best and not get locked away?

I'm all over the place.

At the same time though I'm happy, I'm me. Lots of girls I know don't know shit about music. What's the point?

I'm so fat. External exterior shows a complete lack of love. I think I do have a slow metabolism. But let's not get too technical. I'm a fucking pig.

All of this is predictable shit you've heard all before. I'm bored too. I have bored myself senseless.
Fundamentally I'm a twat.

Where is this all going? Rae Earl – who the hell is she and where is she going?

Saturday 29.12.90

10.34 p.m.

MY STARS SAID THAT I shouldn't think so much. So I won't. Goodnight.

Sunday 30.12.90

9.35 p.m.

I RANG MORT TONIGHT. SHE told me she's going abroad on a trip all round South Africa. God I will miss her. It feels like my leg is being cut off. I can't imagine not being able to go down the phone box and ring her up to make sense of all this shit in my head. She always calms me down. She always helps me out. She saves me from shit time after time. How am I going to cope when she's miles and miles away in a country that does not have decent communications?! They've only just let Nelson Mandela out of prison. To be fair they've had more important things on their minds than having a decent phone box network but still . . .

Dear F W De Klerk. Stop being a racist and sort it out.

Everyone is moving on except me because everyone can.

TANGLE
When all is said and done,
Laughter and listening is over,

240

There's just a tangle.
I can give you a belly laugh so big it will hurt,
I can give you my shoulder to cry on,
And listen to any intimacy you can provide,
BUT
When all is said and done,
When the laughter and the listening is over.
There is just a tangle.
All my contemporaries have wonderful togetherness
I know that everyone has a niggling doubt .
But how many of them are covered in bruises,
They created.
How many voices do they have in their head?
The one person who gets it,
Has the least reason to be fucked up.
But I can't hug him, I can't kiss him
I couldn't make love to him.
Because when all is said and done
When all the listening and laughter is over.
There's just a tangle.

I can be full of shit sometimes but I mean it.

Monday 31.12.90

5.35 p.m.

SOMETIMES I CAN'T BELIEVE THIS is me talking.
It is me though. Little arms. Big middle. Screwed up. In
love with a total unobtainable. I've got such a lot to sort
out. I've got to stop all the mental shit and the bingeing. I've
got to grow up. I hate agreeing with Mum but she does

have a point. And Haddock. Oh I love him but he isn't the answer . . . but he could be the reward. Do you know, I don't think I'm going to keep a diary anymore. I think it makes me linger on bad stuff and thoughts and memories that I should just swallow up. I feel I should write a big momentous entry in commemoration but I'm due down the pub with Dobber – even though she bought the latest Bombularina single. Perhaps I need to think less, DO more and buy more novelty singles.

Tuesday 1.1.91

8.57 a.m.
Bollocks. I'd go completely mad without this and Timmy
Mallett needs a REAL mallet over his head. Not a nice soft
one that's to do with a word association game. But diary,
I'm writing less. I have to do more. I've got to sort out
this head and this body. 'Navel gazing' here (my mum's
phrase) is not always helping. Talking doesn't always help
but you're here. I know you're here and thank GOD you're
here.

Good morning 1991! Working on the 2 year 'crap/
good' basis, this year should be a corker because last year
was a total disaster on nearly every level.

When I walked back from Dobber's house at 7.30 a.m.
this morning it was beautiful. It was like everything had
just been born. There was a frost and everything felt new
and that just made me feel happy.

Well at this point I usually burst into a string of
resolutions but this year I'll make things more simple but
more important.

1) Stop being mental. Stop the thoughts. Stop the
   hitting. How, I just don't know.
2) Lose weight. Don't even tell anyone I'm doing
   it. Just do it. So I, a) can have sex b) I don't
   die of a Flora overdose when I'm 32 or
   something.
3) Manage somehow to find a way to get out of
   Stamford without feeling like I'm dying.

4) Stop all my paranoia. All this 'Are you in a mood with me?' shit because if they aren't before they are after hearing all that self-pitying wank.
5) When I do get to Hull have a good time and make the most of it.
6) Whatever crisis happens I may feel terrible but I will handle it as best I possibly can.
7) Don't end up back there in the ward. I can't because the second time they might not let me go.

They are quite general aren't they but if I can get these sorted out then I'm away.

I think the older I get the more I believe in 'Que Sera Sera' and fate and all that.

As to last night, I thought 'oh no it's like Christmas Eve again – nightmare.' But surprisingly the pub was much less busy. Even though I had to queue up outside the Vaults to get in to the Bolt Hole Bar.

Shellboss came for me at about 8.20 p.m. and we went down the bar. I'd had a bit of Pimm's before I started on the vodkas. By the time I got to the Vaults I was getting pleasurably out of it. I got to a good merry stage all night without pushing it and going loony. Had a lovely chat and a laugh with Fig but couldn't talk long because him and Dobber aren't together anymore and I'd throw Fig under a bus for Dobber. In a nice way.

Haddock's girlfriend was in tears. She disappeared. Haddock and me sat there and chatted about everything and then he said to me –

HADDOCK: What do you think 1991 will be like then?

ME: Well, I hope it will be better than last year.

HADDOCK: When you're in Hull you can come over to Leeds for nights out.

ME: (OH GOD, THE THOUGHT IS TOO BEAUTIFUL!!) Yeah. Do you like 'Mull of Kintyre'?

HADDOCK: (LOOKING AT ME LIKE I'M INSANE) Of course I do. Obviously.

ME: What about 'The Frog Chorus'?

HADDOCK: Er . . . BOM BOM BOM aye-a aye Anyway come over if you like.

ME: Yeah I will.

And then we all ended up in the square at midnight with him snogging the face off his girlfriend.

He's not the solution. He could be the reward. I've got to lose weight and not change the subject to Paul McCartney when things get tough.

I think I might be a bit still pissed!

Wednesday 2.1.91

5.40 p.m.

I DON'T KNOW WHAT WOULD make me better. Going away, staying, changing, staying the same. I don't know.

I know Haddock still loves his girlfriend. I know Dobber still loves Fig. I know what was number one at Christmas in 197-bloody-4 ('Lonely This Christmas' by Mud – crap) but I don't know who I am, what I want, if I'm happy or if I'm not.

I know I need a big hug and a ~~Flake~~ Caramel bar.

Friday 4.1.91

5.59 p.m.

I TOLD YOU. I'M NOT writing everyday anymore. It's not helping. Yesterday I went for a massive walk to Tolethorpe.

I've nothing to report at all. Usually at this time I'm depressed. I am not.

Sometimes I can't believe Haddock even exists. He's like the Yeti but a horny version.

But he does exist. There are occasional sightings. I hope I get one before he goes back again.

Tegs has offered me more work in the bar. I love it. We have such a laugh and it's DOING something.

Sunday 6.1.91

12.34 a.m.

J UST COME BACK FROM WORKING in the bar. Oh – it's EPIC! Me and Tegs are now calling ourselves the Bostik sisters because we keep getting stuck in the saloon doors between the kitchen and the bar. And MTV are showing old *Saturday Night Live*'s with Bill Murray, Dan Aykroyd and John Belushi which are brilliant. Only Tegs keeps accusing me of having a crush on MTV presenter Steve Blame – which I DO NOT!

Anyway I was just serving people and Haddock came in. He's come for a drink he said but I swear he'd come to say goodbye. We had a chat (NOT ABOUT Paul

McCartney) about Battered Sausage being well loved up and about Dobber and Fig and then we had a strained over-the-bar hug. I didn't want to let go. Of course I didn't. I never do. He even SMELLS good. He feels GOOD. Oh he FEELS so good – like LIFE! Like MAN! Like something you don't want to let go of. But I did let go. And he left. And I served someone bloody Archers and lemonade. I let go of the best thing in the world to serve someone peachy shit.

Monday 7.1.91

11.03 p.m.
THERE IS GOING TO BE another war. What can I do? What I always think I can do – sit here, pray 100 times, check the gas, think by doing mad stuff I could change it. Stop it. I'd really like to tell Saddam Hussein now just how much shit he is causing in my head.

Even *Coronation Street* was crap tonight. Too much Mavis.

Shit – am I destined to be a Mavis? But Mad Mavis with carrier bags and loads of cats?

Thursday 10.1.91

10.56 p.m.
I'VE JUST BEEN DOWN THE pub with Haddock's girlfriend.

Judas Rae. Haddock's girlfriend is the fat girl's passport to the human equivalent of the Seychelles.

The more she goes on about him the more I'm convinced how alike we are. He covers all his bollocks up with being dry-as-a-bone funny and Mr Moody. They are going to get married. It's a foregone conclusion. I'm not being a bloody bridesmaid I can tell you that for nothing. When they say 'Has anyone got any objections as to whether these two should not be joined in holy matrimony' – YES!! I HAVE A BLOODY HUGE ONE.

When I look at photos of Haddock – YES he is fit BUT he is also a hidden philosopher type. He's so damn wonderful. I can't imagine ever topping him. I mean I KNOW I've only really been in Stamford. OK so I could probably top him but do I want to? Funny as hell, handsome as fuck, smart, great thighs – what more to want?!

BUT his girlfriend is lovely and I'm Queen of Twats Party United.

AND I am not expecting him to fix me anymore. Or save me. He doesn't even know he's meant to. Haddock – see you on the other side of my transformation into the REAL not NUTS me and the THIN me.

Friday 11.1.91

6.34 p.m.

IT'S BEEN A WEIRD SORT of day. I went to Peterborough with Shellboss. Ended up in Wimpy where a bloke was dressed up like a massive Mr Wimpy beefeater. He fell over and because his costume was so big he started rolling down the street. He was saved by two young lads.

I laughed but then felt instantly bad as he was basically a fat person with no control and a stupid hat.

Shellboss was like 'WHY do you need to lose weight before you get a boyfriend. You're fucking fine the way you are. If you want to lose weight, lose it, but don't put your life on hold till you do.' I explained to her that I felt like Mr Wimpy and the unsexiest thing on earth. Who wants to sleep with me – a beefeater? I need to do SOMETHING to make ME feel better about ME.

I need to lose weight.
I need to be rid of the shit.

THEN I need him. Do I want anyone else? No at the moment.

Sometimes I think the shrinks might be right. I got fat because I didn't want to be touched after what happened but, like I told them, I've always been chubby. I've always felt not like a proper girl. Psychiatrists always look for the easy answer. I remember my mum trying to put me in a sundress with like an elasticated top and being horrified. I wanted to wear my brown Charlie's Angels jumpsuit. We had a big argument outside Nan's house.

You see now I'm going over stuff from years ago. Do I feel better? No. Am I in denial? GOD KNOWS. Raking up shit gets you nowhere.

Talking of raking up shit – Iron Maiden are back with some total crap called 'Bring Your Daughter to the Slaughter'. Piss off – there are scarier things in my mum's wardrobe that she won't throw out just in case she can fit in them again – like that crocheted brown and white cardigan.

249

Sunday 13.1.91

12.09 a.m.

THERE WAS A HILARIOUS RUMBLE in the bar
tonight. Men fighting like girls. I got between them
both and told them to stop it. Tegs said I was brilliant. I
knew they wouldn't hit me. I just had that sense that they
wouldn't punch a woman. It's that instinct I have.

8.01 a.m.

I had the strangest dream last night. It was a deep winter
and Haddock's girlfriend told me that Haddock was
down the pub and because she had something to do I
could have dinner with him. Anyway, people kept
interrupting me asking me questions that made no sense
and I kept thinking HADDOCK IS THERE WAITING FOR
ME AND YOU ARE ASKING ME ABOUT FUCKING
ZEBRAS??!! I was supposed to be there at 11 p.m. and
now it's 11.10 p.m. and then MY MUM WOKE ME UP!
So I don't know what the dream meant or where it went!

9.22 p.m.

Back in reality (sort of!) Haddock apparently wants to go
to the Gulf. Haddock told his girlfriend that she was the
only one who could stop him. I did point out the fact he's
not in the Army and unless he goes as a mercenary he
can't go. This is why I'm single. I tell men they are talking
shit. And he is talking shit. What can he do in the Gulf?!
He isn't properly trained and his camouflage gear is not
army issue – it's probably from Burton.

I would also tell Haddock that him dying would make life totally bollocks.

Monday 14.1.91

11.38 p.m.

MUM HAS FOUND OUT THAT I stopped a fight in a bar. WHO TOLD HER THAT?! She went – oh mad doesn't cover it. Apparently I 'could have got myself killed' – MUM IT'S STAMFORD NOT NEW YORK! Then she said 'What happened at the Riverside in Stamford a few years ago – someone was murdered!' Yes that's true BUT I told her I have instincts about people and things that are rarely wrong and I knew it would be OK. Then she said 'Rachel – you also think you can control the war in Kuwait by checking the iron and tapping the door.' Well PERHAPS I CAN!

No – I don't need the doctor. I need to stop talking and start doing.

11.28 p.m.

Why do some men (and it is ALWAYS men) have such power to fuck things up?

There's obviously going to be a war in the Gulf now. And a big one. At least I'm at home. Perhaps that's why I was meant to leave Essex. To be with Mum when it all goes really bad. It's that voice again.

Tuesday 15.1.91

7.23 p.m.

A TRAGIC ANTI-WAR POEM
BEAUTY SECRETS OF WORLD LEADERS EXPOSED

Long ago it was decreed
A mark of evil would be conceived.
It was, its creators toyed
A sign to show who you should avoid.
But ages past and years are lost
And what the mark meant was soon forgot,
And go to the present where two red marks on the
    head
Are simply unfortunate and let no more be said.

Out of his mother's womb he crept
They thought he'd be the one to cancel Third World
    debt,
He'd study Shakespeare's *Julius Caesar*,
And end up marrying Mother Teresa.
'We have such high hopes' his parents said,
'Shame about the mark that is on his head –
But as life goes on and pressure mounts
It's only what's inside that really counts.'

All over the world in every different tongue
The same song of parental love was being sung,

As special babies were born in every part foreign,
With one important factor always in common,
The baldness of their small heads showing a dark
Unexplainable, ugly, mysterious mark.

As seasons passed, the once head bare
Was replaced with a crop of thick native hair.
So no longer could the strange stains be seen
Though they were still there where they'd always
    been
And thus parents forgot all about them focussing
    more
On the progression of the child and what was in
    store.

The boys though young knew their direction,
It was to be the fun and games of election.
And though miles apart, beyond geographical
    confines
They talked of war in their small minds.
Boastful challenges, heroic story
Clever rhetoric, patriotic glory
And they vowed to each other that one future day
In reality the game they would play.

Time moves on, heads still stained,
Campaigns elections, power obtained
And now the boys could really enjoy,
The beauty of their new found toy.
And oh what beauty! Luxury, power and greed,
Satisfaction, happiness, wealth guaranteed.

And no-one has noticed yet, despite much wrath,
That they are leading everyone up the garden path.
But wait! What's this? A middle-aged feature,
The arrival of mid 40s alopecia,
For every man is touched in his life sometime,
With the onset of a receding hairline.

For most this is unfortunate, but a natural event,
That in life leaves not much of a dent,
But to our boys if their head is uncovered
It means their secret would be discovered.
The red marks that graced them and gave them such
    power
Would show up, the situation would turn sour.
The public enlightenment would soon ensure
They'd end washed up on life's political floor.

Squabbling broke out on what should be the plan
To save the knowledge reaching the common man,
'Only one way' said one of the marked
'A complete cover up operation' he barked
'So no-one will ever find out the truth
That we are extremely long in the tooth.'

But all that cover stuff spoke another
How do we share it about amongst each brother?
It will take gallons of paint everyday
To cover the marks that litter our way.
Fighting broke out amongst the gang
And thus the first stirs of war were sang
Over allocation of the strange formation
That is the common women's foundation.

World leaders always keen to keep
Their secrets have gotten in too deep
And now must fight, let us not mock,
For control of the world cosmetic stock.
The red mark they only show at their secret
    convention,
World leaders with supposed peace intention,
Remove their wigs and display their head
And plan out the route for their mass dead.

Gorbachev is changing the Russian economy as the
    system stops
You buying foundation in state-owned shops.
And though the recession in the U.S. is foregone,
George Bush is more concerned with the woman
    from Avon.
And Saddam Hussein only invaded to seek
The woman who'd disappeared with his crate of
    Clinique.
So don't fret any wars over religion or oil,
Or some hostile nation treading on another's soil,
Don't believe the crap about issues you're fed,
Every war is over the stuff that covers marks on
    your head.
Thing is they want to send us all to high heaven,
So they can get their hands on all of Boots' Number
    seven.

Is that epically brilliant or epically bollocks? It's anti-
make-up and anti-war. I've done A level English and I've
never read anything like that before.

Thursday 17.1.91

12.03 a.m.

*T*HE BLACK BOX MEGAMIX JUST got cut halfway through on the radio to announce that a BLOODY WAR HAS STARTED. This is how it all started, in *Threads*, with people invading Iraq.

War – what are we fighting for? A couple of leaders. No-one cares about Kuwait. Fuck it. Fuck petrol. I don't want to die for FOUR STAR AT THE PUMPS! REJECT CONVENTION! It's got us nowhere – we should all just start again.

Threads started in Iran. It's all the Middle East. The Russians are friendly now. I've got to calm down.

Mum's not buying loads of tins. Well no more than normal. I don't want to survive a nuclear apocalypse and have to eat Morrisons' tinned salmon forever.

I'm shitting it really.

The house is always full of tins that no-one ever eats.

Friday 18.1.91

11.30 p.m.

*I*T'S WAR. I'M FRIGHTENED TO death of nuclear war. I feel a lot depends on me. I know that's mental. I feel by all the stuff I do I'm showing God I don't want to blow up the world. When I write it I KNOW it's fucked – so why can't I stop?

No. I can't stop it – going for a walk. David Dimbleby can sod off with his predictions.

Saturday 19.1.91

1.23 a.m.

MUM JUST RUSHED DOWN THE stairs and said 'Where the hell have you been?'

We've been here before so I very calmly said 'Mum – I felt a bit unwell so I went for a little walk. Sorry to worry you but I needed it.'

She went off swearing but that was it.

Small steps. Small steps. Small steps.

Sunday 20.1.91

12.08 a.m.

I HAD THE MOST BRILLIANT night down the pub with Ronni and Tegs. We have started to compile a Crappers International tape (based on Erasure's *Crackers International* EP) – it's basically a compilation of stuff that is so bollocks it's brilliant. CHEESE CENTRAL.

'Shaddap You Face' – Joe Dolce
'I've Never Been to Me' – Charlene
'Don't Mess with my Toot Toot' – Denise LaSalle
'The Chicken Song' – Spitting Image
'I Am A Cider Drinker' – The Wurzels
'Kinky Boots' – Patrick Macnee/Honor Blackman
'Car 67' – Driver 67 (though I love this song a bit totally)

'Camouflage' – Stan Ridgway
'All I Wanna Do Is Make Love To You' – Heart
'Figaro' – Brotherhood of Man
'Begin the Beguine' – Julio Iglesias
'Brown Girl in the Ring' – Boney M

I refused to add Sonia on there – there's a difference between crappers and crap.

They are all OFFICIALLY CRAPPERS. I'm making a tape of other shit we like. We are going to play it in the bar when we want people to piss off!

Do you know, bar this bloody awful terribly worrying war, 1991 has been quite, well, good really.

2.14 p.m.
Just did fortune telling with the *British Book of Hit Singles* as I haven't done it in ages. Ask the book a question, flick the book to a random page and point. Just asked about me at Hull – will I stick at it?

I got 'How Will I Know' by Whitney Houston.

Won't do that crap anymore!

Wednesday 23.1.91

9.24 p.m.
E VERYONE WOULD DESPISE ME IF they knew what shit was in my head. I think horrid stuff. But then I'm sorry. I'm sorry about it. I don't want people to really die. Never. Except New Kids on the Block. I don't even want them to die – just suffer a bit.

Thursday 24.1.91

10.14 p.m.

RANG MORT TONIGHT – WE'VE been invited to go
and see Mega Brain Jane at Cambridge University
over the weekend. Mort knows how hard it is for me to go
anywhere I sort of don't know so I'm good with her. Told
Mum – she thinks it's a top idea. It's the only time I'll be
going to Cambridge University! It'll be good to see what
people who have got their shit together are all about.
These are the cleverest, the most confident young people
in the country. If not the entire world. Perhaps I can learn
something – I don't mean about ancient Greece or
medicine. I mean about how not to be such an idiot.

Saturday 26.1.91

0.55 a.m.

CAMBRIDGE UNIVERSITY
Yes – the supposed hotbed of academic brilliance
and tradition has been exposed as a total load of mainly
wankers, pretentious public schoolboys (and I emphasise
the BOYS) and basic TWATS. The first 'friend' of Jane's
that we met just stuck her Vs up at us. WHY?!

The rooms though are bloody gorgeous. Mort just told
me off for farting. Oh I feel like farting. Even if I was a
super brain like Jane I couldn't cope with this place. AND
she's lovely – one of the sweetest, smartest people ever.
She let me copy all her work in year 3 and she partnered

me at tennis when I could not hit a ball for toffee and she was amazing!

Now Mort is reflecting on some of the people we met at Cambridge – 'What a bunch of immature wankers.' I can't imagine, on the strength of 95% of people I met tonight, why anyone would want to come here!

OK, there's the prospect of a brilliant job for life but is that worth AT LEAST 3 years of being with TWATS in TWAT CITY! And then when you do end up in a job is it with people like this because I want to be unemployed forever if it is.

The point is I thought I would see people who had it all together – but they seem to be just as messed up as me. Just in a 'we can pass exams in a better way than you' way.

My life would be bloody all right without the return of the head shit. This week it's felt like it was all returning. I'm so frightened. I don't want to end up like last time. But nobody REALLY knows. Nobody wants to know.

Oh I need Haddock. We talk the same.

NO. I need to meet other people. I need a change. A difference.

I'm spending a lot of time in fields listening to Enigma. It's Gregorian chanting. Now you think I've really lost it but it was number one so the whole of the UK is nuts right now. It's David bloody Dimbleby everyday talking about war. He makes you feel unhinged. You need monks.

Sunday 27.1.91

6.09 p.m.
S ADDAM HUSSEIN IS WITHDRAWING HIS troops
  from Kuwait. I'm pleased for everyone but most
pleased that Dimbleby will now go back to doing
whatever he does when he's not making everyone shit
themselves about war.

Wednesday 30.1.91

6.24 p.m.
S OHO'S 'HIPPYCHICK' IS A WORK of total
  sampling brilliance.
    That is all I want to say today.

Thursday 31.1.91

3.40 p.m.
D EATH TO MY INFERIORITY
      I shall go into my chrysalis and RE-EMERGE!
  Better, Faster, Stronger.

    Now I sound like the Six Million Dollar Man. Wish I
was bionic. I know where I'd run right now. Leeds.

Friday 1.2.91

9.35 p.m.

ADNAN IS GOING BACK TO Morocco again tomorrow. He HAS to. It makes no sense but if he doesn't apparently he'll be breaking some immigration law. Mum has to go to somewhere called Lunar House in Croydon. I think this is to make you prove that you really love someone because no-one would go to Croydon unless they really bloody had to. Even I know that!

I can't help but think it's a bit racist though. If he was from America would they be making this much of a fuss? No! Mrs Thatcher let South African Cape apples in the country all during apartheid. I don't know many black people in the government. In fact I don't know many black people at all.

Shit! Am I a secret racist?! No I live in Lincolnshire which is like living in Britain in 1952. There are hardly any black people. Except Adnan – and that's why we get bones through the door.

Saturday 2.2.91

9.22 p.m.

INFERIORITY
If you ever feel inferior
Remember all the times your shoulder was SODDEN
    with their tears,

262

Remember the kind words oozing from your
    emphatic lips,
Recall the strength you showed in the face of their most
    absurd absurdity and how you pulled them through.
Do not care for the condescension, or the stereotype,
Remember your beauty and never forget
That YOU can be the only one who can consent to
    your inferiority.

Thank you Eleanor Roosevelt.
    I don't know who the hell you are but thank you.
    I always think I can make people feel better. I can't!
Who am I?!

Sunday 3.2.91

7.35 p.m.

THIS IS BEYOND BELIEF.
    THIS CONVERSATION JUST HAPPENED –

MUM: I need you to stay in all day tomorrow.
ME: Why?
MUM: Because the British Telecom man is coming to
put the phone in.
ME: PARDON???
MUM: We're getting a home phone. You do need
one these days and Adnan can ring me.
ME: So all the time through school when I was
desperate for one and we couldn't afford one we
now can because you need to speak to Adnan?!
MUM: And I need to speak to immigration.

I just walked off. I can't believe it! Not having a phone nearly gave me pneumonia from standing in freezing phone boxes, it completely cut me off from my friends, it stunted my social life, it stopped me from ringing *Going Live* and it probably stopped me (as well as being fat and nuts) from getting a boyfriend because as soon as they asked for your phone number and you said 'No – I haven't got one' they thought 'skint' or 'weird' and ran a mile.

BUT NOW we are getting one because MUM HAS AN INTERNATIONAL LOVE LIFE.

Not me – not the REAL teenager with a boyfriend to ring.

Brilliant. Oh and apparently she's thinking of putting a lock on it so I can't ring who I like if I 'abuse' it.

10.45 p.m.
BUT WE'RE GETTING A PHONE!!!! YES!!! No more 'Hurry up you fat bitch.' No more 'Call me back I've only got 20p.' No more 'Jabba – you posh bitch – I need to ring the DHSS. Some of us have real problems.' No more spitting either or the smell of piss! GONE. Finished. I can actually talk to people without being ripped to bits.

Monday 4.2.91

7.12 p.m.
PHONE MAN CAME AT ABOUT 10. It's in. It's white. It's BEAUTIFUL. I've already rung Mort, Dobber, Shellboss, Tegs, Ronni, Battered Sausage, Fig and Haddock's girlfriend to TELL THEM I HAVE A PHONE.

No – I have not given my phone number to Haddock because if he never rang I'd be gutted and if he did ring I'd end up talking nervous shit.

10.13 p.m.
Yes Mum – 3 people have rung me tonight because I actually have friends. I'm sorry that annoys you but I've also had to listen to some of the most vomit-worthy pidgin English love discussions with you and Adnan ever. Just to let you know, what you call my 'adolescent gossip crapping-on' is a lot more mature than 'Love Addy Addy.' VOMIT!

Tuesday 5.2.91

7.23 p.m.
I JUST SPENT AN HOUR on the phone to Mort – which is completely NORMAL. MORT RANG ME – yet Mum starts moaning. I said 'You do realise how a phone works? If someone rings YOU they PAY'. Mum started shouting 'You are monopolising that thing.' This was all in front of Mort! In the end I said 'I'll put the phone down and see if you get any calls.'

11.01 p.m.
NOTHING! No phone calls, Mum. Not even from your husband!

11.28 p.m.
No phone calls for me either though which isn't good considering I've told everyone ever I've got one.

Thursday 7.2.91

11.09 p.m.

OH REALLY CRAPPY NEWS TONIGHT. Tegs is leaving running the bar to go and be a nanny/au pair in Geneva. That bar has been SUCH a laugh. That's another person leaving my life to go and do something I couldn't even consider doing.

Friday 8.2.91

4.10 p.m.

FRAGGLE JUST RANG ME TO see if I would like to go to Peterborough. She's mega down. She was meant to be ringing me back. That was half an hour ago.

5.36 p.m.

Adnan is talking to Mum on the phone. Standing there tapping my watch just seems to make her talk luvvy duvvy crap for longer. I am YET AGAIN missing out because of my mum's erotic nonsense. I wonder if the people who are listening to Adnan are thinking the same thing. There might be a teenager in Morocco right now whose social life is getting totally messed up because of this stupid marriage. Young people of the world TAKE OVER and reclaim our right to love. I'm sorry, so-called grown-ups, if you messed it up – but why should you get to be 19 at nearly 50?!

6.03 p.m.

Just put '3 a.m. Eternal' on. LOUD.

6.23 p.m.

Mum has just been up 'I know what your game is!' I said 'Well since you're acting like a teenager I thought you might appreciate some young music rather than your usual Kenny Ball jazz shit.' I think the combination of swearing and pointing out she is acting like a TOTAL FOOL sent her totally mad because apparently my board is being raised for no reason other than I play my music too loudly and it's all 'BOOM BOOM BOOM BOOM.' My mum really is a completely mature role model for life. PATHETIC!!

Tuesday 12.2.91

11.55 p.m.

DIARY, BEING AS IT'S YOU I'm very sorry I've been neglecting you. I can tell you. It's the old trouble again. Collapse of mind. Totally irrational thoughts. When I have time and space they all rush in. Same shit – that I control everything, that I am God or that God hates me. That I have to hit myself to stop stuff happening.

Mum is right – I do need a job but she's totally wrong about The KLF. That's why it's sometimes difficult to listen to her. She gets some stuff SO not right.

Thursday 14.2.91

10.12 p.m.

I HAVE SENT MYSELF A Valentine in my head today. It's one from Haddock OBVIOUSLY. Change the Mel and Kim song 'Respectable' to 'Predictable' and you have MY song.

> *Dear Rae. If I could get my head enough out of my perfect arse I could see you were perfect for me. In every way. Unfortunately my head IS up my perfect arse and therefore I am unable to go out with you/do you/at least help all the terrible shit that is swimming round your head.*
>
> *However when I wake up from the twat coma I am in we will be together.*
>
> *Love Haddock.*

WHAT IS LOVE? (No – NOT the Howard Jones version)
I think love is pretty cruel,
I don't believe it's blind.
It can see the things it wants to see
It can detect a miniskirt a mile off.
A pretty face, a skinny waist
It can't see within this head
If it could it would not love
It would run like hell
So I bind her up behind closed doors
I cut myself and pray on floors
I keep her secret.

She leaks out sometimes
I see how people react.
I bottle her up.

I'm not well. I know I'm not but I have to save myself.

But there's hope. THERE'S HOPE. Bloody hell the new
Rick Astley single is AMAZING. Seriously. People CAN
change. One minute you're a Stock Aitken Waterman tea
boy doing total pop cheese then you go REAL SOUL BOY
GOSPEL!!! It's called 'Cry for Help'. That's not why I like
it by the way. I like it because it's brilliant and you can
reinvent yourself.

I'm not basing my life on Rick Astley but music CAN
lead.

Friday 15.2.91

8.26 p.m.
Ode to me
Good evening, many of you will know me as the
Rather round thing that shouts a lot.
Or perhaps even as the big lump,
With pretty things scattered around.
Not many of you could understand
The mind torture that condemns me
Not many can rectify the fear with the funny
The serious with the silly.

Oh stop writing bollocks poetry and do something.

Saturday 16.2.91

6.12 p.m.

IT'S STRANGE REALLY. SATURDAY NIGHTS were formerly things of such immense brilliance and action and now they are tragic.

10.12 p.m.

Mum was really down tonight. She just sat in the chair looking miserable and a bit out of it. HELLO??!! I do know what lonely is. I do get it. It can't be easy having your husband so far away from you and not even knowing if he will get in the country permanently because you live in the Lincolnshire apartheid system. I stayed in with her and watched *Bergerac* and *Don't Wait Up*. She can't say I don't love her – I bloody hate *Bergerac* and I would rather have a barium enema again than watch Nigel Havers arguing with his dad about golf – or some other middle-class toss.

Meanwhile other people are having lives like I used to have. In pubs. Drinking. Laughing. Snogging. My life should not be based around John Nettles.

But I made Mum smile. That's good. She seems down. I hate her a lot of the time but she's . . . she's OK really.

Sunday 17.2.91

9.35 a.m.

> Bitter Fat Thing
> You know the sort

Large. On *Kilroy* every time the show is about
Size.
I'm JUST the same. It's not fat I think
It's attitude.
Fat women have great lives
But I'm a fat apology.
Big fat joke.

5.45 p.m.
Ronni came round tonight. She's going to Leeds
tomorrow because she's going to uni there next year.
She wanted to see if I wanted to go with her. She's got
some stuff to sort out before she's travels across
Africa. Across AFRICA! East to West, Rwanda,
Ethiopia, Mali – all of them I think and more. Places
Kate Adie goes to. These are my friends. Amazing,
brave, together and I'm watching bloody *Bergerac* with
my mum.

Yes I'm going to Leeds. Ronni is lovely and YES – I
might bump into him. Big city but you never know.

What will I say if I do?

Monday 18.2.91

9.34 p.m.
I'VE HAD A BRILLIANT DAY. We got Hereward
Radio ALL the way up to Doncaster but when we rang
the DJ to tell him he didn't seem that impressed. It felt
good though – getting something from home all that way.
I need to feel like things aren't too far away. Even radio. I
know that's mad.

I couldn't get over Leeds – it's really pretty! The way Amos in *Emmerdale Farm* talks about it you think it would be hell! It's got all these amazing posh massive shopping arcades and it's nothing like Sheffield.

No – I didn't see Haddock. Of course I didn't. I have Haddock radar too – I get this prickly feeling if he's within a mile of me. Plus what WOULD I say to him if I did? I looked everywhere except for the ladies bogs. He was nowhere but it's good to have seen where he moves about. Where he drinks. Where he eats. Where he breathes – how pathetic do I sound?

I think I'm a bit angry at the moment. Living on dreams. Eating massive sandwiches. Wishing it all away. If I was to write everyday in this diary it would sound like the book Jack Nicholson writes in *The Shining*. The same line OVER and OVER and OVER. And Jack Nicholson in *The Shining* has totally gone MAD. Put me in a hotel, close it down for winter and let me get better. No freaky ghosts though thank you. Got enough creepy crap in my head to last me a lifetime.

Tuesday 19.2.91

8.45 p.m.
I WENT FOR A COFFEE with Haddock's girlfriend today. I didn't mention I'd been to Leeds as I would have got total interrogation and I just can't face Haddock talk at the moment unless it's Haddock talk with myself and involves unspeakable hot rudeness. Anyway we were just coming past the Co-op in the car and we saw this old lady fall over on the ice. She split her chin REALLY badly.

We ended up taking her to Stamford casualty, waiting whilst she got stitched up and then taking her home. I feel bad writing this but I was actually grateful something EXCITING had happened. Bugger me. That's how shit my life has got – a pensioner's facial stitches are worth a diary entry. Forget world travel and exotic sex Rae – let's have a good session in Stamford Hospital with a Red Cross cup of tea and some gardening magazines. No – I do not want to know how to get better mulch. Bloody hell – this is what my life is reduced to. It's old people and mulch by day, bingeing on cheese and chocolate by night, mad stuff crawling round my head like insects at 2 in the morning and waving goodbye to people who aren't mental and CAN do stuff.

Feet on the radiator. 'Loaded' by Primal Scream. Better.

Thursday 21.2.91

10.10 p.m.

WRITING THIS SEEMS – IT seems like a joke but Mum will tell you it happened.

I went down to the newsagents down Green Lane tonight to wait for the *Stamford Mercury*. Just for something to do really. Mum sat there chatting to her mate and, no word of a lie, her Labrador cocked its leg up against me and pissed on my jeans.

It was like it KNEW I felt like shit. Mum said 'Take it as a compliment – you have got skinny lamp post legs.' This is true. There is no weight on my legs. I do look slightly like a ladybird but being pissed on by a dog? I can't go any lower than this. Perhaps it's a sign.

No, perhaps the sign is my one decent pair of jeans need a good wash.

At least I know what Labradors think of me. Funny how I've been called a 'fat dog' a million times on Green Lane and now I get pissed on by an actual dog. I think I might prefer it.

Friday 22.2.91

9.23 a.m.

BLOODY HELL! HADDOCK'S GIRLFRIEND AND me are in the paper! There's an entire article 'Woman Seeks Good Samaritans'. I told Mum it was us. She said 'Rachel – you must come forward!' No way! I help old people with their minor injuries whilst the rest of my mates do actually amazing things like shagging and expeditions or both. She just wants to boost her Morrisons profile. I can now be the daughter who saves old women rather than the nutter who stays at university for just one week and can't get a job.

Saturday 23.2.91

11.50 p.m.

RONNI'S LAST SATURDAY BEFORE SHE goes across Africa! We had a great time. I'd made her this big card. It took me ages! She looked dead chuffed but then she said 'I'm a bit nervous about going.' I said 'But you'll have a fantastic time. You are as tough as hell. You'll be fine.'

And it's true, she is.

There goes another one. Nearly everyone has gone now. Me and Haddock's girlfriend are the only ones left and even she is working!

Why can't I tell myself that I am worth something like I tell others? Why does a dog pissing on my leg send me into the spiral? There's this sense that I am NOTHING. The psychiatrist used to tell me to look in a mirror and tell yourself 'I'm beautiful and good' – but you just feel like a twat. They also told me to pretend the man who molested me was in a chair and tell him how angry I am. What good would that do?! I don't even want to think about it. I want to burn and punch myself when I think about that. Do these people even know what they are doing when they tell you to do this stuff? How hard it is? IT HAPPENED. I can't unmake it. What would be the best therapy? Punching the evil sod in the knob! I don't think you're allowed to do that police-wise. I don't even know where he is. It's probably a good thing. There's a queue to physically hurt him – Mum, Dad, my brothers would all like a go.

It doesn't undo it though. You'd feel good for a second then there's just the emptiness. It's like the bingeing. After the chocolate there's the wrappers.

I need to do something now.

Because the fixers haven't fixed it and they can't.

Sod it. I'm going to start the diet.

Sunday 24.2.91

10.45 a.m.

I'M STARTING THE DIET TOMORROW. Monday is ALWAYS the day to start a diet!

I'm not telling a soul I'm doing it except Mum. I've seen women try to sabotage other women's diets. 'Don't get too thin!' 'You're looking gaunt!', 'You're not as much fun as you used to be.' – I've heard it all. It means don't get too pretty. You're competition. Stuff that. Live with it. I want to lose weight.

I'm doing Rosemary Conley's Metabolic Booster Diet. There's the lazy cook's plan. I've asked Mum if we can have a Chinese tonight before I start because I have a feeling that battered sweet and sour chicken, prawn crackers, special fried rice and beef in black bean sauce is NOT on the Rosemary list.

Monday 25.2.91

8.23 a.m.

THIS IS THE FIRST DAY of the diet. I hope I don't lose my sense of humour. Are thin women less funny? Perhaps they don't have to try so hard. Perhaps I could be the first funny skinny woman ever.

I CAN do 4 Ryvitas with Cup-a-Soup and a Lean Cuisine. I know it's only day one but I CAN do this. I went for a walk with 'Flashdance' – if I end up looking like Jennifer Beals that will be perfect. Not wearing leg warmers though love – this is the 90s!

Tuesday 26.2.91

10.19 p.m.
THE 25TH AND I DIDN'T even realise. I'm 19 years old and I've had 2 snogs. I've never had a boyfriend and at this rate I doubt I ever will.

BUT I stuck to the diet again today. 4 pieces of fruit. A cold tin of small baked beans. More Ryvita. Lean Cuisine. Yoghurt. I can't see any massive difference yet but I don't stay long in front of a mirror. THAT is not me. That reflection is someone else.

Wednesday 27.2.91

11.32 p.m.
HADDOCK'S GIRLFRIEND TODAY ACCUSED ME of being snappy and cutting. Yes – that's because I'm jealous of you and the face that THE LOVELIEST MAN ON THE PLANET LOVES YOU and I AM SO BLOODY HUNGRY I COULD EAT HADDOCK. Battered and human variety.

Vic Reeves is bloody hilarious.

God I want Haddock (human not battered)

Perhaps I don't. Fact is I've been spending a lot of time with me recently and I've realised I deserve a break. I deserve to be nice to me. And I HAVE to make myself DO stuff. GO places. Perhaps not Africa but Leicester and stuff.

I can be a full and whole person without the biscuits.

That sounds all Oprah Winfrey but it's true.

Oh no, is my potential thinness turning me into a twat?

Saturday 2.3.91

12.35 p.m.

DOBBER IS UP FOR HER mum's 40th birthday. On Sunday I am going back with her to Canterbury. It's a big deal and I'm slightly worried about it because a) It's miles away b) How do I stick to the diet when we are on a session? Apparently vodka and diet Coke. Anyway I'm going. The vodka will probably help.

Sunday 3.3.91

12.06 a.m.

HAD THE WEIRDEST AND MOST brilliant night at Dobber's mum's 40th birthday. This bloke kept saying 'Rae – you are such a child of the 60s.' I didn't think I was but when I was doing my GCSE's I used to listen to 'Woodstock' by Matthews' Southern Comfort and think I was going to drop out. Perhaps I was born in the wrong era. The 80s were so body fascist – it was all Jane Fonda and leotards riding up your bum. Even skinny people in the 60s wore kaftans and loose clothing.

Haddock's girlfriend went to see him in Leeds. Apparently he's now a bit in love with himself. Isn't that good though? I would love to be a bit in love with myself. Oh and he's coming back next weekend. Dear Rosemary

Conley. Can you metabolic boost me into losing 4 stone in 7 days? No. I didn't think so.

11.15 p.m.
Fucking hell. Do you know what Haddock's girlfriend said to Dobber?! – 'Haddock might try to get off with you in the summer because he wants to make me jealous and you're the only one of my friends he likes.'

I will show all the shits.

They are not shits. They just have NO IDEA how I feel. None of them. And they love me. The biggest twat in my life is ME.

Monday 4.3.91

11.45 p.m.
1) At university you can get pissed on any night in the week. Like school. It's brilliant.
2) At university drinks are cheap. REALLY cheap. In a way wrong cheap because you drink shitloads.
3) Dobber is lying on the floor with a stomach that looks like 'Alien' is about to burst out of it.
4) I don't think I need to call an ambulance. I've seen her like this before. She gets up the next day, has a full fried breakfast and can do an A level a day later.
5) Not many men here. Apparently the 'ratio' isn't very good. Too many teachers. Don't get into teaching if you are a woman and want sex.
6) I'm not having a panic attack AND I had a plain jacket potato for tea. No butter, just beans.

7) No-one mentioned I have lost any weight.
8) Just realised none of them know me except for Dobber who tonight drank Baileys and Rolling Rock cider. She can probably see about 3 of me now all of different sizes.

Tuesday 5.3.91

6.35 p.m.
I HAD AN EXCELLENT TIME with Dobber and I didn't have to rush home. I know I was only there a day but that's progress.

7.37 p.m.
Mum has told me she has to go to Hull on Thursday for an immigration meeting?!! This makes no sense whatsoever but apparently that's our nearest branch. It's about getting Adnan in the country forever and would I come for moral support? Yes. I will. It will be nice to see Hull again.

I just hope I don't get there and decide that it's a shithole. I can't do an Essex again. Perhaps I can do a one week tour of every university in the country. The Fresher Week Nutter Fuck Up tour!

No – Hull is my fate. I feel it as much as I feel the other stuff I'm certain about, like I need to be thinner to do Haddock, that The Smiths will never be beaten, like I would genuinely blow up the back catalogue of The Beatles rather than Abba if I had to – I know, I KNOW. BUT ALL OF IT IS HERE INSIDE ME. And it's not the mental bit. It's the RIGHT bit.

Wednesday 6.3.91

6.13 p.m.

MUM IS VERY IMPRESSED BECAUSE I know where we have to go in Hull. Yes – it's only a little walk from the station. Perhaps I have been here before. I mean reincarnated. Me and Hull. It's odd. Why Hull?

8.22 p.m.
Just went mad in my room to Nomad's 'Devotion'. You can't beat a shimmy and it's better than some stupid aerobic tape. No – I can't do two side steps in my bedroom let alone a full grapevine with swinging arms because it's tiny. I can however go off my tits freestyle to somebody rapping about Maggie Thatcher getting shafted.

Thursday 7.3.91

9.37 p.m.

NEXT TIME I WANT TO kill my mum I have to remember what happened today.

We got to Hull (I still love it – it feels like home – I can't even explain why) and we were waiting to see the immigration official. Right – this is going to sound really bad but the bloke is a ~~Flid~~ thalidomide victim. Should you even call them victims? I don't know. His hands were basically attached to his bloody shoulders. He had no arms. Anyway I'm a bit in shock. My Mum however just walks in and shakes his hand which is sort of on his shoulder with no problem at all. She did it like it is the most natural thing in the world. It was . . . amazing. I think even the man was a bit surprised. I can't really explain it. I just know 99% of people would be freaked out but to Mum it was just . . . she was brilliant.

She answered all his questions in her posh voice which was a bit annoying but she explained Dad and the gay 2nd husband very well. Then at the end she shook his hand again.

When we were walking away to get the train I said 'Mum – you were dead good in there.' I mean it was almost like a lesson in people handling. She was totally cool about it though. She said 'I just saw a person, Rachel.'

How can this person who is a complete selfish cow also be so totally wonderful?

Apparently, though, Hitler was nice to his dogs.

Am I a disability racist? I was a bit shocked at my reaction. That's weird because I watch *See Hear* and loads of weird shows on BBC2 about the handicapped.

Perhaps I am deeply horrible. I judge people on their looks – especially if they have no arms. They judge me on being fat. It serves me right. Only I can change. Mine was caused by eating like a pig, not doing stuff about the shit in my head and being a weak idiot. His was caused by doctors and the medical profession making a massive mess of things before he was even born. Who got the worst deal? Not me.

Friday 8.3.91

9.12 p.m.
JUST WATCHED LAST NIGHT'S *TOP of the Pops*.
Ned's Atomic Dustbin – 'Happy'. Fine. Living Colour
– 'Love Rears Its Ugly Head'. Great song. 'The Stonk' by
Hale and Pace – I know it's for charity but it's
DREADFUL. Roxette – 'Joyride'. Please get pursued by the
police and plough into a tree.

The Clash are at number one with a song that's ten
years old. Yet more evidence that music is running out of
ideas.

And Haddock is NOT coming back this weekend.

So it's a bit like Christmas has been cancelled.

I'm sticking to the diet though. Two Jaffa Cakes have
become the saviour of my life. And I CAN stop at two.
That's the weird thing.

Monday 11.3.91

8.39 p.m.
BIGGEST SHOCK TELEPHONE CALL OF my life
today. Tegs rang and said come to Switzerland. I've got
you a job looking after kids and cleaning a house. But I can't.
I'm too scared. I can't cope away. THAT far away. Canterbury
was a challenge. And Switzerland is full of Toblerones.

Friday 15.3.91

7.13 p.m.

NOTHING TO TELL YOU. I feel ill. Not so much in my head. In my throat. Perhaps fewer chins makes things more susceptible to cold.

Saturday 16.3.91

9.12 a.m.

MUM SAYS MY TONSILS ARE up. I'll have to go to the doctors. They apparently look bad. It's good Haddock is not coming back this weekend as I look like a bullfrog. And if you kiss me I won't turn into a princess. You'll just get this shit virus.

Monday 18.3.91

9.24 a.m.

THERE ARE NO DOCTOR'S APPOINTMENTS today. I can be 'an emergency' tomorrow. Yes. That will do. AS I CAN BARELY TALK, EAT OR BREATHE.

Tuesday 19.3.91

4.35 p.m.

TODAY A WANKER BEARDY DOCTOR told me I was morbidly obese. How exactly does that affect my tonsils? Am I so bloated that they are sore too? How do you lose pounds off your tonsils? I told him I was losing weight. He said 'good' and gave me some antibiotics. The weird thing is after he said that I have never, NEVER wanted to eat something more. It's almost like an act of FUCK YOU! If anyone was stocking a Cornetto now I would have 12 of them but as my throat is so sore I don't even fancy them. HOW IS THAT HELPFUL?! YOU ARE MORBIDLY OBESE? Tell you what GP face – you look like bloody Dr Mopp from *Camberwick Green* and you may like to consider updating your image you arrogant shit. Just make me better and SOD OFF. Bet he went to Cambridge.

I hate even comparing him to Dr Mopp because he was lovely and always had time for people – even for Mrs Honeyman when her baby had paint on its face and she thought he had measles.

Friday 22.3.91

7.13 p.m.

NOT BETTER. I'M PROBABLY DYING. No, diary, nothing else has happened except my imminent death from tonsillitis.

Saturday 23.3.91

10.12 p.m.

I FEEL BETTER. YES MUM I am going down the pub tomorrow. No Mum I won't drink as I know it will ruin the antibiotics PLUS I'm on a diet. The world's most secret diet that no-one can ask me about/moan at me about/try to mess up because they don't want me to be my best.

Sunday 24.3.91

10.17 p.m.

F IG IS BACK FROM POLY. HE'S NOTICED I'VE LOST WEIGHT. FINALLY SOMEONE!! We haven't got scales at home because I think Mum fears them and I'm too embarrassed to go into Boots yet BUT it's working!

That said – no-one in the pub jumped on top of me so I've got a way to go yet.

I told him it was the tonsillitis. It's not. It's my amazing willpower over Jaffa Cakes and my new found love of Ski yoghurts.

It's not a love really. It's a means to an end. Or a Haddock.

Wednesday 27.3.91

9.55 p.m.

FIG WANTS TO GO OUT with Dobber again.
I'd go out with Dobber if I was a boy.

I'm keeping it together. I walk everyday with music.
Miles and miles. Either to Tolethorpe, Toll Bar and back
again or to the fourth Meadows with compilation tapes
on my personal stereo. Burns up calories and I can think.

I still hit myself because I can't get the thoughts out of
my head . . . If I think 'die' I hit myself and it cancels it
out with God.

It's sense.

It's not sense but it's sense to me.

It's funny I never wanted to write it but now I think
sod it. It's only you diary. Why not? I didn't tell the
shrinks as much as I write here.

Some were OK but the psychiatrist who said I was
punishing Mum for what happened was talking SHIT. It
was NOTHING to do with her. Random evil paedophiles
are no-one's fault but random evil paedophiles. I knew
that at 12, thank you. It just fucked me up. My mum was
brilliant. All my family were. That was having a go at me
AND Mum. I was right to threaten him with throwing a
typewriter at him. Though in the long run I don't think
this made him particularly warm to me! HA HA HA!

Piss off with you GCSE psychology. I was mad before
the pervert came along. I know it. I don't remember a
time when I wasn't. They always pick up on the obvious
stuff – of course it was horrible but my head has always

been horrible. No 8 year old should be terrified of malaria when they live in Lincolnshire. At least nuclear war makes more sense. Or made more sense. Thank you Mr Gorbachev.

You see – nothing to do. I'm going into things here that I can't fix. My brain needs something. That number one wall chart that I made or type up my record collection again (without throwing the typewriter at the shrink). The diet is helping. It's something to focus on. A list to tick.

'You Got the Love' by The Source and Candi Staton is blowing my head off it's that good. There's also this Banderas song called 'This Is Your Life' which is fantastic but it's asking me every question in the lyrics that I can't answer. Then it keeps reminding me in the chorus that 'This is your life'. I KNOW!! I'M BLOODY TRYING TO SORT IT!!

Friday 29.3.91

7.42 p.m.

TODAY I SPOKE TO MY dead great granddad for half an hour. I said I know World War One must have been just dreadful and I feel bad asking this but can you help me out? I know being in the Somme and watching young men being butchered to shit makes my life look like the best thing ever but I just need a break. I need something to go right. Give me the power to stick at things. You were in a trench. You survived. Give me what I need to get through this and not go mad.

I've never shoplifted because of my great granddad. He was in no-man's-land about to nick a gold ring off a

German and the German opened his eyes. He said that was God telling him not to thieve.

Actually I think it was just the German dying. Probably horribly.

Perhaps the whole family were mad. I'm just the strengthened version of it. I'm the bottle of nuts-squash without the water.

Does talking to dead people make you mad? Doris Stokes made a career out of it and no-one made her go to group therapy and work with clay. I better not tell anyone though. They are all waiting. Looking for the signs.

Saturday 30.3.91

5.32 p.m.

I GOT STUCK BY THE gas fire today for ages. Why don't they make gas fires you can unplug? If you press plugs in your palm you know you've turned them off. When you leave the house you can see the imprint of the plug. There's no comfort with gas.

Sunday 31.3.91

3.14 p.m.

A SKED MUM TODAY IF WE really need gas. Why can't we just have electric? Apparently it's the boiler and Mum likes to see a proper flame when she's cooking. Yes – because my mental health is less important than seeing fire when you're doing your baked beans.

7.34 p.m.

'Crazy For You' by Madonna is back in the charts! It's like the universe wants to remind me that every end of every disco in the 1980s was spent in the toilets hiding from rejection.

Well – the diet is still going well. Odd. I don't feel like eating much sometimes. I don't feel like getting out of bed sometimes. I like being asleep. That's my main interest.

Wednesday 3.4.91

11.10 p.m.

MY MOTHER TALKS BASIC CRAP the majority of the time but she's right about one thing. I'm going mad here.

1) Wasting all I've got.
2) Mind collapse.

I partly live for *Vic Reeves Big Night Out*. My brother told me about it. It's brilliant.

Vic and Bob
Vic and Bob I'm glad you're here
Because the dole cheques are wrapped around my
  mind
Sent it round the twist
So I'll slip a plum underneath a viper

Very Poor.

Thursday 4.4.91

10.23 p.m.

MORT CAME UP WITH THIS fantastic idea when I rang her tonight. UNESCO (the education part of the United Nations) do these trips to Poland. You go there and teach English in a boarding school and then tour across the place. Mort and me can do it when she comes back from South Africa. Yes. It scares me to the point where I can barely breathe but I'm sick of being here left behind as the nuts one. I can't risk another mess. I have to do something and Mort makes me feel safe. She wouldn't let me die. It's for a month. I know. The most I managed away on my own before without my mum is five days but . . . I have to do it. And Mort is there. She is with me. So I'm going for it. Poland has only just stopped being communist so God knows what it's like but . . . have to try. Have to learn to get out and not feel like I'm dying. And there's no InterCity trains back from Poland. Once I'm there, I'm there. With Lech Walesa and . . . I can't think of anyone else famous that is Polish. I think I need £200. I'll get it somehow.

Poland. Bloody hell. I can't even believe you can get to Poland now.

Friday 5.4.91

11.22 p.m.

> Soon my Wednesday nights will be so grim,
> With my hanky I will sob,

To turn on 10.30 on Channel 4
And there will be no Vic and Bob

Had THE most horrendous experience ever tonight.
Shelboss rang me up and took me out for a curry with
her boyfriend (Cancerian, incisive gent type). Anyway he
bought his mate. It was a bit double-date-feely but I
wasn't attracted to him at all. THEN my brother came in
the Indian (WHY DOES STAMFORD ONLY HAVE ONE
INDIAN TAKEAWAY??!!) and said Hello and this bloke
made a phallic joke in front of my brother! It was
TOTAL death from social embarrassment. A nightmare. I
just feel so prickly and uncomfortable with the whole
men thing.

Told Shellboss about Poland. She thinks it's a great
idea.

So does Mum.

Everyone does.

I do but I'm shitting it.

Perhaps life IS just shitting it a lot of the time. You
have to just get over it. With a bloody paper bag.

Saturday 6.4.91

F IG AND DOBBER ARE WELL loved up again. Good
– I like them both and Dobber deserves to be happy.

Loads of people back down the pub tonight. Lots of
'what are you doing Rae?' Er . . . I'm GOING TO POLAND.
Finally I have an answer better than 'I'm sitting in fields
listening to Morrissey thinking about sex with Haddock
and writing poetry that you will never get to see.'

A few people asked if I had lost weight. I told them I'd had tonsillitis for a very long time. How long can I use that excuse before I have to admit I'm on a proper massive sex goddess diet?

Sunday 7.4.91

11.44 p.m.
I JUST WATCHED THE BEST thing with Mum – *Prime Suspect*. Basically Helen Mirren is this detective trying to solve this murder and rape case and the men working with her treat her like shit BUT she just carries on tough as nails. It was bloody FANTASTIC. She was completely amazing. Mum said 'That's how it is Rach – men give you crap, you come back tougher.' I have no desire to be a policewoman as I nearly vomit when I stub my toe but what a show. UP YOURS SEXIST SHITS! Second part on tomorrow.

Monday 8.4.91

11.37 p.m.
PRIME SUSPECT I SWEAR WAS the best television programme I have ever seen. At the end when she caught the total bastard all the blokes working with Helen Mirren had to admit that they had been totally wrong about her and they sang her a song. It was . . . oh I couldn't look away. TENSE! Even Mum had to admit that it made *Bergerac* look like *Noddy*. The most dangerous person in *Bergerac* is Liza Goddard! She was married to

Alvin Stardust and was on *Give Us a Clue* for years. That
says it all!

Tuesday 9.4.91

9.12 p.m.
I HAVE TO ADMIT NOW I might be slightly sick of 8
ounce jacket potatoes. It's the weighing them that is the
complete pain in the backside. You look like a right
weirdo in the Co-op trying to get ones that are exactly
right.

I'm not giving up though.

I have also started doing Cynthia Kereluk's *Everyday
Workout* on the Lifestyle Channel. I look like a total tit
doing it so I shut the curtains.

Wednesday 10.4.91

M UM HAS BEEN INFORMED THAT I'm 'shutting
curtains a lot'. No I'm not joking. Some people
round here have that little to do that they report on
curtain and blind movements.

I told her I was doing aerobics, that I didn't have a
decent sports bra and my breasts were bouncing
everywhere.

That completely ended the conversation. If there is one
thing my mum fears or is jealous of it's my tits. She
would not want there to be an Edinburgh Road boob
bounce display under any circumstances.

Thursday 11.4.91

6.12 p.m.

N O MUM – I HAVE no desire to watch a recording of *The Darling Buds of May* on video with you. As far as I can see it's mainly about eating really nice farmhouse food round a really big farmhouse table. That's not good for the diet. Also it's Del Boy trying to have sex with his TV wife. That might be good for the diet.

Friday 12.4.91

1.11 p.m.

I 'M TRYING TO FILL IN a form to go to Poland. I've just mucked it up which is ridiculous as I actually REALLY want to do this.

If you could groan I know you would. You know – no. I am not going to write it anymore. I haven't seen Haddock for 6 months. He's meant to be out tonight. He could have grown two heads and a tail by now and turned into a total twat features. But I'm in KNOTS at the thought.

11.45 p.m.

Where do I start? God, life is funny. I mean – you just can't predict it.

Battered Sausage and Fig came round first. It was brilliant to see them both. Dobber and me were having a real laugh in the Vaults and then Haddock flies in and

just completely ignores me. I mean – COMPLETELY. Mr
Pissy Arse. Battered Sausage said 'Aren't you going to
speak to Haddock?' No – why should I go over and see
him? Of course I wanted to but WHY SHOULD I? I'm not
chasing him. No. Bloody no. If he wants to play silly
buggers then oh – I'm crying. Everybody was so lovely
and the ONE person you want to just be thrilled to see
you and NOTICE YOUR weight loss decides this is the
night he is going to act like a total knob end. Then he . . .
Oh pissed off. Write more tomorrow.

Saturday 13.4.91

9.45 a.m.
SEEING HADDOCK JUST THREW ME completely.
And then ALL he eventually did was speak to bloody
Dobber about his on/off girlfriend. Had she heard
anything? Did she know anything? He grunted at me. It
was like April 1989 again. The grunt. The gorgeous idiot.
Only I know that's not him now. Which makes it even
worse.

Sunday 14.4.91

10.13 a.m.
HADDOCK JUST KNOCKED ON THE front door.
My heart leapt ten foot in the air like his eyebrow. I
kept casual though.
  CONVERSATION AS FOLLOWS. IT BEGGARS BELIEF.

HADDOCK: Is Battered Sausage here?

ME: No, he's not.

HADDOCK: See you then.

ME: Er . . . Haddock. Have I . . .

HADDOCK: Rae I really can't talk right now.

BYE THEN. SOD OFF YOU.

I didn't say that. I just said 'Bye!' He ran off. I slammed the door. I slammed the door in a way that it was BLOODY OBVIOUS that I was totally and utterly PISSED OFF.

And I put it all back in the box called Haddock.

I haven't got an actual box called Haddock. There's just stuff under the mattress. I mean in my mental head box called Haddock.

I haven't got a heart to smash anymore. I'm surprised I've got any circulation left.

9.12 p.m.

I can't seem to explain to Mum that *The Darling Buds of May* will not make me feel better right now. She says 'But it was lovely watching *Prime Suspect* together.' Yes it was. Watching a woman solve a horrible murder against the odds was brilliant. A massive family being happy in Kent is not going to improve my mood.

She's still waiting to hear about Adnan coming back to the country. She wants me to take her mind off it I think but . . . let Ma Larkin and her stupid pies and ridiculously idyllic lifestyle where everyone fancies her despite her being massive be a distraction. I'm sick of being everyone's clown.

Monday 15.4.91

8.13 a.m.

GOT AN INTERVIEW AT THE Chequers Inn tomorrow for a bar job.

Tuesday 16.4.91

11.14 a.m.

I'M JUST DOWN THE MEADOWS.
　　Well, just went for an interview at the Chequers Inn. I think I'll pass on that one. The landlord was a bit of a humourless sod. I've noticed that people actually don't want a discussion in life they just want to TELL YOU SHIT. I'll get called a jibber but who gives a toss?! I think most people I am friends with have that opinion of me anyway and whether it's true or not I doubt I can change it.

　　Anyway back to more important issues than jobs – Haddock. It's weird all that time I was worried about using his girlfriend but actually both of them were using me. Inadvertently. I don't think they did it deliberately. But I've been their total marriage guidance counsellor. Serves me right. Now I'm not needed amymore and

FUCK!
FUCK!

Was just writing that and Haddock appeared from behind me. Thank God I moved this quick.

Conversation as follows

HADDOCK: Hello.
ME: Hello.
HADDOCK: Sorry I've been bit off. I've had a lot on and there's stuff I want to say to you.
ME: Yeah. No worries Haddock. I've got to go actually I've got a job interview (LIE – BUT SOD YOU!)
HADDOCK: Oh OK. Well, see you soon then.

He looked a bit upset. GOOD. I can hurt people too.

Then I went.

7.20 p.m.
Now I feel like shit. Well done Rae. Another stellar performance from the lady the *Stamford Mercury* is calling 'this region's most massive crashed and burned buggered up mess up merchant'.

It didn't say that but it would if it was doing a special report on idiots.

Wednesday 17.4.91

5.13 p.m.
WHY WAS I SUCH A bitch to him?
    Because he hurt ME! You can't just pick people up and drop them when you feel like it Haddock.

I suppose you can when you have absolutely no idea that they are completely in love with you and that you are living on sodding Ryvitas, Slim a Soups and apples so one day you can snog them. THE SECRET SACRIFICES THAT I AM MAKING! I can't remember the last time I had a Twix.

Thursday 18.4.91

8.12 p.m.
JUST WATCHED *TOP OF THE Pops.* I love the Chesney Hawkes song and I love his mole. It shows imperfection is beautiful. In fact I want the mole of Chesney. I might draw it on with a biro.

James' 'Sit Down' is a work of genius but Zucchero and Paul Young need to sort it out. What a load of Radio 2 drivel. Something about being without a woman. Here's a tip Zucchero – lay off the crisps. That's what I've had to do. But he's Italian, famous and male so women will be queuing up anyway to share his pizza. What never ceases to amaze me is how unfair life is. I'm fat and can't get one piece of action. Zucchero is probably having a pepperoni pizza 3 times a day and models are cavorting round his table in feathers. I wish I was a man.

No – I don't. I just wish I could be a PROPER woman.

Friday 19.4.91

7.34 p.m.
I WENT OVER TO MORT'S. She goes away for ages to South Africa tomorrow. I got a bit emotional. She was like 'I'll be back before you know it' but she won't be.

She's there for ages. We are definitely going to Poland together but that's miles off and in the meantime – oh . . . not being able to ring her. For the good things. For the bad things. For the REALLY bad things. There's no-one else I can just say I'm in a mess to without them threatening me with places and tablets and things I can't handle.

That's not her problem though. It's not Haddock's either. They can't fix me.

Anyway I hugged her goodbye and said have a wonderful trip but I really wanted to say 'stay by the phone and don't go and would you like a piece of privet?'

That's our private joke thing. Privet. No it's not funny to anyone else and neither is calling each other Feint and Margin in a Cornish accent – but that's what best mates are partly for. Crap jokes that no-one else gets.

Sunday 21.4.91

7.36 p.m.
WHAT THE HELL AM I going to do without Mort?

Monday 22.4.91

12.23 p.m.
SOMETIMES I KNOW I'M MAD. Nutty as a fruitcake. Yet there is nothing I can do about it. There is nothing I can do to stop my brain saying if the ITV

schools logo I am following goes to the top left corner of the screen then I am going to die.

When I write it I feel a bit better because when I read it back it sounds completely mad doesn't it?

Tuesday 23.4.91

11.02 p.m.

NIGHTMARE.
Got a majorly shit job. It's packing cat food on a gangmaster system. Our team get paid by piece. I've got to get up at 6.15 a.m. tomorrow to be picked up by a minibus to put bloody lids on gourmet cat food. Fuck posh cats. White is happy with Whiskas and she's fussy. Why aren't they?!

Wednesday 24.4.91

8.06 p.m.

WOKE UP AT 6 A.M. We all had to pile onto this minibus that was just groaning with misery. People grunted at me like Haddock in a bad mood. A chorus of Haddocks but not as good looking or as lovely. We eventually got to this dreadful place in the Fens at 8.30 a.m.

They showed me the work. You stand round a table and put lids on cat food as quickly as you can. There's no radio on and you do it for about 8 hours. Not even I can have sex fantasies to get me through 8 hours of lids on cat food. Anyway, then they decided they didn't want me. CHEERS! YES!!!! The gangmaster drove me back from somewhere dreadful near Wisbech and said 'Don't worry, duck – I'll sort you out something next week.' No please don't. I didn't say that but no – please don't. Not ever.

Monday 29.4.91

9.35 p.m.

TONIGHT DAVID ICKE WHO USED to be the Sports presenter on BBC *Breakfast* and the most normal person in the world went on *Wogan* and started going on about all sorts of mad shit. That he was the Son of God, that evil was in control and that there was going to be loads of natural disasters.

Now people were laughing and it was funny because he used to read the football results but seriously I was saying stuff TOTALLY less weird than that when I was put in a psychiatric ward and I wasn't wearing a turquoise tracksuit either.

The point is – who is mad and who isn't? And do you get to avoid shrinks and psychiatric wards if you've worked with Selina Scott and Frank Bough?!

Tuesday 30.4.91

7.23 a.m.

JUST ASKED MUM IF I'VE ever been more mad than David Icke. She just got cross and said 'Rachel – forget David Icke and move on.'

Usual answer with added David Icke. The thing is I think I am still madder than David Icke. I just hide it better.

I am dreading telling the bloke I don't want a job when he rings. I can't work with cat food though. It's a sick thought.

6.23 p.m.
He STILL hasn't rung. LONG may that continue!

Wednesday 1.5.91

11.42 a.m.
THE POSH CAT LID GANGMASTER bloke rang. I pretended I couldn't hear him. Then I had to ring back. His wife answered and I told her that I didn't want the job because 'I'd sorted something out else'. I haven't. I hope they don't tell the Jobcentre. They won't. They are too busy making Tiddles and his upper-class feline mates happy.

7.24 p.m.
Everybody is still talking about David Icke. Mum says now whenever something goes wrong at Morrisons people say 'Oh David Icke was right!' I said 'What if he's ill though like I was ill?' Mum said 'ill people don't go on *Wogan*. It was attention seeking.'

How do we actually know that ill people don't go on *Wogan*?

Thursday 2.5.91

10.32 a.m.

MUM HAS JUST BEEN TOLD that Adnan is allowed to stay in the U.K. FOREVER. He is coming back NEXT week. She's really pleased and I'm thrilled because she's completely forgotten about the cat lid job!

5.45 p.m.

I'm going to be in Gooseberry Land again though. At least you can escape Gooseberry Land. Cat Lid Land was like a prison. Mum does go all different when Adnan comes though. All luvvy duvvy and slightly goo-horrific.

Friday 3.5.91

4.32 p.m.

HOW DO YOU KEEP YOUR personality but be someone's girlfriend/wife?

Sorry this diary is full of random thoughts and David Icke at the moment.

Saturday 4.5.91

11.58 p.m.

A TOTAL INJUSTICE AND A TOTAL fiasco at Eurovision tonight. I honestly might never watch it again. The French had this beautiful sort of Arabic song

– which is probably how Adnan should sound like if he could sing. The Swedes just had this uptempo mess which sounded like something Sinitta would sing. It was a tie but because of some stupid rule the Swedish Sinitta won. Honestly if I was France now I would invade Sweden. The Italian hosts were all over the shop, our song was UTTER bollocks. Trying to be 'Feed the World' with a blonde in a short skirt. We used to be GOOD at this??!! What has gone wrong. Even Terry Wogan was getting annoyed – and he was patient with David Icke!

Tuesday 7.5.91

7.13 p.m.

WHEN I HAVEN'T BEEN WRITING it's like – it's a numbness. I don't feel anything. Or there's a panic. Or I just don't want to talk.

Today I just want to tell you that the diet is going really well. My jeans are hanging off me. I don't feel sexy yet though. I don't look sexy either but there's definitely less of me. A bit less mess.

Wednesday 8.5.91

5.14 p.m.

I'VE APPLIED TO BE ON Hereward Radio's Norwich and Peterborough Cash Counter Quiz. Even Mum says it's worth a go. I'd be on the radio everyday for a week and I could win up to £200. It would help me pay for Poland for a start.

Thursday 9.5.91

9.13 p.m.

ADNAN IS BACK. GREAT FOR Mum but sadly I couldn't go mad to 'Last Train to Transcentral' by The KLF as he was watching *Top of the Pops* too. Still, his version of Cher's 'The Shoop Shoop Song' was an interesting listen.

Friday 10.5.91

6.13 p.m.

I HAVE FOUND THE CARTOON 'Citizen Sid' in one of the adverts in the *Stamford Citizen* now for over a year. I have entered the competition every week. I HAVE NEVER WON. It's only to win a fiver but that's not the point. I am the unluckiest person in the world ever.

Saturday 11.5.91

11.46 p.m.

YOU KNOW THAT DOOR IN the Vaults marked 'Private' near the toilet opposite the kitchen? It's just a cupboard full of lemons.

That's how interesting my Saturday night was.

Monday 13.5.91

12.11 p.m.

I THREW HADDOCK'S PLANT IN the cupboard. I
can't look at it anymore.

It's time to lose some emotional weight as well as some
real weight.

Of course if I had real balls I'd put it in the bin
completely but . . . that's letting go of something I just
can't let go of yet.

What am I thinking though? No letters. No phone calls
(he could get my number if he really wanted it) and when
he does come here we go back a year to the grunting. And
still I'm holding on. Praying. Wishing. Hoping. Checking
things. But I'd be doing that anyway about something.
Don't think you're that special Haddock. You're not.

Well you are but not . . . All that started before you. It
all started . . . I can't remember it not being part of life.
Perhaps I was just born with it.

Tuesday 14.5.91

12.11 p.m.

I GOT A LETTER FROM Mort today. She's having a
fantastic time. It cheered me up immensely because
she's having a good laugh (unselfishly) and she's nearly
home (completely selfishly).

I'm lonely. I've felt lonely before at the end of parties
and stuff when everyone is tonguing everyone else but

this is different. This is total loneliness. It's like being stranded underneath your duvet. I'm a bit thinner but still huge. I thought with every pound I lost I'd lose something bad in my head I suppose. That was . . . how much fat is in my head anyway? How much ugly is in my head? If they made me into Kylie tomorrow would I still stick matches in my arms because I thought I looked terrible and was an awful person? I'd look like a right twat on *Top of the Pops* with burn marks up my arms. Explain that one to *Smash Hits* – 'I had a nasty cooker accident.'

I'd be fooling nobody.

Am I fooling anyone anyway? Does everyone realise I'm sad but just not know what to do so it's easier to stay away or pretend it's not happening or are they really that thick?

Sod it all – Gary Clail of On-U Sound System – 'Human Nature'. That's a great song and he said in *Smash Hits* that he lost loads of weight. It can be done. You can lose the pounds but not your soul. I don't want to be a floozy who laughs at shit jokes.

Friday 17.5.91

11.09 a.m.
I JUST GOT A CALL FROM PAUL COYTE – breakfast presenter at Hereward Radio. I'M ON THE CASH COUNTER QUIZ ALL NEXT WEEK!! I thought he was joking at first but it's happening! I'm really nervous but really excited. I could win so much money. My heart was pumping like mad. I can't wait to tell Mum. By the end of

next week in the Greater Peterborough area I will be bloody famous thank you.

12.08 p.m.
I just told Adnan about the Cash Counter quiz. He didn't really get it but he offered to make me a cheese toastie. I was tempted but Rosemary Conley basically says cheese is the anti-Christ unless it's part of a Lean Cuisine beef lasagne topping.

7.12 p.m.
Mum cannot quite believe it about the Cash Counter quiz. She is really impressed. I told her I was quite nervous. She said 'Rachel – you were made for this. It's general knowledge and talking crap – right up your street.' Then she winked. For her that's a massive compliment.

Sunday 19.5.91

11.51 p.m.
CAN'T SLEEP FOR NERVES. THOUSANDS of people listen to Hereward Radio. Well all of Morrisons does.

Monday 20.5.91

5.32 a.m.
I'M NOT ON FOR ANOTHER hour but I can't sleep. I can't eat before I go on. I don't want to do a burpy voice thing on air.

8.22 a.m.

That went REALLY well. Even Mum said I was good! Paul Coyte asked me what the money was for. I said going to Poland and then we had a chat about that and then I GOT ALL THE QUESTIONS right.

Anyway I've got to go to Peterborough tomorrow to get my passport photos done for Poland. So it's down to Woolies today. Yes – I'm dreading it. Why can't I still fly on my mum's passport? That's because you are 19 Rae. You're an adult. It's not how I thought it would be. It's arse.

7.55 p.m.

Shit. I'm still huge. Massive. I look 40 not 19. I wouldn't shag me. MASSIVE face. 27 chins and I've been on a diet for how long? How much longer?!

Tuesday 21.5.91

8.55 p.m.

GOT ALL THE QUESTIONS RIGHT again! AND Mum said I was bright and not boring like most of the people who go on there. It was 'Apples, Staples or Nipples' today. You had to guess whether the thing Paul Coyte said had 'apples, staples or nipples'. He said 'Playboy' which could have both but I went with staples as if I said nipples on air Mum would say I was 'lowering the tone'.

7.05 p.m.

Went to Peterborough to get my passport sorted. I need proof of travel to get one in one day so when me and Mort go to the meeting in London about Poland I'll have to get something then. It's a pain in the arse BUT as I was coming across the bridge from the railway station into Queensgate I think I saw Paul Coyte leaving Hereward! I'll ask him tomorrow. He's sort of like a celebrity friend now.

Wednesday 22.5.91

9.01 p.m.

I THINK I'M GETTING EVEN better at this radio thing. Just before we went live to air today I said to Paul Coyte I think I saw you yesterday. He said let's talk about that on air. So he said 'So you think you saw me yesterday' and I said 'Yeah – you were totally denim clad and looked a bit like Shakin' Stevens.' He said 'Yes – that was me' and really laughed. That was good. What was less good is that I got my first question wrong. He said 'How many eyes does the Cyclops have?' and I said '3.' Of course it's 1. Never mind. I'm still earning loads for basically doing nothing.

I think I really like radio! HA HA HA!

Thursday 23.5.91

8.54 a.m.
WE HAD A GOOD LAUGH on the radio again today. It whizzes by when you're on. Mum's friend Sadie told her she thought I was a natural. I've always loved radio. I had my own radio station in my bedroom when I was 11 and made tapes with jingles and everything. I've always wanted to be a radio presenter. I've shown years of dedication. I hope this has made Mum wake up that my ambitions are completely realistic and that I can do STUFF.

Friday 24.5.91

9.13 a.m.
LAST DAY ON HEREWARD FM but it was fantastic. Paul Coyte introduced me by saying 'She's caused a storm! People have been saying to me – who is that girl you've got on this week? She's really good.' Anyway I ended up winning £178 which will very nearly pay completely for Poland.

God I love Paul Coyte – he was such a love and so nice. He really put me at ease and he said hello to loads of people at the end – mainly because he hates it when people say 'Hello to anyone who knows me.' Well that is a stupid bloody phrase.

Saturday 25.5.91

10.35 a.m.

I HAVE DECIDED RADIO IS definitely for me –

1) It seems to suit people who are loud and weird.
2) I genuinely think I could be better than Jakki Brambles.
3) I can basically tell you every highest chart position and the lyrics of every song of the past 30 years. Even the stuff in French like 'Joe Le Taxi' by Vanessa Paradis.
4) NO-ONE CAN SEE YOU on radio.
5) I can DEFINITELY present *Top of the Pops* better than Anthea Turner.

Sunday 26.5.91

7.42 p.m.

I SAT DOWN WITH MUM today and said 'Do I need to go to university if I really know what I want to do?' Mum said 'Look Rach – getting a degree gives you something to fall back on for the rest of your life and doesn't Hull have its own student radio station? You can get good there and then go on Radio 1.'

She's right. I do need a degree. I think I was just trying to chicken out of moving again. I'm scared. I can't really do Radio 1 from Stamford either though can I?

9.13 p.m.

Just realised Mum didn't freak out when I said I wasn't sure about university. I MUST have been good at the radio.

Friday 31.5.91

11.10 a.m.

BLOODY HELL!! POSTCARD FROM HADDOCK!!

Dear Rae,
Hear you are the new Simon Bates. If you get rich can I have a new moped please?
See you in the summer. Love Haddock X

It's wonderful, it's perfect but it's also torture because I've seen the passport photos. I'm still not in his league. I'm still not pretty enough. I'm still the lump. The lump that doesn't know how to wear a dress, or to be touched or . . . Oh I'm just not ready. Perhaps I AM the problem. I am thought of. I am loved but I piss it all away because I'm . . . Oh you know it all. You've heard it all. It's ME. I'M THE PROBLEM and I'm not putting it all down again because YOU know it and I know it.

Saturday 1.6.91

6.38 p.m.

I'M DOWN AGAIN. IN FACT I'm pancake flat. It's the anticlimax I suppose. The massive up of the radio, the amazing postcard from Haddock out of the blue. All the hope and possibility and now life returns to normal and reality. The lack of money. The dreadful passport photo. I could take it again I suppose but would it be any better? The fear of going to Poland and university. The fear of NOT going to Poland and university. Oh . . . SODDING THE WORST NUMBER ONE EVER. Color Me Badd's 'I Wanna Sex You Up'. If bloody Haddock offered to sex me up I would tell him to bollocks. What a pile of TOTAL EXCREMENT and one of them has a perm. SORT IT OUT.

Sunday 2.6.91

6.54 p.m.

THE PHONE RANG ABOUT 11.55 a.m. This really weird voice said 'Will you accept this reverse charge call from Cape Town' or something! MORT!! OF COURSE I said 'YES!' She is having a BRILLIANT time, she had her passport nicked but it's all sorted! She was telling me about all the blokes she has met, all the things she has seen – it sounds amazing BUT she still sounds like my Mort. I'm so relieved because I thought all this foreign stuff could change things between us. It hasn't though. We gassed on for ages. This may end up being a bit of a problem because God knows how much a reverse charge call from South Africa costs. Quite a bit I imagine. It's not fair though because Adnan is allowed to occasionally ring his family in Morocco to ask them quick questions and Mort is MY family. She's like a sister to me.

Mum will go mad when she sees the bill. Hopefully I'll be in Poland! Lech Walesa will protect me from the wrath of Mum. He stood up to communist nutters – but can he stand up to her? Is my mum scarier than Stalin when she goes mad? No. Not now I'm 19. She has limited powers. What's the worst she can do? Throw away my Smurfs? I can live without Papa Smurf now. I can even live without the one that's a chimney sweep and has its own little brush. These are the things of childhood. I am beyond them.

She could sell my records but she knows I would genuinely never talk to her again. My vinyl – it's part of me. I might still hide it though.

I'm feeling . . . better. Up. I might go into Boots and see how much I've lost. I'll wait till it's quiet though.

Actually I love my Smurfs too and my Britains model stable and all my horses. I better hide everything.

Thursday 13.6.91

10.30 p.m.

JUST AS THE THOUGHTS GET better and I feel more happy, optimistic – just a few sentences can send me hurtling back. I always think my thoughts are gone but they are just lying dormant.

Got a phone call at 9 p.m. It was Battered Sausage. He said come to Exeter and the End of the Year Ball thing. My initial response – excitement, butterflies but after the euphoria comes the inevitable practicalities.

1) Absolutely NO money. Barclays WANK have taken my Connect Card off me. This is just because I never put my student grant in there

(because I never got it!) AND because I went £54
overdrawn. Oh big deal. They treated me like I
was a criminal. No. John DeLorean. Denis Nielsen.
THEY are criminals. Barclays WANK need to get
some perspective. It's FIFTY FOUR QUID not five
million. I rang Dad and he paid it off. He wasn't
happy about it – he said 'You should bank with
the Midland anyway.' Thanks for that Dad. When
I actually ever get some money I may consider it.

2) I have NOTHING to wear. They don't do ball
dresses in aged 19, losing weight but still bloody
fat.

3) I'd be a gooseberry anyway because Battered
Sausage has got a permanent woman. She's
pretty, rich, loaded, probably clever as hell. Oh
– I'm not ready. I want to shove people up the
bum. I want to make a glide-in beautiful Oscar
red carpet entrance. Not a stomp, stomp, stomp
elephant entrance.

Mort is back on Saturday. Thank GOD.

I'm currently sitting at my desk with the window wide
open because apparently there is going to be an Aurora
e.g. loads of flashing mad lights in the sky but all I can
see is darkness except for Mrs Bark still working. It's now
11.15 p.m. She gets up at 4! Does the woman ever sleep?!

Mrs Bark has gone to bed she's in her pink nightdress.
And if she complains to Mum about me looking – CLOSE
YOUR BLOODY CURTAINS!

Saturday 15.6.91

9.12 a.m.

MORT'S BACK!!! SHE LANDED THIS morning at 6 a.m. or something. I wonder when it's OK to ring.

10.45 a.m.

Apparently she's really jet lagged and asleep! Fine but I want to speak to her Mr Mort. I think asking him to wake her though would be a bit selfish so I'll wait till tomorrow.

Sunday 16.6.91

3.12 p.m.

JUST SPOKE TO MORT FOR ages. It's OK now she's just in Oasby to talk to her forever. She asked me about Poland. I said 'Yeah – I'm really looking forward to it.' She said 'I know but I bet you are shitting yourself a bit.' I told her I totally was. There is rabies in central Europe, what if I get appendicitis or meningitis or we have a car crash or they decide they want to be communist again and we are stuck there forever? Mort said 'Rae – it's going to be OK and I am there.' She's right. It won't stop me being in a total state but Mort knows me and she can calm me down. I wish she was going to Hull but she's way smarter than me and she's going to St Andrews. I could never go there even if I was mega-brain because it's in another country!! It's a 6 hour train journey. SIX HOURS. If you have a panic attack there and need to get home you would have to call the coastguard and use their helicopter.

What if I lose it in Poland though? I can't think they are used to mad people. Well they are – they used to run the country! I mean mad people like me.

It's going to be OK

It IS going to be OK

I am going to take control like the psychiatrist says. I'm going to listen to music, go for a walk and keep it together.

I must take loads of batteries. So I'm never in a no music situation. Mum can use her staff discount card and completely empty the Duracell rack.

Monday 17.6.91

1.32 p.m.

ACCORDING TO SOURCES 'IN THE know' the phone bill will arrive next week bringing with it –

1) One reverse charge call from South Africa.
2) About 3 half hour conversations with Dobber in Canterbury.
3) A few calls to Battered Sausage in Exeter. They are long because they have to go and get him from his room.

Tuesday 18.6.91

6.12 p.m.

MUM SAID TO ME TODAY 'Go and weigh yourself Rach – you've lost a lot of weight. Everybody is saying so. Go to Boots and see how well you've done. I'll give you the 20p.'

My jeans <u>are</u> hanging off me. Well I can't really wear them anymore. Leggings are good.

Perhaps I should do it.

People are saying lovely things to me. I don't write them here. It's seems big headed and I still feel . . . I don't feel right. I don't feel like the woman I thought I would feel. I still want to be in my jeans. Just I need a belt these days.

Actually if I go to Boots and show Mum how much weight I've lost it might slightly take the sting out of the phone bill.

Wednesday 19.6.91

7.12 p.m.

I WENT TO BOOTS AT about 10.30 this morning. It's before the lunch rush but after all the pensioners have got their blood pressure medicines.

Anyway I am 11 stone 6.

I have lost THREE stone.

That's MASSIVE.

Three stone.

When I told Mum she said 'Rachel – that is FANTASTIC. You must be so proud!'

I told her yes.

Yes. No. I'm just thinner. I still feel fat in my head. I still feel like the . . . thing. The ugly thing. Deep inside I want to be sexy but I'm lost. Perhaps I just need to lose more. Get more normal sized and THAT'S when it all happens. That's when you just become like the other girls – that prettiness, that woman thing. Not the Rae in-between thing.

But I'll still have a mad head. I'll just have a mad head in a size 12 dress.

Ignore me. I can't cope with any change even if it's good.

Thursday 20.6.91

9.23 p.m.

WHEN IS HADDOCK COMING BACK? I would like to see his reaction to all this.

Why am I waiting on a bloody man who has NEVER snogged me just bloody confused me?

Top of the Pops tonight featured a song called 'People Are Still Having Sex'.

1) People are actually making money from stating the bloody obvious and putting a dance track behind it.
2) It was LAME. It was hardly Frankie talking about gay orgasms.
3) I am NOT having sex.

Friday 21.6.91

I SENT HULL ACCOMMODATION OFF. It took about an hour to check it. Aristotle told me which one to go for – Ferens. It's a traditional hall so you get your food BUT it's on the Lawns complex in Cottingham so it's near the student bar.

Why can't I just send things off. I'm always convinced I've written 'Fuck you!' on things. I get random people in the post office to check and pretend it's to check if people can read my handwriting.

I write it. It's NUTS. I can't stop it though. WHY?!

It's the year's longest day. I'm starving for longer.

At least this diet is working – but for what?

I'm less out of breath but Etam is still out of reach.

Sunday 23.6.91

11.45 p.m.

TODAY IS THE SORT OF day when I'd rather be just about anyone instead of me. My head is . . . it's like a fire not even the best pop can put out. I'm so scared of having Breakdown Number 2. That makes it sound like a film! It would be a shit sequel. It would be exactly the same as the first one. I'd be convinced I was dying, hurting myself, hurting others, rambling for hours and hours whilst psychiatrists encouraged me to talk about my experiences with people at least twice my age. What good does talking do? Does it really fix things? They bury

dead people for a reason. Why can't we just bury bad
things and memories too? Raking it up. What is it like
when a man touches you and you're a kid and you don't
want him to? When he scrapes his hand across your groin
LIKE IT'S HIS. Well clearly Mr Twat Psychiatrist it's
FUCKING AWFUL. Is this a trick question? Now let's
throw a beanbag at someone else and make them answer
a horrible question.

Balls to it. Balls to HIM. I bloody LOVE MEN. I bloody
love them. There are good ones everywhere.

Writing. Not talking. THAT makes me feel better. Now
FUCK OFF Dr Tossface with your silly theories.

Oh he was only trying to help.

Ignore me. I'm in a foul mood. Color Me Badd are still
number one.

Tuesday 25.6.91

8.23 p.m.

I'M SO SCARED OF FUCKING up the good things in
my life. I just feel everyone is growing out of me.

To make this situation better I really should stop going
on about how good *Take Hart* was compared to *Art
Attack*. Rae – NO-ONE OVER THE AGE OF 12 CARES.

Friday 28.6.91

9.35 p.m.

I AM AT MORT'S HOUSE because we have a meeting
tomorrow in London about Poland. She's worked out

where we are going as I have no clue. She's brilliant with maps. She's brilliant with everything. She has a fantastic tan and she has bought me the best present ever – some Nelson Mandela drink coasters! They are FANTASTIC! I will never use them. They are too good!

Every time you are down you have to remember that life can get better. Nelson Mandela used to be in prison. Now he is a hero and something you can put your cup of tea on. THINGS CHANGE.

Saturday 29.6.91

10.34 p.m.
THE POLAND MEETING SEEMED TO go quite well. We will be going to a place called Świdnica. It's quite near the German border. The team we are going with seem lovely – you get paired up with a teacher and you do the lessons together. I've got a brilliant lady called Angela – she's from Hull. HULL! Tell me that place isn't my destiny?! It pops up everywhere. I made a few jokes in the group sessions that people laughed at. We've been told the country is in a transitional state and very different to what we are used to. We need to take batteries and torches, shower gel – everything really. They don't really get vegetarians so they will mainly live on eggs. If you want to phone home you have to go to a special place in town and book the call.

Yes. Inside I am beyond panic BUT Angela is from Hull. That's telling me something. And Mort is always going to be there. If I can stick this I can prove everyone wrong. Everyone. Hardly anyone in Stamford has been to

Poland – it's all Torremolinos, or skiing in Italy or Florida. If I do this . . . Even writing it is hard but I can start to put the fuck up away. The nightmare away. I can become what I need to be. And I can lose weight, go Interrailing with Haddock without a panic attack and do it on every train in Europe – and now there's no Iron Curtain in even more countries!

That last bit was a joke – I just need to calm myself with thoughts of Haddock-based sex adventures.

Sunday 30.6.91

11.00 p.m.

POLAND SOUNDS AMAZING BUT WHAT if my crazy neurotic-ness fucks things up.

NO. STOP THINKING OF IT.

Jason Donovan is number one. Drippy thing from *Joseph* but he looks GORGEOUS as hell in his multi-coloured dream coat.

Monday 1.7.91

8.28 p.m.

THE SUN IS SHINING, THE radio is blaring and summer 91 has arrived in splendid form! Whether or not the next three months (is that all?!) can live up to today's weather is another thing. I hope they can.

Thursday 4.7.91

12.46 a.m.
YOU KNOW SHELLBOSS WAS REJECTED today from somewhere she really wanted to go to and I could say absolutely nothing constructive whatsoever. The girl has helped me through endless horrible stuff, especially this year, and I think I just ended upsetting her more.

God I'm a twat. It should actually be a massive banner over my head: Rae is a twat.

'Rae is a twat' fits the *Blankety Blank* theme tune perfectly.

Friday 5.7.91

11.45 p.m.
I THINK EVERYONE IS BACK. Tomorrow. I haven't seen people for ages. It will be amazing to see their reactions to me being less of a fat cow.

It will be BEYOND wonderful if Haddock is out.

Mum says I've got to start taking compliments and then started saying stuff like 'I think sometimes Rachel I've been too hard on you. I've just didn't want you to get a big head. There's nothing worse than a big head.'

There are far worse things than having a big head and being arrogant but it was not time to start a row. The phone bill hasn't arrived yet.

It was ALMOST an apology for being a dictator mother.

Sunday 7.7.91

3.09 a.m.

WHAT A NIGHT.
REACTIONS TO MY WEIGHT LOSS FROM
PEOPLE WHO HAVEN'T SEEN ME IN AGES –

<u>Dobber</u> – 'You look amazing, but you did anyway!' (she's just lovely).
<u>Battered Sausage</u> – 'LESS BIG RAZZA!' (predictable but half a compliment).
<u>Fig</u> – 'You've lost shitloads of weight. I've put some on. It's all the kebabs.' (He has – but he's still good looking and very sweet).

Then Haddock's girlfriend came in the Vaults. Now she's been around for months so she's sort of seen my weight disappear and she's been really kind about it but she was followed by HADDOCK.

I swear when you haven't seen him for ages he . . . HE GETS MORE GOOD LOOKING. It's like he's taking horny pills or something or I'm just UTTERLY LOVED UP TO THE POINT OF NEAR HEART ATTACK.

He walked in just as Kenny Thomas' 'Thinking About Your Love' was playing on the Vaults jukebox. Me and that jukebox are psychically linked – shit song but lyrics spot on.

I quickly put Carter the Unstoppable Sex Machine's 'Sheriff Fatman' on.

He didn't spot us at first. Then I swore he did a double take and waved. Eventually he came over. It's the eyes.

328

They are like chocolate. A lovely non fattening chocolate. Like Thornton's Continental but with zero calories.

Can you tell I'm hungry?

Anyway he looked me straight in the eye and dry-as-a-bone said 'Have you seen Rae?' and winked.

I said 'Piss off – I will have you know I am Rae of which you speak. I've just not been eating so many crisps.'

Then he goes 'Looking good young lady.'

Looking good young lady. It's hard to come back from that.

And I said 'Well you look knackered' (HE DIDN'T – HE LOOKED BEYOND BEAUTY).

He then told me he'd been 'burning the candle at both ends' and is going to work all summer. I said I was going to Poland at the end of the month. He just sniffed and said 'Well we better have a good time while we can then.'

Then we all went to Olivers and we all WENT FOR IT. He still dances like a god.

Now I'm tired but I can't sleep. I don't think I can sleep again.

Monday 8.7.91

10.20 p.m.

I WAS TEMPTED BY A pizza tonight that Adnan was scoffing but I have never been so committed to sticking to this. I can do it. I'VE DONE IT and I'm keeping doing it. The weekend proved it.

God – I hope the Poles still have food queues and rations. Oh that's an awful thought. I just don't want to get there and put on loads of weight.

Wednesday 10.7.91

9.30 p.m.

IF I'M NOT WRITING MUCH in this diary it's because NOTHING AT ALL is going on.

Diets are boring. Weighing out Special K (25 grams!) is dull but essential.

I am totally living for the weekends and of viewings of you know who.

Saturday 13.7.91

11.23 p.m.

HADDOCK WAS WORKING TONIGHT. I very nearly had a Pukka Pie and chips in commiseration. The Model Fish Bar smells like SEX when you haven't been there in a long time but I resisted. I would feel like crap afterwards and just at the time I feel the loss of my virginity nearing more than ever before.

Sunday 14.7.91

10.23 p.m.

DON'T I WRITE TOTAL SHIT at times?

Tuesday 16.7.91

4.55 p.m.

MY MUM IS UNDER THE complete control of the all-eating Adnan. It's very sad – for such a strong woman she disintegrates in relationships. She's a right pathetic cow. She waits on his every word. Perhaps it's her generation. That's the only way they know how to be with men.

And before you say, if I married Haddock I would not moon all over him night and day and wait on his every word and wish. He'd certainly do the washing up, wash his own underpants and do the cooking. I don't mind doing the hoovering and the driving everywhere. It would be a very equal relationship IF WE EVER GOT OUT OF BED!

Can you imagine if people knew about this?! The world would explode!! His girlfriend certainly would! HA HA HA!!! Even if I do ever go out with him I'm not telling him all this. I know it's a bit . . . full on.

Wednesday 17.7.91

11.34 p.m.

THOUGHTS HAVE BEEN BLOODY AWFUL today.

You never forget being a gooseberry. You never forgive either – both the people who made you one (not their fault) and yourself (YOUR fault).

I want to save the world but I haven't worked out a way to save myself yet.

Today it was quite funny/tragic really. I had a bad thought on the way back home, swiped myself hard around my face and two people were behind me. I realised all the tramps and 'nutters' I used to avoid and I had become one!

A street nutter.

If my writing is slightly all over the place it's because I'm trying to avoid watching a woman on TV who's having a facelift.

I got into the hall of residence I wanted at Hull which was a severe relief.

I can't stand staying in my room on a night as lovely as this. I want to be a part of it.

Thursday 18.7.91

4.39 a.m.

IT'S PISSING IT DOWN WITH rain. I hope it does it like this on Saturday night as Battered Sausage reckons he is sleeping down the Meadows!

Having trouble sleeping. Keep thinking about Poland. Can I stick it?

I love 'Get Ready!' by Roachford. Says so much of what I want to say. Asks all the questions too.

It was 49p in the bargain bin at Woolworths. Criminal really.

Sunday 21.7.91

3.45 a.m.

JUST HAD THE LAST SATURDAY night before Mort and me go to Poland.

Battered Sausage's girlfriend bought him the Bryan Adams number one single shit. We took the piss for 3 hours tonight! We managed to work 'Everything I Do I Do It For You' into nearly every sentence we said to him. IT WAS EPIC.

Haddock and me chatted for ages. When he said goodbye he gave me a big hug and said 'Now be careful and don't you be running off with a Pole.'

I told him I wouldn't. I didn't tell him a photo of him was coming with me to Poland.

It is.

Wednesday 24.7.91

7.46 p.m.

ALL OF US HAVE GOT to do a special lecture in Poland on British Culture. Naturally I have picked music. They've got a video player there so I am going to take a recording of *The Rock 'n' Roll Years* to show them AND I have drawn pictures of hippies and punks. Apparently they didn't have hardly any Western music and they have only just got MTV.

I would NOT have survived if I had been born in Poland. No way.

Thursday 25.7.91

10.12 p.m.

MY SUITCASE IS PACKED. I'M at Mort's house now because Mr Mort is driving us to Heathrow tomorrow. I have bought every medicine and drug known to man. I basically emptied Boots today. I don't think I'll need corn plasters but I've got some. Nan had corns – not 19 year olds!

Please, PLEASE GOD let me be able to cope with this. Please don't let me go mental. Please let me keep it together and not go mad in a foreign country.

Friday 26.7.91

6.49 p.m.

HERE I AM ON BOARD a LOT Polish Airlines plane. It's so cramped it's unbelievable and my ears are killing me. Mort – a quick word.

Hello!

Thank you.

Food is about to be served! Lovely can't wait for this one. I'm sitting next to a skydiver. I'd hate to be a stewardess – still I suppose it's an escape from Eastern Europe isn't it? I can't see anything outside the window.

I like Poland already for one thing. There are 18,400

Polish zlotys to the pound. For the first time in my life I feel rich.

I feel a bit mad but OK. There's a lot going on.

Saturday 27.7.91

1.20 a.m. Polish time
12.20 a.m. GMT
I'M GOING TO DO POLISH time from now on. It's too confusing otherwise.

POLAND!! Well we landed after mass turbulence and then we discovered that some of the people's luggage was still at Heathrow! I started singing 'Travelling Light' but everyone death stared me so I stopped.

Now at a hotel in Krakow and we have to get up at 7.30 a.m. tomorrow to see some salt mines! MINES!! A MINE. I can't get out of it though. Deep breaths.

We stopped off at this really weird place. It seemed like a primary school that they had opened specially. We had some aniseedy bread, herb tea, fish and an onion. AN ONION??!! This place is harsh. I left the fish WELL alone.

I am TOTALLY knackered. Everyone is really nice though.

Sunday 28.7.91

11.55 p.m.
ŚWIDNICA SCHOOL CAMP, POLAND. I am in a room with 3 manic Poles – actually one is a wild child, one is a smoker and one keeps laughing at just air.

They are all TOTALLY gorgeous. They seem to have mainly lived on raw onion. This is not a surprise.

The salt mine today was one of the most amazing things I have ever seen. Going down I very nearly had a panic attack but Mort sensed it and grabbed my arm. I was OK. Once we were down there it was incredible – cathedrals, altars, chandeliers all made from salt and a tennis court! The only downer was apparently the Nazis made people work down there and some people died. Probably loads. Nobody Polish seems to like anyone German.

Anyway lessons start tomorrow. I'm a bit nervous but Angela knows exactly what she is doing and I am just going to follow her.

CLASSIC group of people – Steve the leader, Mark, Ian, Chris – sound as a pound Vix, Mary, Julie – it's like I've known them years.

Monday 29.7.91

10.12 p.m.
WE HAD A BRILLIANT LESSON today. Angela is a great teacher. We did 'introducing ourselves' and where we came from. Some of the people there already speak brilliant English and this one girl told us she was from a farm and after Chernobyl happened loads of strange animals got born. It was genuinely one of the best stories I have ever heard.

I had a full on panic attack tonight. It was partly the Chernobyl story I think. It's the sort of thing I love but also the sort of thing that reminds me of accidents, disasters and death. I think I scared Vix a bit but Mort told her I had the occasional funny do and she's lovely. She's not treating me any differently. Perhaps people who aren't from small-town-small-mind Stamford are a little more accepting of weirdoes.

Apparently there is a staffroom that is full of drink. We are allowed in it tomorrow.

Tuesday 30.7.91

6.45 p.m.
THE POLES HAD TO EXPLAIN to us today that the sausages that we are eating every morning are covered in plastic and we are meant to remove the plastic before we eat the sausages!

HA HA HA! None of us realised.

It's weird – normally the thought of having a tummy full of Eastern European plastic would make me feel completely insane. But everyone else is OK and so am I. Plus I feel I'm sort of representing Britain. I know it's not the Olympics or anything but I need to look positive.

The communal showers are not good. There's one right at the end that is private. I'm waiting for that one. We all are though!

11.12 p.m.
Just been in the staffroom.

Polish vodka has a piece of long grass in it and is not like in the Vaults.

What a night. I think I just sang 'Waterloo' all the way through on a table.

Wednesday 31.7.91

4.57 p.m.

I DID SING 'WATERLOO' ALL the way through on a table but the Poles loved it. Mort confirmed over breakfast. The Poles do not take Abba for granted like everyone else. I didn't think they even had Abba!!

I did my pop lecture today. It went down a storm. The students had loads of questions – How many people were punks? Did punks go to school? Did I still know any punks? Basically I am in Poland teaching Punk. I think I could do this for a living but I don't think there's a big call for it in Lincolnshire.

10.55 p.m.

The Poles don't have gravy. They appear to have melted butter. I'm a bit worried I am putting on weight. There is a nurse on camp so I will find her tomorrow and ask her if she can weigh me.

Thursday 1.8.91

4.32 p.m.

I FOUND THE NURSE. SHE is the scariest woman I have ever met. She was hard as nails with a moustache. I took Agniezska to translate for me. Eventually she put me on these ancient scales and said I was 70 kilos. That's about 11 stone I think so I THINK I have lost more weight. I thanked her very much but she just grunted. I bet she was Polish KGB or something.

11.11 p.m.
A manic Pole wants the light on to do something so I'm just doing a quick update. Tonight we had a bit of a disco and this one gorgeous Polish girl started doing this well pervy dance to 'Rush Rush' by Paula Abdul. All the boys, in fact ALL the girls were staring – she is now called 'Rush Rush'. She has lost her Polish name. Which was probably Agnieszska, Magda or Paulina! There don't seem to be many different Polish first names AND all the boys are called Bogdan or Tomek!

Friday 2.8.91

11.16 p.m.
FREDDY IS ON THE PULL with Agsomething. SHARKING!!

This camp is brilliant. Mort and me are having such a laugh and I'm not homesick at all. You meet different men too and you think . . . Well there is an international world of men.

I'm not marrying a Pole though. They all get to 40 and look like Benny Hill. Mind you so do the women – HA HA HA!

That's not fair. I'm just being silly. Everyone is lovely.

I've got to get up at 6 o'clock in the morning to go to Wroclaw. We are trying to explain the word 'sharking' – they don't understand it.

Saturday 3.8.91

11.45 p.m.

ON THE BUS TO WROCLAW today Tomek taught us this Polish song about beer. Basically it's called 'Peeva' and it's saying 'Barman please I would like more beer'. It's brilliant. I also now know the Polish for 'You stupid spectacled snake – I hate you.' They have a word for a person that acts like a snake and wears glasses. What a language!

I'm having some bad moments but there is so much distraction I – well I hate to say it but Mum is partly right. I need to be doing stuff and to be with people. It doesn't stop the mess but it hoovers it up for a while.

I've made a decision. I'm not going to go to ring Mum whilst I'm here. I will send her a postcard.

Reasons why –

1) You have to book international phone calls at a place that looks like it is still run by the KGB.
2) I don't want to spend the wages I am getting here on trying to call her and then just get Adnan. I'd have to talk to him out of politeness but it would be weird.
3) Since the Berlin Wall came down you can get pirate cassette tapes in Świdnica for the equivalent of 40p!! Me and Mort went mad!! I got *The Sisters of Mercy, The Best of the Stranglers* and loads of other stuff. We've been told not to

show them off though because to the Poles that is still quite a luxury.

Sunday 4.8.91

10.15 p.m.

B IT EMBARRASSING TODAY FOR BRITAIN.
Firstly the Poles thrashed and I mean THRASHED us at football. Then we went into the gym and they showed us all these wonderful folk dances. They have real meaning. They are the way the people courted and the way that people met and fell in love. Some were even about rebelling against the Russians. They were beautiful and intricate.

Then they asked us if we could show them our folk dances.

What could we do? After a mad conflab we showed them the Hokey Cokey and the The Conga by Black Lace.

The Poles loved it but bloody hell did Britain look piss poor!

Monday 5.8.91

5.12 p.m.

I 'M SAT IN THE MIDDLE of a Polish field. It's so quiet it's totally brilliant.

I love Poland it's amazing. I do feel the mad bits but I'm managing them.

I had a lovely conversation with Chris last night. He said that at the meeting in London I had made loads of unfunny jokes that bombed and he went home to his mum and said 'I can't spend weeks with her.' But then he said 'you are really funny and sweet.' Then Mark said 'I think you are the most sensitive person on this camp.' I am transparent. Then he hugged me and when I tried to shrug him off he went 'Fucking just give me a hug' and I did.

I am the host of 'Polish Blind Date' night tomorrow.

Tuesday 6.8.91

11.34 p.m.

I AM CILLA BLACK IN Świdnica. That's all you need to know.

Plus I can't write anymore because of that vodka. It's lethal. I think it's got a buffalo on the front or something.

Thursday 8.8.91

8.45 p.m.

H ILARIOUS TURN OF EVENTS! I have suspected concussion and it's all because of a Bagpuss impression. Me and Laura were weeing ourselves at Mark's Bagpuss yawn and we bumped heads and then my eye swelled up. Then I sort of fainted. Actually I think it was being pissed and a bit of panic. Anyway because we are their 'guests' the Poles didn't want to take any chances and this morning I was sent in a Polish ambulance to hospital. It was a Volvo estate sort of car with a stretcher in the back! I got more injuries on the way! I was rolling all over the place. Anyway NO JOKE there were BATS in the waiting room of casualty. The doctor spoke perfect English and prescribed bed rest for a day. He told us he'd been up for 24 hours. Polish doctors work bloody HARD. He'd probably been trying to get the bats out of casualty. That's the weird thing – no-one seemed that bothered.

Friday 9.8.91

11.30 p.m.
I'M IN BED LISTENING TO my Victoria Wood tape 'resting'. I can't believe I'm saying this but I'd prefer to be teaching. We are doing a fashion show next week. Angela says it's a great way to learn verbs and colours if you're learning English. Plus there's a fancy dress party tomorrow night. I don't want to miss that.

The scary nurse is going to assess me later.

7.34 p.m.
The scary nurse says I'm fine to resume activities tomorrow. Well I think she did. She said 'You OK.' Then I pointed at the scales and she weighed me again. I was the same. I'm wondering if her scales say 70 kilos for everyone but I am not going to argue with her! She is like a Bond villain with knives in her shoes.

Saturday 10.8.91

11.22 p.m.

THE FANCY DRESS PARTY WAS fantastic. Maria went as the Statue of Liberty. Mark actually painted himself blue and went as a Smurf. He looked brilliant. I just zipped myself slightly in my suitcase and went as a suitcase. The highlight of the night though was 'Rush Rush' doing 'Rush Rush' again.

I am glad Haddock is not here to see me as a piece of luggage.

Haddock.

In any nation he's a lovely thought. I have to say I haven't thought about him quite so much since I've been here.

Sunday 11.8.91

4.56 p.m.

MARK CAN'T GET THE BLUE paint off himself. He is worried he is going to look like a Smurf forever.

I've moved on to Polish sangria stuff. The vodka was actually in danger of killing me.

Monday 12.8.91

8.55 p.m.

WE ARE PAUSING FOR A word from OTTO!

Rae dear friend!

Thanks God I met you at this camp. You're incredibly good at taking it easy and I'll never forget you.

When I met people from Britain I always got the impression thet they pretend all the time but after I met you I'm no longer sure about it. You've really natural! Keep it up!

What you told me gave me some stuff to think about!

You are good table tennis but you should work on your backhand – you haven't quite got it yet.

If there is anything you'd like to have (that you haven't got yet, which is not much I'm sure) don't hesitate to tell me about it. I'd even jump up to the sky to get one of the stars and give it to you. You're really worth it!

My English may be not the best yet but I'm able to speak my mind almost fully so I won't take this advice of yours (as to changing to Polish in my diary).

As anything else you wrote me goes – I'll seriously think about it.

And believe me, your head should be decorated with real stars.

Otto X

I have no idea what I said to him or told him what to do
– I was pissed.

Tuesday 13.8.91

10.45 p.m.

WE DID THE FASHION SHOW today. Angela is FAB at her job. Britain should send her everywhere in the world to teach. Everyone would love us.

It's the end of school on Thursday (I can't believe it – it feels like I've always been here, in a good way). Anyway we have to do a show. We are doing the Time Warp – mainly because it's easy to create Rocky Horror costumes with bin bags. Plus we all know the words!

Wednesday 14.8.91

11.35 p.m.

I WALKED PAST THE NURSE'S office today and she dragged me in. She put me on the scales and it was 68! I've lost 2 pounds. God knows how. I've been eating a lot of cucumber and onion and dancing a lot. Perhaps that's it. Anyway she SMILED and said 'Dobry' which means good in Polish. MAJOR victory for Polish/British relations!

Thursday 15.8.91

11.24 p.m.

WE DID THE ROCKY HORROR. The Poles seemed to like it. They like everything though. They are the loveliest, friendliest bunch of people in the world. It's an amazing place. Seriously, I feel quite emotional about saying goodbye to people tomorrow. REALLY emotional. I know that sounds daft because I've only known them for days but it's all been so intense and – shit – I'm crying – it's been the thing I've sort of needed. Bloody Poland. Whoever would have thought it. And I've made it and not fucked it up. Yet. No but I won't. Mort has been amazing. Just right like she always is and I've done something WELL.

Friday 16.8.91

12.39 p.m.

MOST OF THE STUDENTS WENT this morning. Everyone cried. Grown men were crying. This time and place has been brilliant. Then an odd thing happened. GiGi told me that scary nurse wanted to see me. I went there and the nurse started saying stuff in Polish. GiGi said it was difficult to translate but basically the nurse wanted me to know that I was 'sort of special'. I gave the nurse a hug. I'm much more huggy after Poland. And then the nurse went. It freaks me out. I will never see her again. Most of these people I will never see again.

We are getting an early night tonight.

9.45 p.m.

> Poland
> You have changed me
> I am slightly less nuts
> The side of me I used to be so resentful of
> I am becoming most proud of
> I can be sensitive
> I can be silly
> The part of me I tried to eradicate
> Has come forward
> And it's a great part of me.

Saturday 17.8.91

4.49 a.m.

IF MY WRITING IS CRAP it's because I'm writing in the dark on the way to Auschwitz. We are going to Auschwitz. I know! Last summer I'm watching *War and Remembrance* and this summer, today, I am going there.

10.12 p.m.

We are staying a youth hostel in Oświęcim. It's the town near Auschwitz. The Poles don't like you to call it Auschwitz – for very understandable reasons.

What I saw today. Cabinets of children's shoes taken from them before they were gassed. Cabinets of hair shaved off prisoners. Cabinets of suitcases of people who thought they were being relocated then were gassed. Actual gas canisters. Words. There are no words. In fact there's apparently a famous quote 'After Auschwitz – no poetry.' Nothing matters. Nothing beautiful exists.

I just know for all my life, for the rest of my life if anyone is a Nazi I will fucking, FUCKING hate them.

Even that sounds lame. You can't write about it. You can't even . . . Just have to make sure it doesn't happen again in any way you can.

Sunday 18.8.91

6.45 p.m.

AFTER YESTERDAY WE ALL FELT really down. Rightly. Anyway we ended up in this mountain range. It was beautiful. We went up this very unsafe chairlift but the view was worth it! Then later we saw this little metal barrier that said 'Republic of Czechoslovakia'. It looked like something you get in a car park. Anyway I said 'Let's go and visit another country' so we all joined arms, started singing the theme tune to *Heidi* and skipped into Czechoslovakia. It was brilliant until about 5 soldiers with sub-machine guns – I AM NOT JOKING – appeared from nowhere and we LEGGED it back NOT singing the theme tune to *Heidi*. What were we thinking??!!

Anyway I have not caused an international incident and I am not dead.

I feel bad having fun after Auschwitz. I don't think I'll ever get over that place. Should you even get over that place?!!

Monday 19.8.91

7.12 p.m.

WE ARE ON OUR WAY to Warsaw but apparently there is something going on in Russia. A state of emergency there or something?! The rumour is all the borders are closing and everything is going hardcore communist again. In Poland too!! I do love this place but I don't want to be stuck here forever. Shitting hell!!

Mort says to calm down. We don't know what is really going on and we are currently on a bus and can't do anything. Then she said 'Do you fancy a packet of crisps?' which is an in-joke we have about an old Central TV community service announcement.

Mort can always calm me down.

11.10 p.m.
We are in a hotel in Warsaw. I can't hear any war and there are no soldiers anywhere.

I controlled a panic. Only with Mort and the thought of crisps though.

Tuesday 20.8.91

6.12 p.m.

APPARENTLY THE THING IN RUSSIA is nothing. There's tanks and stuff but no borders are closing and we are not going to be stuck here forever.

Today we had a tour of Warsaw where we saw this completely horrible building that Stalin had built as a present for the Polish people called the Palace of Culture and Science. The tour guide said that Stalin basically put it there to remind 'the Polish people to behave'. Then she showed us this Polish postcard that had a cartoon of God on it pointing to Europe. It said (in Polish) 'Proof that God has a sense of humour – he put Poland between Russia and Germany!'

I have to say I can understand why the Poles still aren't keen on Germany and Russia.

Does that make me a racist? I never, NEVER want to be any kind of Nazi.

We also had to go and see the Polish Education department to be thanked or something. The man (who looked like Lech Walesa) thanked us and that was it.

Now we are going to have a party in the hotel! VODKA TONIGHT! Last day in Poland tomorrow.

Wednesday 21.8.91

1.12 a.m.

I JUST WANT TO SAY the Irish people in our group are the most amazing people at starting parties with sing-songs ever. Mary and Mark in particular. Once they start EVERYONE joins in. Angela started singing 'When a Child Is Born' by Johnny Mathis. It was fantastic.

I'm pissed but I've also had Polish crisps so I am fine.

8.12 a.m.

I am not fine. I am dying. We are looking round the square today on foot. God help us.

7.13 p.m.

We had lunch in the Old Town Market Place which is pretty and looks like it's old but actually the Germans bombed the shit out of it and it had to be completely rebuilt. It was still lovely and then Mort and me found this mad shop. It had a letter from Eric Clapton on the wall and some pendants that bring you different things if you wear them. I chose 'Self love and healing'. I'm never taking it off. It's copper, round and a bit ugly but it's Poland and it's . . . just been the most. I can't put it into words. I can hide the thoughts. I can do normal stuff and strangers and foreigners quite like me. I feel different. I feel like this was . . . Oh I just LOVE POLAND. It's the most special place. It's the place that has sort of . . . saved me. I know that sounds mad. I think I'm still pissed. It's that vodka. I don't think it ever leaves your system

Another party tonight. Chris says he's not going to bed. NONE of us are!

Thursday 22.8.91

9.45 a.m.

ON A LOT POLISH AIRLINES plane. We were put on the plane last and the airport official said 'Lots of you are drunk.' We were! We had been drinking and singing all night. But she let us on and we have all been served – a sausage!!

Goodbye Poland. Now I'm dreading Heathrow. It's going to be very hard to say goodbye to the people who have made this so brilliant.

6.10 p.m.
Back home. Heathrow was hard. EVERYONE cried and hugged but we've all said we'll keep in touch.

I walked down to see Mum at work in Morrisons. I didn't wear shoes. I couldn't be arsed. Mum looked so pleased to see me but she did say 'Why didn't you call me?' and 'Where's your shoes?'

I told her I'd had a brilliant time and loved it. She said 'Rachel – I'm pleased you're back safe and I'm pleased you had a great time.'

9.12 p.m.
Just found out bloody Bryan Adams is still number one!!

Friday 23.8.91

6.54 p.m.
I'VE SLEPT NEARLY ALL TODAY.
Just rang Dobber – apparently no-one is out tonight or tomorrow as everyone is working.

It will sound melodramatic and bollocks but Poland has changed me.

I feel changed.

Monday 26.8.91

6.35 p.m.

I'M ON A BUS TO St Albans with Battered Sausage. God knows why.

I'm in a state of confusion. Before Poland I was screwed-up, loud, fat occasionally-funny Rae, now I'm half that and half I don't know what.

7.35 p.m.

I think we choose the friends we deserve. That's why I chose Battered Sausage. We just take the piss out of each other ALL THE TIME. It's lovely and friendly but sometimes you want a chat about serious stuff. I do love him but all he wanted to know about Poland was 'How fit the birds were' and 'How good the beer was'. I told him the women were gorgeous and the beer was cheap. He said 'I'll book my seat now!'

Oh Haddock – just stop working and let me see how I feel about you now.

Thursday 29.8.91

HAD A BRILLIANT DAY AT Polly's seeing everyone. Only I'm totally out of step with the charts. Everyone is singing 'I'm Too Sexy' – apparently it's a song! Never heard it!

Sunday 1.9.91

2.15 a.m.

SO POLAND HAS HELPED MANY things. What has it not helped? Loving Haddock.

1. Gave me a massive hug when he saw me.
2. Said 'I've quite missed you' and winked.
3. Looked unbelievable in a STRAW HAT. YES. THAT is the level of horn we are talking about.
4. Asked me if I'd met any fit Polish men. I said 'a few.'
5, Bought me a drink of vodka – so it felt like 'I was still on holiday'.

Oh I need to get away from him. He is cruel and lingering hope that will never come true.

Saturday 7.9.91

9.12 p.m.

LOOK DIARY – HERE'S THE deal. I'm not writing when I'm just numb. And I've been just numb. I can't even be bothered to wash half the time. Mum says it's because Poland was such an adventure and I came back to the same old stuff. No-one else has changed. I'm still the same to them. I can't wait to get away now. With nothing to do except wait for university the thoughts get bad again and I just get stuck and I feel I'm going backwards again to the old Rae. Perhaps I'm not the problem. Perhaps Stamford is. The way I'm remembered. The way people see me. Oh I don't know anymore.

No-one is out tonight again. Looks like no-one will be out again till the 28th and that's my last Saturday night in Stamford. Everyone stop Summer jobs and come and discuss Warsaw with me!

Thursday 12.9.91

11.45 p.m.

I LOST IT TONIGHT.

I went down Green Lane shops to get some milk and the twats on the wall said 'You're still a fat bitch.'

The thing is this is basically how Nazi Germany started with just name calling and so I said 'Fuck you – you shit. You'll still be sitting on that wall being a fucking cock to people when you're 50 because you haven't got the balls or brain to do anything else and if you lay a finger on me I will get my brother to beat the living shit out of you!'

Now it was wrong to put my brother in a fight situation without telling him but I was too angry to think straight. All the twats went 'Ohhhh – hark at her. Doesn't SHE think she's something?!' I just got the milk and went home. FUCK THEM. I'm not taking shit anymore. I don't care if they think I'm fat. NEWS FLASH GREEN LANE TWATS – I DON'T WANT TO SLEEP WITH THICKO NASTY SHITS AND I DON'T CARE WHAT YOU THINK OF ME.

Monday 16.9.91

5.47 p.m.

JUST SAW MORT FOR THE last physical time before she goes to St Andrews. I don't think I will see her till Christmas now but you never know. I have the best, funniest, kindest best mate you could ever want.

All my entries seem so dramatic but it really is all coming to an end this time. I feel a bit of panic. I get the mad thoughts but if I can do Poland then I can do Hull.

Thursday 26.9.91

4.10 p.m.

NO MUM – I DO not need an Oxford Mathematics set. I'm doing English Language and Literature at university and my need for a protractor is thankfully gone. But it's a kind thought.

Buy me some bloody sexy bras though. (No I didn't say that.)

Sunday 29.9.91

3.23 a.m.

THE LAST SATURDAY STAMFORD NIGHT. Not ever – but for a long time.

Battered Sausage has threatened to come and see me in Hull to check out the 'Northern Slices and flange situation'. I may not give him my address! Dobber was lovely and said she'd try to make it up but it's miles from Canterbury. I said we'd go 'Stammy Gad Mad' at Christmas.

And Haddock? Haddock said 'I'm only in Leeds. Come over for a beer.' Bloody hell Haddock – if only you knew! I want more than a bloody Carlsberg. Then he hugged me after Olivers and left.

Ronni is in Leeds too. I could go over and see her and – oh that's terrible. But I can't just go over and see him. That's . . . That's like admitting it ALL. All this Haddock-based madness.

I don't know what to do. Just go to Hull and have a good time, lose more weight, buy better knickers and see.

Thursday 3.10.91

10.24 p.m.
I JUST WEIGHED MYSELF AT Boots. I am 10 stone 12! So the Polish nurse's scales were right!

Friday 4.10.91

8.28 p.m.
THE END OF MY YEAR off. The end of an era. Leaving Stamford tomorrow for Hull.

I could go on forever and I frequently do but I'll just say this. I have been blessed with so many things but I have the best mates in the world and I can make some new ones too!

We've gone from down and out to actual progression and there's always hope.

Sunday 6.10.91

12.31 a.m.

CURRENTLY SAT IN E11, FERENS Hall room with Saul. He lives across the way and is very Welsh. He's rolling a joint. I'm not having any but he is lovely. Next door is a classic called Mish. Leaving Essex was the best thing I ever did. A second-year burst in and started to rifle through my underwear earlier. I told him to bollocks. He apologised and left. I'm not having people looking at my bras. Especially as they are SHIT. As soon as I get my grant I'm going sexy bitch.

I can be happy here I think. I think I can stay.

8.10 p.m.

BLOODY HELL! Bryan Adams is STILL number one. This is a bloody piss take now. I'm going down the union.

WHAT HAPPENED NEXT . . .

I'M THINKING YOU ARE PROBABLY after a happy ending. You want me to lose loads of weight, stop being loopy and marry Haddock. Or at least get a snog off him.

There is a happy ending. But it might not be the one you want.

In fact some of you may have skipped here just to find out what happens with Haddock. Turn back and read ALL of it. I had to go through it you know. It's the least you can do.

Anyway . . .

Let's go through things one by one.

My weight. My weight went up and down. I was 14 and a half stone. I was eight and a half stone. I've been every size and every pound in-between. You know what – being skinny solved NOTHING except the fact I fitted in a pair of size 10 velvet hot pants from TopShop for 2 weeks in 1992 (It was a rave thing). Weight is a number that I choose to react to. I've been skinny with a lousy man and fat with a lovely man. Does it make you feel better when you lose weight? It might. Will it solve all the problems you had with your self-confidence and men in the first place – no. The number on the scales can move but trust me – your head can stay in exactly the same place. Sort your head out before you sort anything else out.

I didn't have the therapy I really needed till I was 28. I found a wonderful counsellor and we worked together for

two years. Do I still have anxiety and OCD? Yes.
Sometimes. It's a bit like being an alcoholic. It's always
there and it will come and bite you on the arse when
you're stressed or when you least expect it. But I manage
it and I'm never afraid to ask for help. Nor should you be.
Your doctor has heard worse. We are all a little bit mad.

My mum says I can tell you this now. She's a manic
depressive. She hates the term bipolar. It doesn't sum up
for her the amazing highs and terrible lows. By the time I
was born she'd already had shock treatment for it. The
signs were there. By anyone's standards marrying a
Moroccan bodybuilder and having him tattooed on your
bottom not long after divorcing your gay second husband
is rather . . . manic. In her words she was 'on one'. I've
seen her brilliant manias and I've seen the price she pays
with her depressions. She's a fantastic woman who KNEW
that I would need a challenging life to keep me well. She
has been and continues to be a wonderful mother –
though she still drives me mad. She has supported me in
telling my story and in everything I do. As have my
brothers and my dad. He's only got one leg now after
smoking 40 cigarettes a day for over 60 years. It wasn't
the fags though he says. It was years of working in drafty
factories that upset his veins.

There's no point arguing. He's 76. Just get him 20 John
Player Special.

What else? The man who molested me went to prison for
abusing other girls in an historic abuse case. The police
were brilliant. You shouldn't be scared to talk to them
either. And if it has happened to you I'm so, so sorry.
What happened to me was really minor but it affected me

greatly. I shiver when I think of people who go through sustained, serious abuse but it's never too late to stop people. Talk to someone.

I'm still best friends with Mort. We've been through it all together. I borrowed her birth plan just like I copied her history homework. Some friendships are just magic aren't they? Dobber is still one of my dearest friends on earth and Battered Sausage is still gloriously Battered Sausage. So many other people in this book are still in my life and they make it brilliant.

And so to Haddock.

The thing about Haddock was – he was the opposite of everything I was, yet he <u>seemed</u> to feel exactly the same way. Where I was fat, he was thin. Where I was plain as day, he was handsome as hell (I'm looking at the pictures now and he was. He was fit, and frankly he didn't know it). Yet he appeared sometimes to be as troubled as me. This is all assumption. As much as he was my friend, he was also a TOTAL fantasy figure. Perhaps I read it all wrong at the time, but there seemed to be something deep-rooted that he didn't like about himself at the time. I can tell you now, apart from the usual atypical adolescent failings, there was nothing to dislike. There really wasn't.

Time passes. You know what it's like. You lose touch. I doubt the poor bloke could even remember my name. He was a big part of my life; but in his I doubt I caused as much as a ripple.

I thought about him from time to time. I went to Leeds and I hoped I would bump into him. I didn't. There were no deliberate Haddock stalking trips, but I was there at the same time that he was, plenty of times. I was always seeing other people. More often than not, I wanted to see him more than the people I was actually seeing. I didn't call him though, because calling him up out of the blue would have just been too weird. I lived in fear of him guessing – because that would have been the worst rejection of all. I walked round Leeds hoping he'd save me from messes I'd got into but he never appeared. Probably a good thing.

Sometimes in the early 90s we were at the same parties, but we never really talked. We just said 'hello' and took the mickey out of each other.

There was one time at Fig's house. I think. I say I think because I might have read it wrong, but I think he might have tried to get off with me. It was a sleepover. 1994? Christmas time. I was drunk. He was drunk. We were in Fig's front room. Fig and Dobber were snogging. Battered Sausage was snoring. Haddock and me were having a play fight. Then it went weird. I remember saying the words 'No, let's just stay friends' or some other clichéd nonsense. Perhaps he hadn't really tried. My little insecure fat girl reached up and said 'It's bloody Haddock – of course he didn't try to kiss you.' He stayed on the floor. My inner insecure fat girl dragged me back alone to the sofa.

Lame. Lame. LAME. YES I KNOW. I REGRET IT. I was scared to my bones but perhaps I had read it wrong and perhaps some things are never meant to be.

I stayed awake for hours. I heard his heavy breathing. I looked at him in a heap. I thought about how much he made me laugh every time I saw him. I thought about his kindness. Understated. Real. I'd had a long term relationship by this point. It had been fairly disastrous.

Here was someone four years on that I still thought about. I still liked him. I really liked him. He was single. I was single.

I stayed rooted to the sofa.

And that was that.

Haddock fell from my life like sand through my fingers, like Bros from the charts.

These things happen. Who gives the Berlin Wall a second thought these days?! Things that were enormous parts of our life get forgotten. Once Haddock had been everything . . . and then he was almost nothing.

The diaries themselves followed me round everywhere. To halls of residence, to houses shared with other students, to flats shared with lovers. They came with me wherever I went. I never looked at them. I just never wanted them to be found by other prying, piss-taking eyes. I didn't want other people to see my excruciating tales of unrequited love, of madness and of sexual frustration. I kept them with me simply to keep them safe. Every November 5th I meant to put them on the bonfire. I just never got round to it.

And that was that. Again.

Until . . .

I had a funny feeling about Nottingham. On a train on the way to that interview at the University of Sheffield in late 1990, we pulled up at platform 4 of Nottingham station. I had to catch my breath. I will never be able to explain why, but I had a feeling. It was not specific, but it was overwhelming.

Six years later, almost by accident, I ended up there. Everything happened in Nottingham for me, long after everything in this diary had ceased to be relevant. Friends, lovers, job. That city and me just clicked. And it's where I met my husband Kevin. Quite frankly the best bloke in the world. You wouldn't be reading any of this if it wasn't for him. He stopped me from throwing all the diaries out and encouraged me to share them.

One Saturday night in late 2000 or early 2001 (I can't remember the date but I remember the events like it was yesterday), I was walking back to our flat with Kev in the centre of the city. Nottingham on a Saturday is packed with hen parties, stag parties, drunk teenagers, and merry twenty-somethings. It's manic – you walk against a tide of people whatever direction you are going in. We were walking across by the Theatre Royal when I saw him: a face among a million other faces. I hadn't seen him for years. I have no idea why he was there. He didn't live there. I shouted out his name. He hadn't changed much. I think in a perverse way I had wanted him to have morphed into a minger – a balding, middle-aged stereotype. He hadn't.

Conversation went as thus:

ME: HADDOCK!
HADDOCK: Oh my God – Rae Earl!
(HUG)
ME: I'd like to introduce you to my husband Kevin
– he's Australian!
HADDOCK: (to Kev) You've got a good one there . . .

I said something I can't remember, then he said:

HADDOCK: Come for a drink?

ME: Mate, I have to go – I'm working at 6 a.m.

HAD: Please come . . .

ME: Sorry mate – I've got to go . . . See you soon.

He disappeared and mumbled something.

That was the last time I saw him.

'You've got a good one there'

'You've got a good one there'

'You've got a good one there'

It was throwaway . . . but it felt like one of the biggest compliments of all time.

I couldn't sleep that night. I had to explain to Kev about Haddock.

Kev said: 'Why?! Oh WHY didn't you go for a drink with him and tell him what he had meant to you?!'

But I couldn't. It belonged to another age. What was I going to say? 'Hello Haddock. How's life? By the way I was in love with you when I was 17? You made me feel better about myself at a time when hardly anything else did? You have still got the best arse I have ever seen'?

Besides . . . the Haddock I bumped into isn't the Haddock I knew, or even the Haddock I thought I knew. The Haddock I knew now has his own happy ending. I know this because when the first book came out I had to ring him up and warn him what was about to be revealed. That was an interesting conversation. He genuinely had no idea. Anyway Haddock finally realised he was a handsome, witty sod, with a great backside. He put any demons he had to bed, married a fantastic woman and has lovely children. And no – he is not an insurance salesman. He does something as I suspected far more wonderful than that. But don't go looking for him. He's very private. He wants to stay anonymous and I think that's bloody right. Let's leave him to the contented, great life he deserves.

Anyway, seeing Haddock in Nottingham that time set me on the world's biggest nostalgia trip. I dug out these diaries. They were still in a 'Walkers Newsagents of Stamford' bag and shoved between my GCSE certificates and a shoebox full of Smurfs (Mum never threw them out). I read them cover to shabby cover.

They tackle everything I felt about my life then; but there's one thing that seems to come out of them. One 'something' that is behind all of my diaries. It's a something I thought was exclusive to me at the time, but it wasn't. It was relevant then and it's still relevant now. It underpins all of this and everybody mentioned in the diaries.

We all feel fat, ugly and bad about ourselves sometimes. Irrespective of what we really are. And if we've got any sense we do two things. Firstly we love ourselves and that's our responsibility. Then we find people and things that make us feel even better about ourselves. Because most of us are the same – all we want to be is loved.

It's what I was looking for, it's what Haddock was looking for, what my mum was trying to find, what all my friends were looking for. Even the ones at school you think have it all sorted don't. I know that because after the first diary was published they wrote to me and told me that they felt like I did then. We are all just after being loved and appreciated. Fat, thin, gay, straight, male or female.

I'm sorry. It sounds like the worst kind of generalised American chat-show gush – but it's true. I believe it.

Anyway that really is it. My diaries have been published and adapted for TV and this Bonfire Night I really do intend to burn them.

And I don't mind telling you about it all because I suspect you've felt some of the same things . . .

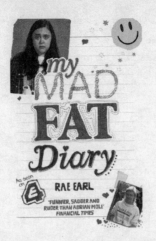

Read the prequel to *My Madder Fatter Diary*,
MY MAD FAT DIARY

It's 1989 and Rae is a fat, boy-mad 17-year-old girl,
living in Stamford, Lincolnshire with her mum and
their deaf white cat in a council house with a mint
off-green bath suite and a larder Rae can't keep
away from. This is the hilarious and touching real-
life diary she kept during that fateful year . . .

My Fat, Mad Teenage Diary evokes a vanished time
when Charles and Di are still together, the Berlin
Wall is up, Kylie is expected to disappear from the
charts at any moment and its £1 for a Snakebite and
Black in the Vaults pub. *My Mad Fat Diary* will
appeal to anyone who's lived through the 1980s. But
it will also strike a chord with anyone who's ever
been a confused, lonely teenager who clashes with
their mother, takes themselves VERY seriously and
has no idea how hilarious they are.